They Came to Nashville

They Came to Nashville

Marshall Chapman

Foreword by Peter Guralnick

The Country Music Foundation Press

Vanderbilt University Press

Nashville

Published by Vanderbilt University Press
and the Country Music Foundation Press
Nashville, Tennessee 37235
First edition 2010

This book is printed on acid-free paper
made from 30% post-consumer recycled content.
Manufactured in the United States of America

Frontispiece: Cover of Marshall's Opry program
from her first night in Nashville, January 28, 1967
(courtesy of Gaylord Entertainment)

Library of Congress Cataloging-in-Publication Data

Chapman, Marshall.
They came to Nashville / Marshall Chapman ;
foreword by Peter Guralnick.
p. cm.
Includes index.
ISBN 978-0-8265-1735-7 (cloth : alk. paper)
1. Country musicians—Tennessee—Nashville—Interviews.
2. Rock musicians—Tennessee—Nashville—Interviews.
I. Title.
ML394.C52 2010
781.642092′276855—dc22
[B]   2010000113

Contents

Foreword

ANYONE WHO HAS EVER SEEN HER on stage knows that Marshall Chapman is a force of nature. But then anyone who has ever read her on the page can attest to the same force of impact. There are differences, to be sure, but the one element that ties the two experiences together is Marshall herself. She follows the imperative that Ray Charles and Lowman Pauling laid down musically, *Tell the truth*. This carries with it all kinds of potential for squirm and discomfiture, but her truth is neither cruel nor sentimental—I think "quirky" might be the best way of describing it—it's a truth that links passion and whimsicality in a way that few artists I can think of, musical or otherwise, have yet to assay.

Like *Goodbye, Little Rock and Roller*, Marshall's memoir of song, *They Came to Nashville* is a tribute to the virtues of digression and divagation—and I don't mean that as any kind of a backhanded compliment. Sometimes—maybe most of the time—the best way to get to a place, the best way to get at complex truths, is not by a straight line but by recognizing, by *appreciating* all the forks in the road along the way. If Marshall didn't follow the dictates of her imagination, for all we know she might have stayed in Spartanburg, South Carolina, where, it's true, she did get to see Elvis Presley perform sitting in the "colored" section of the Carolina Theatre with her family's maid, Cora, when she was just seven.

It was a formative experience. But so was nearly everything else. "Making love for the first time (first orgasm, you name it)," as she said in one interview. Hearing Willie Nelson for the first time. Writing her first song. Writing her latest song. Writing her first book. Acting in her first movie. And so on. The wonderful thing about Marshall is how welcoming of each experience she is—in all of its serendipitous complications, all of its multifarious possibilities—and how eager, and scrupulous, she is to get on with the business of communicating it. In this book she encourages others to embrace a similar breadth, a similar randomness, in the questions she asks, in her receptivity to the answers, in her explicit complicity with her interview subjects. She's even got me doing it. When was the first time I came to Nashville? Or more to the point, how did the two of *us* ever come to meet? It wasn't through Lee Smith, though it could have been, since Lee is everyone's soul mate, and the musical *Good Ol' Girls*, a collaboration between Lee and Marshall, the novelist Jill McCorkle, and songwriter Matraca Berg, is yet another of Marshall's remarkable collective enterprises. Marshall at one point was holding out for the likelihood of a long-ago dinner party for Emmylou Harris at Chuck and Beth Flood's (see page 60)—but that wasn't it either. Different dinner parties. I cling to the almost certainly manufactured memory of meeting her in the parking lot at Maude's—with, somehow, both Phil Walden and Pete Drake in the picture. Doubtful. We might just as well settle on Jack Clement, whose antic spirit deserves a memoir of its own, something Jack, a visitor from Alpha Centauri, has been promising for years. The point is, *it doesn't matter*. Like everyone in this book, somehow or other we got there. And the getting there—and the stories about getting there—is all that matters.

Reading *They Came to Nashville* can set off that kind of thinking in anyone's mind. It's a form of free association that, as anyone who has ever tried to marshal their thoughts knows (sorry), doesn't necessarily come easy—and it certainly isn't free. Marshall's lifetime of incidental adventure, both on and off the stage, can be instructive—but more to the point, it can be thought- and, more important, *feeling*-provoking, as every subject of Marshall's scrutiny, from longtime Love Slave (Marshall's band) and Straitjacket (his own) Eddie Angel to Kris Kristofferson and Willie Nelson, discovers. You'll never get such a skewed and true perspective on the odd turns that life can take as you will from these free-flowing explorations. And yet at the heart of it all is just that, Marshall's heartfelt dedication and devotion to—well, to the truth. To its depth and diversity and inexplicable mystery, to its real-life entertainment value, if you will.

See for yourself. Discover the pleasures (*and* truths) of the purely anecdotal, the modernity of the digressive. But most of all revel in the variety of human experience, not to mention the variety of *each* human experience. And don't miss the opportunity of adding to it if and when Marshall comes to your hometown—with or without her Love Slaves.

—Peter Guralnick

Oh, driver!
For God's sake catch that light, for
There comes a time for us all
when we want to begin a new life.

—Robert Penn Warren

I thought Nashville was the roughest
But I know I've said the same
about them all

—Willie Nelson

Prologue

THE NIGHT I MET BILLY JOE SHAVER, my hair caught on fire. I kid you not. The year was 1971. The place was Nashville, Tennessee.

We were all at a party at Jack and Liz Williams's house. Jack and Liz were a couple of expatriate songwriters from Texas, part of a vibrant underground Nashville music scene. (Jack went on to fame and fortune starring in the original Broadway production of *Sweeney Todd*. Liz was the first female songwriter I ever met.) The party was your typical early '70s party, with lots of smoke, beer, laughter, and music. You just never knew who might show up.

I was standing in the living room, minding my own business, when someone approached me with this cowboy-looking guy.

"Hey, Marshall! Meet Billy Joe Shaver. Billy's a songwriter from Texas."

Actually, I wasn't standing. Leaning would be a more accurate description. I was leaning against the mantelpiece in the living room where—unbeknownst to me—several sunken candles were burning. Even though I was in a semi-altered state, I vividly recall this encounter. Because no sooner had this person said, "Hi, Marshall! Meet Billy Joe Shaver," than Billy Joe's usually crinkly eyes became big as saucers. Like he'd just seen a ghost. And in that instant, I heard a faint crackling sound, followed by the unmistakable smell of burning human hair. It wasn't until people started shouting and beating me about the head that I realized my hair was on fire. As it turned out, I lost about a third in the back, leaving a crater of charred split ends from hell.

I've been told this was Billy Joe's first night in Nashville. But even if it wasn't, I'm sure something equally bizarre transpired. That's just the way it is here in Music City USA. Because Nashville is a music center—like London, New York, Austin, and Los Angeles—it has always been a magnet for dreamers, iconoclasts, poets, pickers, and prophets from all over. I've lived here forty years and can count on one hand the number of natives I've met. It's true. The great majority of us are from somewhere else.

Lately, I've been thinking a lot about this—why anyone would pick up and leave everything they've ever known to pursue a dream. What were they looking for? What were they running away from? What did they imagine would happen?

When you're young, you don't think about it. You just do it. Now that I'm older, whenever I think back to the young girl I was—inexperienced but ready, innocent, wild, and full of dreams—I'm amazed at the energy and gumption it took to pursue this path I've chosen.

Over the past few years, whenever I've found myself at a dinner party or just kicking back with artist/musician friends, I can't help it. I start asking all sorts of questions, encouraging them to talk about what brought them to Nashville.

These are the stories.

Kris Kristofferson

THE FIRST TIME I SAW KRIS KRISTOFFERSON was in somebody's room at the old Ramada Inn on the James Robertson Parkway in downtown Nashville. I had gone there with Jack Clement and Walter Forbes. It may have been DJ Week 1968. I was a nineteen-year-old sophomore at Vanderbilt University. I remember there were other people milling about the room. And a certain electricity in the air.

A scruffy-looking guy was sitting on the end of a bed playing a guitar, singing a song he had written. Every time he got to the part that went "La de-dah de-dah de-dah-dah / La de-dah de-dah . . ." everybody in the room began singing along, including me. But I was thinking, *Man, those are pretty dumb lyrics. I guess he just couldn't think of any words for that part.* But the people in the room seemed mightily impressed with this scruffy-looking guy with deep-set eyes that seemed to look at nobody, yet saw all. Then I heard someone whisper *Kris Kristofferson* and figured that must be his name. Sounded like a pretty cool name for such a scruffy-looking guy.

Now mind you, I was *just* becoming aware that people wrote songs in Nashville, Tennessee. That somebody would actually sit down and think about his or her life, or things like "freedom" and "injustice," then write a song about it. I was so young and naïve, I wasn't thinking about much. Until that night, I probably thought Stephen Foster had written every song that ever was, other than "The Star-Spangled Banner," which I knew was written by Francis Scott Key. Until that night, I had always equated Nashville with Porter Wagoner and the Wilburn Brothers and the Grand Ole Opry. But that night at the Ramada Inn, in a room full of strangers and some guy named Kristofferson singing a song about Bobby McGee, I came to realize that Nashville was also a place where people came to write songs. People you did not necessarily see on TV. And some of them actually made a living at it. It was a revelation.

I don't remember meeting Kristofferson that night. At least I hope not, seeing as this was pre–Kent State, which meant I was wearing the uniform du jour of the "TVC" (Typical Vanderbilt Coed)—a tweed Villager skirt with McMullen blouse, knee socks, and Bass Weejuns. After Kent State, of course, everything changed, including the clothes we wore. After that, it was bell-bottom jeans, black turtlenecks, sandals, and my favorite accessory of all—a blue suede choker with a gold nuclear disarmament peace symbol pinned on the front. While purchasing the choker and pin at a head shop near Vanderbilt, I remember thinking, *Boy, Mother sure would hate seeing this peace symbol on my neck.* And that somehow made me happy.

The next time I saw Kristofferson was about two years later. Ironically, I was again with Cowboy Jack Clement and Walter Forbes. I wrote about Jack in my first book, so if you want to know about him, then read it . . . or google him, whichever suits your fancy. Suffice it to say, Jack was at the controls at Sun Records when Jerry Lee Lewis recorded "Great Balls of Fire" and "Whole Lot of Shakin' Going On." Fifty years later, Jack would sing his "West Canterbury Subdivision Blues" at my wedding. Everything in between and since has been fairly well documented, but somebody needs to write the book. (You listenin', Cowboy?)

As for my connection with Walter Forbes, I'd met him the spring I was sixteen years old in Hollywood Beach, Florida. I'd gone there with my father for the annual ATMI (American Textile Manufacturers Institute) convention. Usually Mother would accompany Daddy to these events, but she hadn't felt up to it that year, so Dad ended up taking me. It was my first time to fly on a commercial jet, so I was pretty excited. Plus I got to skip school. But the fact that he had asked me to go was beyond special.

One night after dinner, Dad said, "Walter Forbes Sr.'s having some friends up to hear his son play guitar. You want to go?" Sounded good to me, so up the elevator we went to Mr. Forbes Sr.'s suite at the Hollywood Beach Hotel, which is where we were all staying. As we walked in, the first thing I noticed was this guy in a white dinner jacket, playing a Martin guitar, singing songs about mules and slaves and things

Marshall and Kris Kristofferson backstage at the Ryman Auditorium,
Jan. 27, 2010

you just didn't talk about in the proper South Carolina society I grew
up in. Plus, the guy had crinkly blue eyes and the biggest, whitest teeth
I'd ever seen. He looked right at me and smiled when he sang, and being sixteen years old, I was smitten.

I came to learn that Walter Forbes had recorded two albums for
RCA that Chet Atkins produced. That he and his wife Kitty had moved
to Nashville so Walter could pursue a career in music. A few years before, Walter's only brother had been killed in a gun accident, which

only increased the family pressure for Walter to succeed. So when the uncertainties of a life in music became all too real, Walter returned to Chattanooga to work in the family business. The Forbeses were textile people like my family. Everybody in the textile business knew each other. My grandfather, who'd died that previous winter, had been good friends with Mr. Forbes Sr.

About a week after my father and I were back in Spartanburg, a package arrived in the mail from Chattanooga. Inside was a record album entitled *Chattanooga Arts Festival featuring Walter Forbes and the Revived Virginia Minstrels*. It was inscribed, "To Marshall, Very first copy, Love, Walter." After I read the inscription, I shrieked and burst into tears. My parents thought I'd gone off the deep end. Understand, I come from a long line of Presbyterians—often referred to as "The Frozen Chosen"—so my behavior was surprising, even to me. After I calmed down, Dad showed me the two RCA albums Walter had sent him a couple of years before. I spent the next few months learning to play every song on those albums.

After that, there were summer visits to the Forbes home on Lookout Mountain. I was hoping Walter would teach me more about the guitar, but he said, "Nope. There's someone here who's much better than me—Norman Blake." So I ended up taking three lessons from Norman Blake on the second floor of an old brick building in downtown Chattanooga. I remember carrying my guitar up a long flight of worn wooden stairs to a room with an electric fan whirring back and forth in an open window. But the summertime heat never bothered me. I was too focused on Norman Blake and learning to play the guitar. I remember how exhilarating it felt, the first time I was able to simultaneously play bass notes with my thumb and melody notes with my fingers on songs like "Home, Sweet Home" and Elizabeth Cotten's classic "Freight Train." My mother had driven me to Chattanooga that first trip, and I can still see her sitting there reading or knitting while Norman Blake taught me guitar. Those were the only guitar lessons I ever had. After that, I just picked things up on my own.

That same trip, I remember being at Walter and Kitty's, watching Walter fill shotgun shells with bird shot using this little machine he had in his basement. I was just standing there watching him. There was music playing on the stereo, and every now and then, one of us would say something. I remember Walter asking if I had thought about college. I told him I had, but had no idea where I wanted to go, or even if I wanted to go. Most of the women in my family had gone to Converse College in Spartanburg.

"You want to go to Vanderbilt," Walter said emphatically.

"What's Vanderbilt?" I asked.

"It's in Nashville, and that's where you want to go."

After that, whenever anybody asked me where I was going to college, I always said, "Vanderbilt."

My parents were hoping I would go to a small, southern, liberal-arts women's college like Agnes Scott, Hollins, or Sweet Briar. They weren't particularly thrilled about my obsession with Vanderbilt. Like many people in South Carolina, they considered anything west of the Blue Ridge Mountains "just plain uncivilized." I remember Mother saying, "But we don't *know* anybody in Nashville." I was thinking, *Exactly. And that's why I'm going!* Also, after two years at an all-girls boarding school in a midsized town in North Carolina, I was ready for a change.

So the first time I came to Nashville was to look at Vanderbilt with my mother. We flew out Friday, January 27, 1967, during my senior year in high school. Riding in from the airport, I remember how gray everything seemed—the crags of limestone on either side of the road, so different from the green pines and rolling red clay hills back home. Mother and I stayed at the old Anchor Motel on West End Avenue. That first morning, we had breakfast at Miss Martha's Restaurant across the street. Mother picked it out because it had her name. Mother was born Martha Lenoir Cloud, but everybody called her Martha.

A Vanderbilt coed named Carmi Carmichael showed me around. I'd known Carmi from Spartanburg. Her family had lived just up the street from my family on Connecticut Avenue while her father was president of Converse College. On Saturday afternoon, Carmi took me to a basketball game at Memorial Gym to watch the Vanderbilt men play Mississippi State. We arrived early and sat in the back row of the student section. By tip-off, the gym was packed. I had never experienced so much excitement. After a sluggish first half, Vanderbilt won convincingly enough, 79–64.

That evening, Carmi and I drove downtown to see the Grand Ole Opry in the old Ryman Auditorium. Our seats were on the main floor just under the balcony. I remember somebody spilling a Coke in the balcony and it dripping down to where we were sitting. I also remember a large woman nursing a baby in the pew in front of us. I'd never seen a woman nurse a baby in public—or in private, for that matter—so I was somewhat taken aback. I was thinking, *Boy, it's a good thing Mother didn't come. Mother would not approve of bare bosoms in public, baby or no baby.* Other than that, I just remember how down-home everything was—musicians and friends and hangers-on wandering on and off the stage, while the show just kept on going. It was like being on a train. And I loved the commercials and how they were part of the show—especially the song about Martha White's Self-Rising Flour with Hot Rize Plus. And Bobby Bare singing "Detroit City" while women rushed to the stage with their cameras flashing.

That previous fall, I had applied to Vanderbilt, Emory, Hollins, and Converse. By spring, I was accepted at all four. But thanks to Walter Forbes, there was never any doubt in my mind as to where I would go.

I arrived on the Vanderbilt campus in the fall of 1967. Not long after I'd settled in, I got a call from Walter, who was in town visiting Cowboy Jack Clement. They were in a bar out on White Bridge Road called the Hound's Tooth. It was Walter, Jack, and Bill Hall. They were having a few drinks, so I took a cab out to meet them. It was my first time to ride in a cab alone *and* my first encounter with someone in the Nashville music business. I've often wondered whether it was God or the Devil smiling on me that night. Probably a little of both. Anyway, a few weeks later, I received in the mail a couple of Stoneman Family records ("featuring Dancing Donna") from Bill Hall, also known as the Colonel. Cowboy? The Colonel? Men back home didn't have names like this. Men back home had names like James, John, and Roger. This Cowboy guy and the Colonel . . . they were making records, for chrissakes! No way any fraternity boy was going to compete with this.

By the way, I just called Jack to ask how Bill Hall got his nickname. "He had to be called something," Jack replied. "Cowboy was already taken."

MUSIC ROW IS ONLY TWO BLOCKS from Vanderbilt, but back then it might as well have been on the moon. That night I first saw Kristofferson, Walter had picked me up at my dorm to take me

7:30 – 8:00 – LUZIANNE
BILL ANDERSON
SKEETER DAVIS
GEORGE HAMILTON, IV
DEL WOOD
JIM EDWARD BROWN
COUSIN JODY

8:00 – 8:30 – MARTHA WHITE
BILLY WALKER
CHARLIE LOUVIN
JUSTIN TUBB
OSBORNE BROTHERS
CROOK BROTHERS
STRINGBEAN
MARGIE BOWES

8:30 – 9:00 – STEPHENS
BOBBY LORD
THE CARLISLES
BOB LUMAN
ARCHIE CAMPBELL
JEAN SHEPARD
BOBBY BARE

9:00 – 9:30 – PET MILK
ROY ACUFF
BILL MONROE
BILLY GRAMMER
LONZO & OSCAR
DOTTIE WEST
FRUIT JAR DRINKERS

9:30 – 10:00 – KELLOGG
HANK SNOW
WILLIS BROTHERS
ROY DRUSKY
JUNE CARTER
MARION WORTH
CARTER FAMILY
CURLY FOX

10:00 – 10:15 – SCHICK
BILL ANDERSON
GEORGE HAMILTON, IV
MARGIE BOWES
STRINGBEAN

10:15 – 10:30 – PURE OIL
JIM EDWARD BROWN
THE CARLISLES
SKEETER DAVIS
COUSIN JODY

10:30 – 10:45 – BUCKLEY'S RECORD SHOP
CHARLIE LOUVIN
JEAN SHEPARD
DEL WOOD

10:45 – 11:00 – NEWPORT
ROY ACUFF
BILLY WALKER
OSBORNE BROTHERS
CROOK BROTHERS

11:00 – 11:30 – COCA-COLA
HANK SNOW
BILL MONROE
JUSTIN TUBB
FRUIT JAR DRINKERS
DOTTIE WEST
BOBBY BARE
SAM & KIRK McGEE

11:30 – 12:00 – LAVA
ROY DRUSKY
LONZO & OSCAR
BILLY GRAMMER
MARION WORTH
BOB LUMAN
CONNIE SMITH
CURLY FOX

Marshall's Opry program from her first night in Nashville, Jan. 28, 1967

downtown to meet up with Cowboy at the Ramada Inn. And that's where we were when Fred Foster came bursting through the door with Kristofferson in tow. After Kris sang "Me and Bobby McGee," Cowboy asked him to sing it again. When he did, Cowboy said matter-of-factly, "That's a hit."

Like I said, the next time I saw Kristofferson, I was again with Cowboy and Walter Forbes. The two of them had picked me up in Jack's black Cadillac to go to a party at Doug Jeffords's house. This was toward the end of my junior year. By then, I was playing music with Vanderbilt classmate Woody Chrisman, who would later join the Grand Ole Opry as a member of Riders in the Sky.

I just received an email from Doug Jeffords in Ireland, and he had this to say: "The party was for a bunch from *The Johnny Cash Show*, plus assorted pickers. I had met Kris almost as soon as he hit town, but really got to know him during the *Cash Show*. Newbury was there, Vince Matthews, and some others. As I recall, you arrived with Clement, who Larry [Larry Murray, head writer for the *Cash Show*] had invited to drop by. You were in your TVC mode, while still looking like a real folkie. I knew immediately that you were someone much more interesting than the Vanderbilt coeds of that era! You looked around for a few minutes, then said, 'Shit! Woody's got to be here,' and departed to return with him."

This was late spring 1970. By then Woody had married and had a child, with another one on the way. He and his young family were living in an attic apartment on Pierce Avenue, where the Vanderbilt Children's Hospital is today. He was in bed with his wife and child when I knocked on their door.

"Hey, Woody!" BAM! BAM! BAM! "Get up! There's a party with some people from *The Johnny Cash Show*. I'm with Jack Clement and Walter Forbes and everybody's playing music!" So Woody got out of bed in his skivvies, grabbed his fiddle, and down the fire escape we went.

Next thing I know, we're pulling into Doug Jeffords's driveway.

Now, I wouldn't see Jeffords again for another twenty-seven years. Not until late one Sunday afternoon in June 1997. My husband Chris had wanted me to see a house being shown in the old Richland–West End neighborhood, but by the time we got there, visiting hours had ended. So I walked up on the porch hoping to get a peek, when I saw two men standing just inside the front door. As the realtor mouthed, "Sorry, we're closed," the other said, "Hey, that's Marshall Chapman. Open the door!" As it turned out, the other man was Doug Jeffords. So Chris and I ended up buying Doug's house, which is where we still live today. It amuses me to think we might never have lived here had I not crashed that party with Walter Forbes, Cowboy Jack Clement, and a snuff-dipping fiddle player wearing nothing but his skivvies.

Anyway, we must've been a sight walking into Doug's house that night. But the strange thing is, I just vaguely remember Mickey Newbury and Kristofferson and Vince Matthews being there, mainly because there were other, larger forces at play. This was just after Kent State, and when Walter (who had served two years in the Marines) said he didn't blame the National Guardsmen for shooting those students, I suddenly felt a seismic shift at my core. And even though I was still a virgin, I lost a big chunk of my innocence that night. The world I had been raised to believe in was not the world I was beginning to see. I looked at clean-shaven Walter, who'd gone back to Chattanooga to live the life of privilege I was raised to live, then glanced at scruffy-looking Kristofferson singing, "Freedom's just another word for nothing left to lose," and thought, *You can't have it both ways, Marshall. You're either free and open and sensitive to the world, or you're not.* And though I may not have been aware of it at the time, my soul was casting its lot with the scruffy-looking guys.

I'VE RUN INTO KRISTOFFERSON MANY times since those two nights from my Vanderbilt days—BMI parties, onstage at Tipitina's, backstage at the Troubadour, and so forth. Then there was that all-nighter in somebody's room at the King of the Road Motor Inn in Nashville. Kris was holding court with Billy Joe Shaver, me, Willie Nelson, Waylon Jennings, and Sammi Smith in attendance. Well, initially it was Kris, Billy Joe, Willie, and me. Sammi Smith came padding down from her room later on. Then *way* later on, Waylon just sort of blew into the room like a cyclone.

As I recall, Kris had been scheduled for an early morning appearance on a local TV show. But as the time for his scheduled appearance drew near, it became more and more apparent that nobody in this room would be making a scheduled appearance *anywhere*, much less on a local TV show. It wasn't that anybody was incapable, mind you, it's just that nobody wanted to leave. Then somebody turned on the TV to the station. At first, the show's host—looking television perfect—was going on and on about the fabulously talented Kris Kristofferson who was due to arrive any minute, and that's when we all started laughing. By the time the talking heads realized that Mr. Kristofferson would indeed *not* be making an appearance on their early morning TV show, we were rolling on the floor. It was an outlaw moment, for sure.

Before I go any further, let's get one thing straight. Men may not understand this, and I'm not sure I understand it, and even Kris may not be aware of it, but Kris Kristofferson has "it." By "it," I mean this: every woman I know—including level-headed women with no interest in pop culture, movie stars, or Hall of Fame songwriters—seems to go absolutely gaga for Kris Kristofferson. I've been observing this phenomenon for years, and I'll admit, I am not completely immune myself. I may have thought Kris a "scruffy-looking guy" when I first laid eyes on him forty years ago, but his "it" stock seems to have risen with the years. Case in point: in 1986, I was at a low point in my life. So one night, to cheer myself up, I ventured out to hear Delbert McClinton at a new club in Nashville called Music Row. The club was located on—you guessed it—Music Row. Anyway, it was a fun night. Bruce Channel, Tanya Tucker, and Will Lee from the Letterman show all sat in with Delbert's band. Delbert and I had recently recorded a duet of a song I wrote with Will Jennings called "Rockabilly Sweethearts." So when Delbert asked me to come out onstage and sing it, I, of course, obliged.

Later, while the band was loading up for New Orleans, I was talking to Wendy Goldstein, Delbert's wife and manager. Wendy must have sensed that I was blue. "Why don't you come to New Orleans with us?" she said. "Delbert and I are flying down in the morning. You can fly with us. We're going down a day early to see a new musical at the old Toulouse Theater. Allen Toussaint wrote the music. Delbert's playing Tipitina's the next night. What do you say?" Sounded good to me. So the next day, I'm on an early morning flight to New Orleans with Delbert and Wendy.

As we were checking into our hotel near the Quarter, I couldn't help but notice the scene in the lobby. It was like a circus. Everywhere you looked, there were people with tattoos all over their bodies, greeting other people with tattoos. People disrobing to show off their tattoos. I saw one man drop his trousers, while everyone around him was oohing and aahing over a particular detail. It didn't matter *where* a tattoo was located. These people were here to admire art. You never saw such a scene. At first, I thought we'd stumbled upon a Hell's Angels convention, then quickly realized not all were biker types. In fact, many defied classification. I saw one little old lady in a pink linen shift, wearing espadrilles and pearls, who—other than the tattoos covering both her arms—could've passed for a member of the Junior League. As it turned out, the National Tattoo Association was holding its ninth annual convention in our hotel.

So I'm standing there watching this scene, getting ready to take the elevator up, when Wendy says, "Oh, by the way, Kristofferson's playing Tipitina's tonight. We'll probably go there after the play."

Once in my room, I tried taking a nap, but my mind was too bothered with everything going on in my life. For the past year, I had been trying to extricate myself from an agonizing relationship. It had gotten to the point where I was finding it difficult to go out, like there was a neon sign on my forehead flashing WOMAN IN PAIN! WOMAN IN PAIN! everywhere I went. I was feeling way too vulnerable and I didn't like it. *Buck up, Marshall. Just put on a good face, girl. Come on, you can do it!* Finally, I got up and bathed and dressed.

Just as I was about to leave my room to meet Delbert and Wendy in the lobby, I walked over and stood at the window. A flock of birds was flying high in the sky. And in that moment, I began to pray. *Oh God, if I run into Kristofferson tonight, please help me see him as the sensitive human being You created, and not the sex symbol I'm trying to make him out to be in my mind. I would really appreciate it. Thank you. Amen.*

Of course, we ended up going to Tipitina's and Kris was there, playing with his band—a seasoned group that included Billy Swan and Stephen Bruton. The place was packed. And the women were out in full force. And I don't mean run-of-the-mill snuff queens. I watched with interest as a group of extremely well-heeled women cavorted about in front of the stage. "That's the governor's wife," somebody pointed out, " . . . with a bunch of her friends." By the end of the show, they were throwing jewelry, their underwear, calling cards with phone numbers, you name it. I mean, Kris was up there singing about Jesus, Gandhi, and Martin Luther King, and all this is going on.

Then Kris brought Delbert out to sing "Dust My Broom." As the band settled into a groove, I turned to the stage manager, pointed to a twelve-string guitar sitting in a stand, and said, "Okay if I play that?" He smiled and gestured gallantly toward the guitar: "Be my guest." So I walked out and picked up the twelve-string and began chunking along in the key of E, my favorite key. It felt good. Almost immediately, the neon sign on my forehead began to fade, until finally, it was gone. After "Dust My Broom," Delbert ambled over and handed me a black Stratocaster, and I proceeded to do "Betty's Bein' Bad" with Kris and Delbert singing *Bad! Bad! Bad!* in the background. We were rocking, having a ball, and Kris could not have been more gracious. After the set, we all went upstairs to Kris's dressing room. It was quite a scene. I was sitting in a chair, taking it all in, when I noticed a familiar-looking sofa in the corner. By then Kris had come over and we were talking.

"See that sofa over there?" I said. "Three years ago, I wrote a song sitting on that sofa."

A silver-tongued devil
With a heart of gold
A killer combination
If the truth be told

"Probably should've given you credit," I said, laughing. We both laughed. I was enjoying myself. It was territory I hadn't visited in a while.

After the show, we rode on Kris's bus back to his hotel. After saying our goodbyes in the lobby, Delbert's road manager, Keith DeArmond, went out front to hail us a cab. There was one on the curb, but the driver was asleep, his head slumped forward on the steering wheel. So Keith tapped on his window. The driver sputtered awake, then drove us back to our hotel.

OKAY. SO LET'S GET ANOTHER THING straight. I have a crush on Kris Kristofferson and I don't care who knows it, including my husband. Being a doctor, he's for anything that keeps my heart rate up. In fact, just the other night, I was asking him about this "it" business. How some people just seem to have "it," while others don't. So what exactly is "it"?

"Pheromones," he said.

"Pheromones?" (I love when he talks that doctor talk.)

"Yeah, women have it, men have it, animals have it, even insects have it. It's an odorless substance that acts on the brain to attract the opposite sex. Nobody knows what human pheromones are. Only that we have them."

Okay, I could go on, but I'm starting to blush. Mark Twain once said, "Man is the only animal that blushes—or needs to." Robert Mitchum once said, "If I die of anything, it'll be of embarrassment."

Sounds like as good a way to go as any. And a good place to stop for now.

A windy day in Malibu
November 5, 2008

So Kris, let's talk about Nashville. You lived there from . . .
From June of 1965 . . . ah . . . actually I went there first on leave from the army—I think at the end of May. I had just come back from Germany. I was supposedly on my way to teach English literature at West Point, and ended up going to Nashville on leave. I spent two weeks there with Cowboy Jack and Marijohn Wilkin and all these people . . . Bobby Bare . . .

So you came to Nashville directly from Germany?
Yeah, with one stop to be briefed at West Point. Then the next day, I went to Nashville and met all these people, and in two weeks, decided to change the direction of my life. I fell totally in love with the people I met and the things they were doing. They were all knocking each other out with songs. The first time I was on Music Row, I had walked up from the hotel where I was staying in downtown Nashville . . .

Do you remember the name of the hotel?
It was . . . *(long pause)* I can't remember now, but I'll tell you later if I think of it. It was a big, tall hotel *(laughs)* . . . ah . . .

The Andrew Jackson?
Could have been that.

The Andrew Jackson was where Roger Miller once worked as an elevator operator.
Yes, yes . . . that was it! Because they told me that. *(laughs)* You got it. And then I *walked* in uniform up to 16th Avenue South—I think on Demonbreun or something—the one that goes all the way up there, and I went in and met Marijohn Wilkin, who was a relative of my platoon leader [Don Kelsey] in Germany. While I was sitting in her

office, Johnny Darrell came over. He had just come onto the charts with his first record, which was "Green Green Grass of Home."

Oh, yeah. Darrell was the first to record that.
That's right. So he was on the charts and we were all celebrating. We went over and listened to it in Jack Clement's office.

Still in your uniform?
I'm still in uniform. Yeah, that's why they called me "Captain Kris" for many moons after that.

So you were a captain [in the army]?
Yeah. Anyway, we're going from Jack's office down to the Professional Club, you remember that? It was a club at the end of Music Row where you had to know the owner or whatever, back before you could buy liquor by the drink. And it was dark inside, and it was only people in the [music] business. If anybody came in who wasn't, they were just ostracized and out. So on the way over there, this guy came out of Cedarwood [music publishing company] and said to Darrell, "Porter's in there covering you right now." Porter Wagoner was recording "Green Green Grass of Home," and Johnny couldn't believe it, because they had offices right opposite each other *(laughs)* on the same hallway. And so for the rest of the night, he was just getting drunk. He felt horrible.

So this is your first night in Nashville *ever*?
First in Nashville ever.

You never came as a kid or anything?
No.

So you're how old, about thirty?
I was twenty-nine. Of course, I knew Nashville because I'd been listening to the Grand Ole Opry since before and after Hank Williams. But I'd never been to Nashville until that night. And then all this stuff was happening at once. I remember Jack and I stayed up the whole night.

That somehow doesn't surprise me.

He was showing me the building right next door, which was Acuff-Rose. Audrey Williams [Hank's widow] had an office in there. So we went in there and ran into Doug Kershaw, who was trying to sell the rights to "Louisiana Man." *(laughs)* I mean, this is my first night in Nashville. I went through two weeks of this. I'm thinking, "This is where I belong!" So then I got out of the army. It was heaven for me. It was hell for the rest of my family. But it was so exciting. I think Bobby Bare was there that night at the Professional Club.

How did you get to Nashville? What mode of transportation?

I flew.

From . . .

Washington, D.C. I had gone from there to New York to see about the West Point thing, and I had to go back to Washington to get out of the army. And I was very lucky to do that.

So what stands out most in your mind about your first twenty-four hours in Nashville?

All I remember is that they were sharing songs. And to me it was so exciting because that's exactly what I wanted to do.

Did you play any of your songs?

In fact, I did. I played one song.

What was it called?

"Vietnam Blues."

Oh, I think I've got a 45 of that somewhere at home. Didn't Chris Gantry record that?

Chris didn't. It was a disc jockey. And then Ralph Emery used to play it all the time. But when I played it that night, Jack [Clement] was the only one that responded to it. He thought it was well written.

So he encouraged you.

Oh, yeah. And I remember he took me down to the train station . . .

Union Station . . .

Yeah. It was just the two of us, and he told me how he used to get on trains and ride down to New Orleans and turn around and ride right back. I'm thinking, "This is one of the freer spirits I've ever run into!" And, of course, he hasn't changed a bit.

That's for sure. Okay, let's take a break.

(Later)

Jack once told me about a letter your mother had written you about this time—a well-written, very articulate letter about how you were throwing your life away coming to Nashville.

Yeah, I showed that letter to Jack. There was a passage in there where she says, "We were amused before, when you used to love Hank Williams, but to find that at the age of twenty-nine that your idol is Johnny Cash. Nobody out here knows anything about him except that he's a drug addict and been in jail for it." And when Jack saw that *(laughs)* he says, "Give me that letter! I'm showing this to John." So he did. And *that's* how I got to be introduced to Johnny Cash. I wasn't there when he gave it to John, or read it to him, but the first time I met John, when I was the janitor over at Columbia [Recording Studio], he said, "It's always great to get a letter from home, isn't it, Kris?" *(laughs)* And we were . . . you know, it's like we had a bond ever since then. And I think that's probably why he was as encouraging to me as he was. He even carried around a set of lyrics I wrote—a song he never recorded—but for a while, he carried it around in his wallet. The song was called "The Golden Idol." Nobody ever recorded it.

What was it about?

I got the idea watching a program on TV. The Aztecs were sacrificing these people. They would build up these little girls and make them like princesses, you know, treat them like royalty, then take them up to the top of a pyramid and kill them. And to me, it was symbolic of what they do to some stars. "They made a golden idol of the girl you used to be / Hanging bangles on your branches like a lonely Christmas tree / They dressed you fit for killing . . ." It was that kind of thing. He just liked the way the words sounded. Anyway though, the fact that I knew he was carrying that around in his wallet was . . .

That had to be encouraging.
Oh, shoot. Johnny Cash?

He was the man.
Yeah.

Okay. So you stayed in Nashville those first two weeks at the Andrew Jackson Hotel . . .
Yeah. And then when I came back to live, it scared Marijohn to death. She had driven me back to the hotel the last night I was there, and when I told her that I was going to come back and write for her, I remember her head just went and hit the steering wheel. She had been being nice because I was Donnie's friend from the army, you know? And she'd been taking me all these places, and now I was going to change my life?

She knew the sacrifice you were making . . .
Well, yeah . . . but she also . . .

. . . and that she was inheriting a stray!
Yeah. Like it was going to be up to *her* to make it worth my while?

I remember reading somewhere, Marijohn saying that a lot of your songs—the early ones, anyway—were real long.
God knows, they weren't commercial at all. None of the ones I had at that time—other than "Vietnam Blues"—ever got recorded. But I knew somehow that Nashville was where I belonged. Because everybody— like Chris Gantry and the guys that were around then—they were all living and dying for writing songs, and passing them to each other, you know. And it was a long process. At first, she [Marijohn] wouldn't even let me record my own demos. *(laughs)* Johnny Duncan sang them.

Marijohn didn't like the way you sang?
Oh, *nobody* liked the way I sang! *(much laughter)* It was thoroughly

drummed into me by then that I was not a singer. And I accepted that without question. The first guy that wanted to record me was . . .

Fred [Foster]?
Nope. It was Billy Sherrill [produced "Stand by Your Man"].

Get out of here!
When I was working over at Columbia, I was all the time giving him my demos to pitch, to get them recorded by people he was recording, and he asked me one day—and it was "The Golden Idol"—he said, "How'd you like to take a shot at recording that? . . . and we'll release it."

Wow . . .
(laughs) And I said, "The janitor gets to . . ."

The Singing Janitor!
Well, yeah. Hey! That's exactly what I think Bucky Wilkin said: "What are you going to be? . . . the Singing Janitor?"

So did you record it?
Yeah, I did. And we tried to cut another one, too. It was "Jesse Younger."

Was it with session guys? . . . like Harold Bradley and those guys?
Yeah. But I knew all those guys because *(laughs)* I'd emptied their ashtrays for two years. And they were all on my side. But it wasn't anything that they [CBS Records] had any way of marketing. I think we sold seven copies. And later when Fred [Foster] wanted me to record, I thought I was still under contract to Billy, and I remember I went and told him Fred wanted to cut a whole album of my songs and wondered if I could get out of the contract, and he said, "Well, let me check it out." And then he said, "You know something? You're not even under contract here. You've got my blessings."

So the next time you come to Nashville, you're coming back to live.
That's right.

Did you come back alone?

I came back alone . . . because my wife . . . there was no way . . .

Nashville wasn't what she'd signed up for.

No. And it's understandable. Because any time I was doing music when I was in Germany in the army, it was always something horrible for her to have to go through. Because I'd be down getting drunk at the Enlisted Men's Club or the Rod & Gun Club or wherever we were playing, just getting as drunk as I could to get up the nerve to sing. So when she found out we were going to move to what to her was Hicktown, USA . . . It wasn't the Nashville that you lived in, because you were at Vanderbilt with all the upper class . . .

Well, you know . . . that's how I snuck in.

But where *we* were . . . well, eventually I got the job at Columbia. Although it was not something to be particularly proud of, it was a great job for me. But they [his wife and two children] came back, and I rented a house over near West End somewhere, right behind some school.

Will Campbell said you used to live near his office.

Oh, that was after I broke up with my wife. I moved into a condemned building on Music Row, and he was down below me. The building was owned by a real character, a woman who was sort of the oddball of Music Row. I remember her chewing me out for not fixing the front door at Columbia Records. Kathy Gregory was her name. Her husband, Bobby Gregory, had written "Sunny Side of the Mountain," and she had that written on their garbage can. He was bedridden all the time and she was just nuttier than a fruitcake.

Did you have, like, a room?

I had one big room and a bathroom and a kitchen . . . and holes in the wall bigger than I was. It was really a rough looking place.

Rats?

I never saw any rats. At least not the rodent kind. *(laughs)*

Kris Kristofferson   21

Did you have a bed? Was there, like, a mattress on the floor?
I had a bed.

So the room was furnished.
Aw, jeez, it looked like it'd been hit by . . . One time the police came because Kathy caught somebody trying to steal the clothes I had hanging in my closet, some old army uniforms, nothing really, and, of course, there was stuff all over the floor. Anyway, I went in there—I couldn't tell that anybody had even been in there—and I had to call the police, you know, because Kathy had caught someone carrying my clothes out the door. So when the police came, they said, "Wow, they really trashed the place." And of course, they [the thieves] hadn't touched it! *(laughs)*

People were always staying there, because every other week I was going down and flying helicopters in the Gulf of Mexico. I'd be a week down there, then come back for a week. And while I was gone, people would—either with my consent or not—go in there and stay for a few days. One of them—I can't remember his name now—he was a nice guy, a songwriter, but a total loser, and he found some weed I had brought back from the Gulf. I didn't smoke at that time—I had brought it back to give to Mickey Newbury, who did. Anyway, this guy found the weed, and I guess he got loaded on the bed or something because he burned a *big hole* in the mattress. So the rest of the time I lived there, I had this hole in the mattress which she [Kathy Gregory] had put out with beer.

Yuk!
(laughs) So that's where I lived.

How long did you live there?
Almost two years.

Where on Music Row was it? I guess I could call Will [Campbell] and find out.
You know where Combine [Music] was?

Yeah.
There was one house between us and Combine.

I remember Will had an office on Music Row in the mid- to late '60s. He was sort of the "preacher-at-large" for some organization [Committee of Southern Churchmen] trying to reconcile the civil rights struggle with white southern churches.
Yeah, that was it. But it was a condemned building. And Will's place wasn't a mess like mine was.

Would it be safe to say that in those years, you were not a housekeeper?
Yes. And I've never become one. *(laughs)* But Will Campbell was a hero to me from the first time I met him. And I'm pleased to hear he's writing another book. I remember reading some stuff he'd written that I really liked. Then I heard he was a preacher for the Klan. And I said, "Explain something to me. Maybe I didn't understand the things of yours that I read, because, ah, it just doesn't match." And he said, "Well, Kris, you know, I had heard that you've got a lot of education and that you're a pretty intelligent guy. Can you think of anybody who needs a preacher more?" And I just said, "Well, I guess you're right."

That's Will for you. "If you love one, you've got to love 'em all."
Oh, he is absolutely the only person like him I've ever known.

And that's his whole ministry: it's easy to love people who believe and think like we do. He would march with Dr. King one week, then go baptize the children of Robert Shelton [Grand Dragon of the Klan] the next.
Yeah. He was the real thing, that Will Campbell. Those were interesting times.

Okay. So when you came back to Nashville to live in June of '65, you lived with your wife in the house off West End . . .
. . . until '67.

So she was with you for about two years. Then after she left, you moved to the room above Will's office on Music Row?
That's right.

Were you flying helicopters to oil rigs in the Gulf while you were married?
I did it for one year while I was married. And then I kept flying up until . . . until . . . *(lowers voice)* I had to leave. I was in fact fired. I was breaking their rules against drinking and flying. But that's not the only reason I got fired. I went out with somebody's girlfriend.

Would that somebody have been in a position to fire you?
He was my boss! *(laughs)* I was safe as long as I was working out in the Gulf. Because there's no wine, women, or song out there. But after a couple of years—or right before a couple of years—they moved me onto the ground. I was living in a house they had for pilots. I was going out and raising hell every night, which I couldn't do sixty miles out in the Gulf. So it didn't take me too long to get in too much trouble. That was back when I was writing "Bobby McGee" and all those songs. But anyway, I remember going back to Nashville in March of '69. And when I told Mickey Newbury I'd been fired, he said, "Great! Johnny Cash has got a new TV show up here. And they're all staying at the . . ." I think it was the Ramada Inn.

The one downtown, on the James Robertson Parkway?
Yes.

That's where I met you! Or at least where I heard you sing "Bobby McGee" that night. There were some guys from *The Johnny Cash Show* . . . Larry Murray . . .
Yes. Larry Murray was head of music for the *Cash Show*. Those shows were so great because there were so many different stars coming into town every week—two different shows full of people who had never come to Nashville before. I just saw one of them the other night—Gordon Lightfoot. I just went and saw him up here in northern California.

I remember sitting in the front row of the balcony [at the Ryman]—I went to one taping where they had Tony Joe White, Linda Ronstadt, Neil Young—that's when I heard him [Young] sing "A Man Needs a Maid."
Yeah!

And I wanted to shout, "A woman does, too!"
(big laughs) Yeah. Oh, yeah. Well, it was great times.

It was electric.
It was almost like a God-sent thing for me because it was right when I thought I was going to be sued by my ex for not paying her enough child support. Because I didn't have a source of income anymore. And then all of a sudden, within weeks, I had all those songs cut.

Do you think *The Johnny Cash Show* was the catalyst for that?
Oh, yeah. Because I was really out of the business when I was down there in the Gulf. I'd come back for a week and try and hustle songs. But you had to be there [in Nashville] all the time. So when I told Mickey I'd been fired, he said, "This is great! I've got a room here and we can pitch songs to *everybody*. So we became like—through Larry Murray—the mascots of *The Johnny Cash Show*. And so Linda Ronstadt, Neil Young, Joni Mitchell . . . there was all kinds of stars coming in who'd never been to Nashville while I'd been there.

A friend of mine, Carlana Harwell—she was Carlana Moscheo then—did make-up for the *Cash Show*, and she remembers you just sitting in the make-up room, playing songs for anybody who would listen.
Oh, yeah . . .

'Cause that's where the stars were coming in to get made up. And I'm thinking, "Man, that's smart . . . just go in there and lay it on 'em!"
Can you believe anyone having the audacity? Because I *knew* by this time that I wasn't really a singer like the people I admired, like Lefty

Frizzell and Hank Williams and George Jones . . . real singers, you know? But to have the nerve to subject people . . . when they couldn't move *(laughs)* in a make-up chair or something . . .

Like playing a prison.
Yeah. They can't leave!

I think I've probably got enough here, Kris. I can't think of anything else . . . Okay, one more: how much longer were you in Nashville, after you had the place above Will [Campbell], when everybody started cutting your songs? Were you still in Nashville when Sammi [Smith] cut "Help Me Make It Through the Night" in 1971?
Ah . . . well, I kept the place. I started going on the road in 1970.

Was that when you played the Newport Folk Festival?
Well, that was the beginning of it. *(Papers start blowing off the table. Kris picks them up.)* Vince Matthews and I drove up to that show and when we got there, John [Johnny Cash] asked me to sing two songs during his set. I remember reading an article about the Newport Folk Festival—how Dylan had given John a credibility with an audience he hadn't been exposed to. Dylan idolized John, just like I did. And so he made John a hero up there, okay? Well, John did the same thing for me.

What two songs did you sing?
"Bobby McGee" and "Sunday Morning Coming Down." I remember they didn't want me to sing. I remember the guy saying, "You know, John, you've only got forty minutes up there." And Carl Perkins said—Carl was supposed to open for John, he was playing with him then. Plus there were people who had come to Newport just to hear Carl Perkins—and Carl says, "Hell, just introduce me as the 'late and great'—you can take my place."

What a sweetheart.
Oh, I couldn't believe it! Well, they didn't make him do that. But I got to sing the two songs and they went over very well. So that next

afternoon they asked me to be on one of those songwriter things where they had James Taylor, Joni Mitchell . . . all the big stars that were playing, and I got to get up there with them. And so from then on, I got offers to play—folk festivals mainly. That was in '69. Then, about a year later when I was at Janis's house up in the Bay Area with Bobby Neuwirth, I got an offer from one of the Johnny Cash people again—a girl that had worked with their production company—to open for Linda Ronstadt at the Troubadour. That was in June of '70. From then on, it was just one thing after another.

So how long after that did you live or pay rent in Nashville?
Well, I started to say earlier, but I got sidetracked talking about myself. *(laughs)* But I took off in '70 when I started playing. I remember Janis saying, "Boy, you are gone! You're just going to gypsy on down the road." And it was true. I went from one gig to another. So from '70 on, I was on the road. But I kept my place in Nashville.

So whatever happened to the mattress with the hole in it? Did you buy a new one with the royalties?
Nah . . . I just turned it over! *(laughs)* And it stayed like that for two years. I finally let go of that place in 1972.

So you never stayed there those last two years?
God no, it was horrible.

Yet, you kept paying rent?
(laughs)

Why are you laughing?
Well, the rent was only fifty dollars a month!

So did you keep it, thinking, "All this could disappear and I might have to go back to that room"? Or did you just symbolically want to feel like you were still connected to Nashville?
I don't know. I guess I just . . . wanted to remember.

Mary Gauthier

I MET MARY GAUTHIER IN THE SUMMER of 2007 at a party at Beth Nielsen Chapman's house. Only I wasn't aware I was meeting Mary Gauthier. I thought I was meeting someone named Mary with no last name. Like Cher or Charo. I was making my way through a buffet line of Mediterranean food when someone said, "Hey Marshall, have you met Mary?"

I looked up at the bright-eyed woman standing across from me. "Oh, hi Mary," I said.

At first, I thought maybe she was the cook. She exuded that kind of confidence. It wasn't until later that I realized "Mary" was Mary Gauthier, a critically acclaimed singer-songwriter I'd been hearing about for several years from artist friends in-the-know. Harlan Howard once made the distinction between run-of-the-mill songwriters and those few he considered "dangerous at all times." From everything I'd been hearing, Mary was one of those few.

That night at Beth's, my husband Chris and I retreated with our plates of food to a cozy sunken living-room-type area where we found ourselves in the company of Ashley Cleveland, Mary, and two or three others. As I recall, the food was delicious and the conversation lively, as Ashley regaled us with stories of her recent escapades as a soup kitchen volunteer. At one point, Mary and I engaged in conversation about something, I can't quite remember what—maybe global warming. I found her bright, openhearted, and intense. Usually, I feel like I'm the one who's too intense at social gatherings. It's true. Small talk has never been my forte. But with Mary Gauthier in the room, it was like the intensity quota was filled, and I could just relax and enjoy myself.

One thing I've noticed about Nashville: you hear about some new singer-songwriter moving to town, and you don't run into them for years. Then when you finally meet, it's like—BAM! They're suddenly everywhere! The Village Cleaners, Walgreens, Target, Prince's Hot Chicken off Dickerson Road, you name it. Sure enough, a few days after I met Mary Gauthier, I ran into her at the Produce Place on Murphy Road. After exchanging stories in the parking lot, I warned her I might be stalking her for this book. And now, here we are.

Mary's townhouse
A clear, cold Nashville day
January 9, 2008

So Mary, when did you first hear the word "Nashville"?
Umm . . . I don't remember. But when I ran away from home as a kid, [I] stole my parents' car, which only had AM radio. So there were only country radio stations or gospel-preaching stations, so I stuck to the country radio stations. And I'm sure that's probably when I first started hearing about Nashville. Either that, or it was *The Lynn Anderson Show.* When I was a kid, television would go dark at night. Then when it would come on in the morning, it would come on with the national anthem and then Lynn Anderson on Sunday morning. So it was the national anthem and then, *(sings)* "I beg your pardon / I never promised you a . . ." And then maybe they announced it coming from Nashville, Tennessee.

I remember that show. It was on one of the networks.
So we sat there waiting for it . . . you know . . . waiting for the buzz to go away.

So when you ran away from home, was "home" New Orleans?
Well, I was born in New Orleans, then lived in Baton Rouge as a kid, so I ran away from Baton Rouge.

So you stole your parents' car?
I did.

What age were you?
Fifteen.

That sounds like a book in itself.
It is.

I look forward to reading it. *(laughter)* **What kind of car was it?**
It was one of those station wagons with the fake wood on the side, like a *Brady Bunch* car.

So where'd you go in that car?
You know . . . I . . . it's hard to put all that together. It's a strange story. I stole a car, and . . . and ended up somehow in a detox. I'm not sure exactly how it all came together.

So there were some missing years.
There was some missing stuff, but I ended up in a detox on my sixteenth birthday.

Okay. So how long have you lived here in Nashville?
I moved to Nashville in September 2001.

September 2? Oh, September *of* 2001.
Well, it was *about* September 2, because I didn't have any . . . my stuff wasn't here, and I know I'd just gotten here that first week in September, because when September 11 happened, I didn't have a television to watch it on. And I didn't know anybody, so I stood outside on the sidewalk in Hillsboro Village and watched at that bar . . . you know that bar that has all those televisions in there, where you can stand outside on the sidewalk and watch TV?

Sam's [Sports Bar & Grill]?
Yeah, that's the one.

Um, 2001. So you're a recent arrival.
Yeah.

Mary Gauthier and Marshall at the Bluebird Café, Oct. 10, 2009

Had you ever been here before?
I came here once for Tin Pan South, as a fan.

So how long did you stay in town?
For that?

Yeah.
Well, that's another little story. When I came, it was the day the tornados hit Nashville.

April of 1998? You arrived the day of the tornados?
Yeah, the tornados hit just after I landed.

Would it be safe to say drama has followed you all your life?
My *whole* life . . . *(laughter)* . . . the whole time.

Okay, so you first came to Nashville on an airplane. Where were you flying from?
From Boston.

A commercial airline?
Commercial airline.

Nonstop?
Yeah.

So you get here, and . . . where'd you stay?
Well, that's another whole story. We couldn't get to the hotel we were supposed to get to, because the tornados were hitting.

You say "we." Were you not by yourself?
I was traveling by myself. But I was in a shuttle bus full of people who worked for the airlines—stewardesses and pilots and so forth.

Going to the hotel?
Going to the hotel. We ended up at the Maxwell House . . .

So the tornado had just hit . . .
It was *hitting*. We were rushed out of the shuttle bus into an underground parking lot. So we were in there while the tornados hit, then we got back in the shuttle bus. There were tree limbs down everywhere. We couldn't . . . downtown was pretty maxed out at that point. So we couldn't get to the hotel we were supposed to go to. Nobody knew *where* they were going to go, then somebody radioed that there were a couple of rooms available at the Maxwell House.

So that's where you ended up spending the night?
That's where I ended up spending the night.

How long were you in Nashville?
A couple of days. They did Tin Pan South anyway. So I stayed for the event.

Other than the tornado, is there anything else in particular you remember, that maybe only could have happened in Nashville?
Yeah . . . yeah . . . I remember that Billy Joe and Eddy [Shaver] were supposed to play at Wolfy's, but Wolfy's was destroyed by the tornado, so they moved their gig over to some other place on Broadway. I was walking down the street and just happened to see them there by accident. I just went in, and there was Eddy and Billy Joe.

So you knew who they were?
I knew who they were because of their music, but I'd never seen them in person. So I just sat there and watched them and thought, *Man, I love this town. I'm gonna come here. It's just a matter of time. All I have to do is get out of two restaurants, a bad relationship, and Boston. (laughs)*

That's great . . . yeah, hearing Eddy and Billy Joe. That would inspire *me* to move.
Ahh . . . Eddy was so freakin' *loud*. And Billy Joe loved it. He was just smiling and laughing, and Eddy just got louder and louder and louder, and it was . . . I just remember that, along with the fact that the wall behind where they were playing had just been wiped out by the tornados. It was . . . you know . . . I was *done*. I knew I was coming here.

So you go back to Boston . . .
I go back to Boston with a plan. I'm coming to Nashville.

So . . .
I knew I had to find a way to get out of the restaurant I owned, and divest myself of everything I was connected to in Boston. It was a process that took three years.

So when you came back, did you drive?
Oh yeah.

U-Haul?
Yeah.

By yourself?
By myself.

What kind of car?
Um, nineteen ninety . . . six? . . . Subaru Outback.

What color?
Red . . . and silver.

Silver interior?
Yeah.

Got it.
(We take a break while Mary brews some hot tea—
Earl Grey with agave)

Were you a fan of country music?
Yes.

Who were your favorites growing up?
I always loved Willie. I always loved Merle. I still do and always will
. . . love George Jones . . . and Tammy Wynette . . .

Drama! *(laughs)*
Yeah. I loved the drama people.

George and Tammy, man, when they were together, it was like . . .
fireworks! And of course there was that time she got kidnapped. I
remember going to a Halloween party and my costume was "Tammy
after the Kidnapping." Some people in Nashville didn't think that
was funny.
Okay. So what would you say made you move here? Had you
already started performing in Boston?
Yeah, I had started in the folk scene in Boston. At that point, I had
put out two CDs. They were very southern-tinged. I didn't fit in the
folk scene in Boston, but I knew I didn't want to come to Nashville

prematurely, 'cause somebody early on had told me, "You've got one chance to make a first impression." So I knew I needed to *suck* in Boston—get that out of the way *before* I came to Nashville. I was old enough to know I had some growing to do as an artist, and mountains to climb onstage before I could even begin to be comfortable at it. So I had those three years of working up there. But I knew I was going to come to Nashville, because in my mind—and I still believe this—the best songwriters in the world are in this town. I knew I had to be here. I didn't know if I'd ever even be in the game here, but I knew that I wanted to come here and be a part of being lifted up by other people's greatness. But I didn't want to come here and suck. So I had to kind of wait it out, and get better, and do the road. That's a booming voice that told me, "You've got one chance at a first impression." And so I'm glad I took that to heart.

Like B.B. King once said, "You don't want to make a move too soon."
Exactly.

I was intrigued to see you wrote your first song at age thirty-five. And I thought *I* was a late bloomer. If you would, talk for a minute about getting a late start in music.
Yeah, I owned a couple of restaurants. I worked in restaurants all my life, and then I quit college and moved to Boston for reasons . . . I don't even know why I moved to Boston, but . . .

Where'd you go to college?
I went to LSU. Studied philosophy for six years then realized there was no meaning.

Okay, so you move to Nashville. You're a songwriter. Were you looking for a publishing deal?
Yeah, I came here and I knew I needed a publishing deal. I didn't really know what a publishing deal *was*. Coming from the [Boston] folk scene, people don't make money on copyrights up there; they just make money touring, because the songs aren't commercial enough to

be marketable. But I knew I needed a publishing deal, even though I didn't know what one was. I had taken some classes from Ralph Murphy—he teaches quite a bit—and Murphy became a mentor of sorts. And he'd always talk about Harlan Howard, Harlan Howard, Harlan Howard . . . and he'd quote Harlan, and he'd use Harlan's wise words a lot in his lectures, so all I knew when I came here was Harlan Howard and Ralph Murphy.

Those are two good ones.
So I figured out that I should go knock on the door that said HARLAN HOWARD SONGS. So I did. And I got an appointment—I didn't even know Harlan was dead. I didn't know Harlan. I'd never met Harlan Howard. He had died a few months before. So I went to Harlan Howard Songs and knocked on the door. His widow [Melanie Howard] runs the business, and she let me play her a couple of songs. I'd written one called "I Drink" that got her attention. And we started going back and forth, and I'm not quite sure how this happened, but a year later, I'm sleeping in Harlan Howard's side of the bed.

That's surreal.
It was scary. It was scary . . . 'cause they had this urn thing over . . . like this antique bed frame with this urn thing, and she jokingly said, "Harlan's up there," and I jumped the hell out of that bed! She has little jars with his ashes all over the place. Willie has one on his bus.

(nervous laughter) **You think that helped your songwriting?**
It scared the shit out of me. It was completely intimidating and unfathomable that I lived there . . . this is . . . my story is beyond me.

Well, that's something that could only have happened in Nashville, that's for damn sure.
So it was through Melanie that I got to know Harlan. I got to know his songs. There's five thousand songs in the office that Harlan Howard wrote. And only a couple hundred of them have been recorded. So there's four thousand Harlan Howard songs that the world has not heard—in that office, demoed up. It's like a who's who

. . . I mean, *decades* of different people coming through Nashville are singing them. Everyone from the Judds to Garth Brooks singing demos of the songs Harlan wrote. So I get to know him through Melanie. It's funny . . . he was given away by his mother, and so was I. We both have this orphan heart. Melanie used to say she was put on earth to . . . take care of orphans or something, but she let me listen to all those songs, and I really felt like I got to know him.

Yeah, I met Harlan when I first started out and felt fortunate that he took an interest in my writing. In fact, the very first song I ever wrote I demoed at Wilderness Music, an office he had on 17th Avenue South. I remember while we were recording, someone from the city came by to ask if it was okay for the city to plant a couple of magnolia trees in front of his building, and Harlan says, "Sure. I got nothing against magnolias!" So they planted these little sticks. 'Course now when you drive down there, they're huge! Man, that was thirty-five years ago. *(laughs)* You were in Baton Rouge waiting for *The Lynn Anderson Show* to come on.

Anyway, every time I see those magnolia trees, I think of Harlan. I remember one winter it was real cold—snowing and everything—and Harlan was worried I'd freeze to death. I was always running around without enough clothes on. So one morning, I heard this knocking at my door, and it was Harlan with a red and black lumber jacket he'd bought for me. He said, "Here, wear this. It'll keep you warm."

Yeah, that's that orphan heart. It's a profound thing. He just wanted you to love him. And if any more came of it, I'm sure it would have been no problem! *(laughs)*

Rodney Crowell

IN THE FALL AND WINTER of 1972, Rodney Crowell and I both
happened to work at T.G.I. Friday's on Elliston Place in Nashville. We
weren't there for more than a few months, but I distinctly remember
Rodney. He never said much. In fact, I don't remember him saying
a word the entire time he worked there. Whenever I tried talking to
him, he'd sort of smile at me with those big blue eyes of his. He seemed
friendly enough, but in a spaced-out kind of way.

Rodney was a busboy and I was the seater-greeter. I don't think either of us considered our jobs a career move. We were just trying to pay
the rent, while waiting for some kind of break in the music business.

Being seater-greeter required that I greet customers at the door and
take them to their tables. There I would hand out menus and say, "Your
waiter will be with you in a moment." Friday's was a popular place, and
customers often had to wait to be seated. I remember one time during
lunch rush, Irving Waugh, who was president of WSM, came in with
some business associates. Only I didn't know he was Irving Waugh. I
just saw him as another hungry customer.

"Name please?" I said, holding my pad and pen.

"Waugh," he replied, smiling.

"How do you spell that?"

A few of his friends chuckled. His smile faded, his jaw clenched.

"W-A-U-G-H," he said. (He seemed pissed.)

"Okay, I'll call you when your table's ready. It shouldn't be long."

A few minutes later, I walked over to where he was standing.

"W-A-U-G-H? Your table is ready. This way, please."

A few days later, I got moved from seater-greeter to bartender. The
manager wanted to try, as sort of a promotional gimmick, having female bartenders on Wednesday nights. So I was the first female bar-

tender at T.G.I. Friday's in Nashville, Tennessee. Another entry for my food and beverage resumé.

As a bartender, I was enthusiastic and incompetent. Occasionally, when using the little bar gun that squirted out water, tonic, soda, Coke, or Seven-Up, I would press the wrong button and a Scotch and soda would end up Scotch and tonic. Most of my customers were men, and they seemed to take it all in stride. Often when presenting a drink, I would say, "Hope this isn't too strong for you, sir." I was known for my generosity when it came to mixing the alcohol portion of my drinks, perhaps as compensation for my bar gun deficiencies.

Another one of my responsibilities as seater-greeter was making sure the busboys had properly set the tables. Most of them were fairly adept, if not teachable. But Rodney was hopeless. After bussing a table, he would casually toss down the new silverware like somebody playing pick-up sticks. I remember trying to explain to him about folding the napkin and placing it on the left where the fork goes, and so on. I'd be talking on and on, while Rodney just stared at me with those big, blue, spaced-out eyes, which, of course, made me nervous. I sensed there was a lot going on in that noggin of his, but he wasn't giving anything away.

OVER THE YEARS, I HAVE privately cheered Rodney on while watching him develop as a songwriter, producer, recording artist, and human being. In March 1988, I was at McCabe's, a guitar store and performance hall in Santa Monica, the night he did a show with his then-wife, Rosanne Cash. It was just the two of them, accompanied by Steuart Smith on guitar. Rodney was flying in from somewhere, so the show was a reunion of sorts for the couple. Regardless, he was late, so Rosanne went ahead and started without him. I was sitting in the audience with my good friend Diana Haig, and we're thinking, *Oh my God, what's gonna happen now?* About halfway through the first song, Rodney finally walked out on the stage. I'll never forget the expression on Rosanne's face—a combination of love, relief, and *Where the hell have you been?* The cool thing was she never stopped playing. She just said, "Catch up!" and that was that.

The rest of the show was basically about Rodney working his way back into her good graces. And, man, did he evermore bring out the arsenal! Charm, humor, talent, good looks . . . you name it. The dynamics between them brought to mind a scene from a play I'd seen in New York in 1983—a revival of Noël Coward's *Private Lives*, starring Elizabeth Taylor and Richard Burton. Miss Taylor was reclining on a chaise lounge, minding her own business, when Mr. Burton suddenly reached down and, with both hands, began playfully shaking her bosoms. It was an unscripted moment that took everyone by surprise, including Miss Taylor. I'll never forget the expression on *her* face. It was similar to Rosanne's—love mixed with other things. But in Miss Taylor's case, those "other things" were years of exasperation, combined with disbelief—as in, *I can't fuckin' believe you just did that!*

Anyway, McCabe's was magic. It wasn't so much what anybody said or did—Rodney and Rosanne sang beautifully and the songs were great—but there was something in the air between them. Something you could feel. The electricity coming off the stage was palpable. Whatever it was, it must have been real, because I have heard that their third daughter, Carrie, was conceived later that night.

IN THE 1980S, A BUNCH OF US used to go to our friend Virginia Team's land out on Little Marrowbone Road near Ashland City, just outside of Nashville. The land was about seventy acres of wooded ridges with campsites and a spring-fed pond where people could fish and swim. I called it "Virginia Beach." I remember Rodney and Rosanne and the girls being out there on more than one occasion. I can't remember if they skinny-dipped, but that's what most of us did. It was like an alternative country club.

Once in the early 1990s, I happened to be at the Ace of Clubs in Nashville the night Rodney played with a band that included Kenny Vaughan on lead guitar. I can still hear their version of "Highway 61 Revisited." Those guys raised the roof! Until that night, I'd always considered Rodney a country-folk singer-songwriter. But after that show, I'm thinking, *Damn, that mojo can rock!*

More than any artist of my generation, Rodney seems to have evolved to a place that moves me in a profound way. I have just about worn out "Rock of My Soul" from his *Houston Kid* CD (2001) and "Time to Go Inward" from *Fate's Right Hand* (2003).

During the 2003 Southern Festival of Books, I hosted my annual literary in-the-round at the Bluebird Café. It was me, Matraca Berg,

Marshall and Rodney Crowell at Rodney's house, Jan. 24, 2010

Clyde Edgerton, and Jill McCorkle. At one point, Rodney sat in and read from his work-in-progress memoir. I clearly remember the passage—about him as a twelve-year-old, crashing his bicycle while trying to impress a girl.

More recently, Rodney was here at the house having fried chicken with Chris and me and Dub and Joan Cornett. We were talking about old times, and when I mentioned the table-setting incident from our days at T.G.I. Friday's, Rodney laughed and said, "Aw, Marshall, you know my heart wasn't in bussing those tables."

My house in Nashville
January 16, 2008

So Rodney, let's talk about when you first came to Nashville that August night in 1972. How'd you get here?
In a '65 Chevy Impala.

What color was it?
Baby blue.

What about the interior?
Interior was white and, ah, little bit darker blue—rolled, pleated . . . it was Donivan Cowart's car.

So you didn't have a car?
I had a Nova . . . a Chevy Nova . . . a '69 Chevy Nova. But it wasn't as cool as my first car, which was a '63 Chevy Nova Super Sport with red bucket seats. Three on the column, you know, spoked wheels. A little white job . . . oh, it was great. I later traded it for a new one. But coming to Nashville, we were in Donivan's '65.

Was this your first time in Nashville?
Yeah. We left Houston . . . well, there's the story how we got here. We had gone to Crowley, Louisiana, to make a record with this guy.

You and Donivan?
Me and Donivan. We went to Crowley, Louisiana, to this studio
J.D. Miller owned. It was that studio where they made all those race
records back in the '60s, you know . . . those nasty records . . . you
ever hear any of those?

You mean like "Annie Had a Baby"?
Yeah. "You go down to San Antone / You'll see the same as I do."
They made all those records there. And above the studio was a beauty
shop. What is that stuff they used to . . . that really foul, acrid-
smelling stuff?

**Oh, yeah . . . when you get a permanent . . . it's got ammonia
in it . . . that perm-set stuff.**
Yeah, well, it came through the floors. So we're up there making
a record, just drenched in that smell. But it wasn't really a record.
There was a guy named Pee Wee Whitewing who's a steel guitar
player down there, and he pulled me aside—he was a nice guy—and
he said . . .

Wait a minute. Pee Wee Whitewing? You're making that up.
Pee Wee Whitewing. He was Hank Thompson's steel guitar player.
He lived in Crowley.

Is Crowley near Shreveport?
No, it's down south, between Lake Charles and Lafayette. Anyway,
he says, "Hey Rodney. You think you're making a record, but you're
not." And I said, "No, I'm making a record. You saw me. You were
right there in the studio." And he says, "No, you *think* you're making
a record. But you're not. You'll find out." He said, "This producer,
he's not really a producer. You seem like a pretty nice guy. I just need
to tell you." So I got all huffy and stiff. Anyway, so the producer goes
to Nashville, and he calls me and says, "Okay. I've signed you to a
ten-year recording contract with Columbia Records, and you're going
on the road with Kenny Rogers and the First Edition. You need to
get on up here." I might have had eight hundred dollars on me at the

time, 'cause I was playing . . . I had a steakhouse gig. So I went and bought a brand new D-35 [guitar], and we got in the car and took off. I had about three hundred bucks left.

So you drive back to Houston. Then . . .
We got in the car, took some pills, and drove to Nashville.

Did you stop?
No.

To get gas, right?
Not even to get gas. We were running on fumes and willpower! *(laughter)* But if we stopped, it wasn't for long. We certainly didn't eat. We weren't hungry. We were smoking cigarettes, going to Nashville.

Who did most of the driving?
Donivan. He drove, and I did commentary.

So you were the color commentator.
I was the color commentator: "Well, we just went through Little Rock. You know, I've never been to Little Rock. Hey! Look over there!"
 So we were heading to Nashville as fast as we could go. We couldn't stop, because we were going on the road with Kenny Rogers and the First Edition, and we didn't want them to leave without us! *(laughs)* But we didn't even have any instructions as to where to *go*. I mean, inquiring minds would have said, "Okay, so who do we meet up with when we get to Nashville?" It never occurred to us to think about that. We just got in the car and popped the clutch and took off.

So where did you spend your first night in Nashville?
I'll tell you. Well, the first thing we did when we came in to Nashville off the freeway . . . Here's the image of me and Donivan when we got to Nashville, just grinding our teeth and blaring. We head downtown and slide in sideways. The dust clears, and we get out rubbing our hands together. Then it dawns on us—this was just after dark—"Wait a minute. Where's the welcoming committee? Who do we look for? What do we do?"

The producer from Crowley was there [in Nashville], right?
No. *(laughs)* He had sold our record and the publishing rights for a hundred dollars, then bought himself a bus ticket. So while we were driving up here, he's on a bus going back to Louisiana with a hundred dollars.

So the Kenny Rogers tour never materialized.
(laughs) Yeah, right!

Did you know *anybody* in Nashville?
Not a soul. Did not know a soul. We didn't know anybody. And like I said, we were so excited about our new record deal and going on the road, we didn't bother to ask who we look up. *(laughs)*

How old were you?
Twenty-one. So finally we were sitting around downtown near 2nd Avenue—seems like we hit the river, then got out and walked around a while, saying, "I wonder what we do?" So then we drove back up Broadway to where it becomes West End, then drove on out to Highway 70, where it peels to the right, then turned around. So for about three hours, we just cruised back and forth . . . I mean, we had no sophistication. I don't know that I'd ever stayed in a hotel my whole life.

So you were green.
I was green, you know, a poor white boy. I'd been to college, but . . .

Where'd you go to college?
Stephen F. Austin in Nacogdoches.

How far did you make it through?
Two and a half years. I did a year seriously. The next year and a half, I did *un*seriously. My studies were English. The only thing that I really enjoyed out of college was . . . I started to read, you know, started reading poetry. And I remember reading *The Red Badge of Courage* by Stephen Crane. And some Joseph Conrad. Anyway, so we drove up

and down Broadway and West End maybe ten times. And there was a guy named Chris Grooms that came with us.

Oh, so there were *three* of you.
Yeah, he was this guitar player we knew. Donivan and I were a duo.

So you and Donivan performed together, like in college and stuff?
Yeah.

What was the name of your duo?
Rodney & Donivan!

(laughter) I mean, what else is there? (more laughter)
Yeah, Rodney & Donivan. So the record that we were making was called . . . *Rodney & Donivan*.

Were you writing songs?
Yeah.

Both of you?
Yeah. Anyway, so Chris Grooms came with us. He was this really weird DADGAD guitar player . . . played a lot of Irish . . .

What kind of guitar player?
DADGAD. D-A-D-G-A-D tuning. He was the first guy I'd heard talk about that.

I've never heard of that.
Yeah, all of those guitar players in Ireland, you know, the real students, those Celtic students, they played . . . *(Rodney's cell rings)* I'm only going to get this if it's my daughter. *(It's not)*

Okay. I'm going to guess where you stayed . . . the Anchor Motel.
No, no, that would have been smart. *(laughter)* You know, we had been driving and, let's see, what did we do . . . ? We probably went to the Krystal and got us a Krystal Burger and a Coke. In the end, we drove back out to Highway 70 where it splits. This time we

just kept going to the right. So right about midnight, after driving back and forth, we headed out Highway 70 until we got to a little park on the right-hand side of the road, about where Bellevue Mall is now, or maybe just this side of where it is today. And so we just pulled into this little park, and rolled out and slept in the grass.

Did you have sleeping bags?
Nah . . . well, maybe Chris did.

A pillow?
Nah. I had a guitar case. Probably had . . . I don't even know if I had a suitcase. So I laid down in the grass and slept until I got all dewed up and woke up with the sun, then started to take stock: "Okay. We're here. Now I wonder what's going on?"

Anyway, back in those days, the Parthenon was sort of the hippie, degenerate, itinerant, homeless hangout. So we went there and started asking questions. Then we started looking for girls, you know. So they said, "Well, there's a lake east of here called Percy Priest." So we got some directions and—at the end of the second day—drove out to Percy Priest, found a picnic table. We gathered up some rags, and I think through the course of that day we'd gotten some blankets and stuff. So we went out and I slept on top of a picnic table.

That second night?
Well, for the rest of the summer—through September. It was great because you could take a bath in the lake, plus we had water. The picnic table was right on the lake, right next to the water. So we'd go out there at night. That's where our camp was. Donivan slept in the front seat, Chris slept in the back seat, and I slept on top of the picnic table.

Were you under a tree so the dew wouldn't get on you?
I was under a tree.

Good. I was worried about you.
(*laughter*) Well, my mama would have been. It was great. I mean, I look back on my homeless time as maybe the best time of my life.

Because the system was . . . we figured out the system pretty quickly. And my system was sleep at the lake, get up in the morning, then go to this little drugstore near Cotten Music in Hillsboro Village— breakfast was sixty-nine cents there. And sixty-nine cents at this little café next door to the Red Dog Saloon. Two eggs and toast for sixty-nine cents. So mornings we would come in from out at the lake, you know, sixty-nine-cent breakfast, and then you'd piddle around at the Parthenon all day, then go down to Bishop's Pub and play music at night, you know, pass the hat, get four or five, six dollars. So that was gas back to the lake.

How'd you find out about Bishop's?
Parthenon. Donivan and I would play our songs for the hippies, sitting on the grass at Centennial Park. And the hippies were, you know, they were kind of adoring us, and it was exactly what we wanted. We were trying to get some girl to take us in, you know, play your songs until somebody melts. *(laughs)* And they said, "Wow, we know how you can make some money. Go down to Bishop's Pub and sign up and play and you pass the hat." That was how we discovered Bishop's Pub, which is where the Tin Angel is today. Anyway, so that's what we did. And Tim's [Tim Bishop, the owner] girlfriend took a liking to me. Every night, she would give me a pitcher of beer and a hamburger with, like, a pound of French fries. So I'd go over in the corner and give Donivan half, and we would split the French fries. We had breakfast and dinner wired, then we would play. So that's how we wired Nashville.

Who was playing Bishop's at that time?
Ah . . .

Was Olney there?
Yeah, David Olney, Steve Runkle . . . I mean, at that time . . .

Did George and Arizona Star ever drift in?
George and Arizona . . . Oh yeah. I knew George and Arizona. And there was Bobby David . . .

Oh yeah, I remember him. I haven't thought about him in years. *(laughs)* "Jesus, when you come, please come to Nashville!"

Well, speaking of [Nashville], when was the first time you heard the word "Nashville"?
When I was a wee child, we had Hank Williams records. They were 78s, out of the dust sleeve and scratchy and stuff. My dad was a construction worker, an eighth-grade education, sharecrop farm kid who wound up in Houston, who *really* wanted to go to Nashville to be on the Grand Ole Opry.

So *you* heard about Nashville . . .
When I heard about Nashville, it was with *longing*. It was this thing that somehow my father missed. The Holy Grail was Nashville.

So it was like heaven . . .
Yeah. Nashville was heaven. I was going to Nashville when I was two years old. It wasn't conscious, but the seed was planted. My dad had a little pick-up band, a local band that played a lot around east Houston.

Did he write songs?
No, but he was a *great* singer. Better singer than me.

And he played guitar?
Played guitar. Was a bandleader. He would play those shit-hole honky-tonks on the east side of Houston.

Blood buckets.
Shit-hole blood buckets. And he would go out there—I played drums with him when I was eleven—he'd go out there and strum a big A-chord and say, "Here's a song written by Harlan Howard!" So he already . . . he had the . . .

So he was knowledgeable.
He was knowledgeable. He knew his songs. And he'd announce his songs, and he treated those fourth-class shit-holes . . .

So he loved songs.
He loved songs. And he loved, you know, 'cause I don't know what radio he had as a child, because . . . I mean, they were dirt poor, sharecrop farmers in western Kentucky.

Your father's people?
Yeah. I mean, they were so poor that during the Depression, they lived in a sheep shed. It was Tom Joad in the woods.

So they migrated to Houston to get jobs?
Well, the ship channel and the oil industry there meant you could get menial labor. So that whole crew migrated to Houston from western Kentucky. I think my grandfather went first and got a job as a night watchman. Then my dad went down and drove a truck for an ice company. This was in the day when people still delivered ice by—it was originally by wagon and horse. People didn't have refrigerators; they had *ice*boxes. The ice companies delivered ice, the way the milkmen delivered milk.

I remember a little bit of that.
But anyway, my dad would stand up, and he treated his little shithole shows as if he were Roy Acuff hosting a segment of the Grand Ole Opry. So the way I heard about Nashville, it was nirvana. It was heaven.

So how long have you lived in Nashville?
Well, that first time, I was in Nashville from August of '72 until August of '74. Then I went to Toronto.

Toronto?
Yeah, I was in Toronto four months—from August until Christmas of '74. I was living up there, if you call that living there . . . I was staying with some people. Then I left Toronto, came back to Nashville, got my car and my dog, and we went to Austin. But while I was in Toronto, I met Emmylou. She had heard some of my songs and wanted to record them, so her producer, Brian Ahern, arranged for me

to go to D.C. from Toronto to meet her. Anyway, I lived in Austin less than a month, because Emmylou came and played the Armadillo in the middle of January, and I went and sat in with her at the Armadillo, and after the show, we were backstage and she said, "I'm going to L.A. tomorrow, you want to go?" And I said, "Sh . . . yeah!" She said, "I've got a ticket for you." So I flew *(laughs)* first class to L.A. the next day. I mean the *very* next day. I didn't know I was going. And I stayed there seven years.

So you lived in L.A. seven years. Then you moved back to Nashville, right?
Yeah, I came back on the Fourth of July, 1981.

So you came to Nashville *twice*.
I did. Once on an August night in 1972, and again on the Fourth of July, 1981. Nine years later.

And you've lived here ever since?
Yeah, with the exception of 2001. Claudia and I were in L.A. because she was going to acting school. We lived in L.A. for a year. But we never did get rid of the house here. We knew we were coming back.

Okay. I want to hear about *one thing* that has happened to you while living here, that could *only* have happened in Nashville.
Let's see . . . *(long silence)* Would you rather it be in the early stage, or later on?

It doesn't matter. Maybe early?
The early stage is more . . . you know, earlier in your life is more vivid. I mean, I have some incredibly vivid Johnny Cash stuff. Let's see . . . only in Nashville. Okay, I was living in a house on Acklen Avenue—this was when I was dishwashing over at Friday's, before I was promoted and came under your care *(laughs)* as busboy.

(more laughter) The blind leading the blind.
Yeah. *(laughs)* Oh, but . . .

I remember seeing you and thinking, "That guy's either real smart or retarded."
(laughs) . . . or under the influence.

Stoned as a billy goat.
Stoned as a billy goat. But I was *happy* washing dishes 'cause I could be stoned back there and drinking. I would slip out the back door and smoke pot, then come back in and drain everybody's half-empty drinks, then go back to the house on Acklen just knocked out. And there would be Townes Van Zandt and Guy Clark and Bobby David and all these . . . so when I got promoted—getting promoted was not good for me, because I could hide out washing dishes. So when I got promoted, I . . .

. . . you ran into Miss Quality Control.
Miss Quality Control. *(laughter)* I mean, here was this gorgeous Amazonian woman, who . . . I don't know if you were as *capable* as you seemed, because . . . I mean, you seemed incredibly capable at your job up there as the greeter.

I had this earnest little side.
Well, while you were trying to figure out, "Who is this guy and what's he all about?" I'm sitting there going, "God, this is a gorgeous woman." And I mean, you were so capable and smart and exuded, like . . . you were an educated woman!

Hey, I was a Vanderbilt graduate!
You were a Vanderbilt graduate, and you had that little bit of dilettante to you, that southern charm that Fayssoux Starling has.

Funny you should mention Fayssoux. She and I are from the same hometown.
I knew that.

We still keep in touch.
Well, you and Fayssoux . . . you know, Fayssoux and I . . .

She's still got it.
She has it. And for a while . . . you know, Fayssoux and I had a little
love affair for a while.

Oh, I never knew that.
Yeah, it was . . . I mean, she was so . . . I was in lo—

Fayssoux is gorgeous.
She's gorgeous.

**She's sixty-seven years old and she's *still* gorgeous. She just recorded
her very first album, and now she's playing all the time with this
twenty-seven-year-old guitar player, Brandon Turner. Just last year,
she and Brandon opened for me at the Handlebar in Greenville.**
I was in love with her.

God, she's just great . . . she's . . .
Well, you and Fayssoux have that same kind of . . . Fayssoux is very
articulate. You know, she's an educated woman. And she comes from
that southern aristocracy.

**Yeah, we're from the same . . . *(laughs)* Fayssoux and I have the same
parents!**
You have that same thing . . . you know . . .

**It's so funny hearing you say this, because back then, I was trying
so hard . . . I wanted to be a hippie hanging out in the park. I was
thinking, *(barely audible)* "That guy over there [bussing tables] is a
real artist. You just *want* to be one." You know? Just insecure as hell.
But acting like I could run the CIA!**
(laughs) Well, both of our insecurities met there. I would look at you
and go, "Oh, man, she's got it all together. I mean, I am an *amoeba*!
(peals of laughter) I am a single-celled . . .

**And I'm sitting there going, "He's probably a real artist. He's not
going to talk to you."**
I mean, I was smart as a tack, but at that time, I didn't . . .

You didn't say a word.
I didn't let anybody know it. Like you said, I was taking it all in. I was taking in everything I could. I was probably a lot more cautious then than I am now. But, you know, I was also insecure. I *thought* I knew what I knew, but I needed to check it out before I played my cards. Okay, so where are we? Oh, yeah . . . only in Nashville. Okay. Acklen Avenue, the front porch, and so we're sitting out there . . .

Who was sitting out there?
It was Townes Van Zandt and Guy Clark and Richard Dobson and Skinny Dennis, the upright bass player, and Robin and Linda Williams . . . and this really crazy drummer whose name I can't remember. This kid was crazy.

He might have been playing with me. Back then, I had a crazy drummer that tried to tear up the bar where we played. The bar manager called me late one night after our gig, said our drummer was down there, trying to dismantle the place.
I don't even know if this guy's still alive. But anyway, we're all playing music on the front porch, as if it were a stage. *(laughs)* It was a full-blown hootenanny. Of course, Townes was a bit too accomplished and too well known, but he was sitting there drinking and carrying on, and we had a little record player. So we're all sitting there playing, and here comes this guy walking down the street with a record in his hands. We just kind of watched him come up, and we're playing, and he walks up and says, "Hey, I heard you guys all playing and, ah . . . I just made a record. You want to hear it?" And we went, "Well, yeah, man, we got a record player. It's right here." The record player was plugged inside the front door, but setting there on the porch, right? So he plopped it down—he was kind of a Spanish-looking fellow—a boy, really . . . just a beautiful boy, at the time. And it was Johnny Rodriguez. And the record was "Pass Me By (If You're Only Passing Through)."

Get out of here!
He had gotten an acetate of the record that morning.

"Pass Me By" . . . what a great record! And what a sweet . . .

It was his first record. He didn't know anybody in Nashville. He was walking, and he happened to hear us playing, so he came over to see if we wanted to hear his record. And this *big voice* comes out, singing that great Hillman Hall song, you know . . . *(sings)* "Hey, pass me by . . ." And we all just fell out. We were all *slayed* by this. We're going, "*No shit!* You just made that record *last night?*" And it was Johnny Rodriguez, just walking up off the street. He didn't know anybody, except whoever had fished him out of Texas to make this record 'cause he had that big voice. He didn't know anybody. He was so innocent. Just totally guileless. Anyway . . . that could only have happened in Nashville.

That's a great story. I love that. Okay. One Johnny Cash story, and we're done.

Hmm, just one . . . let's see . . . Okay. Johnny Cash had this guy that worked for him named Sonny, who took care of his boats—Sonny and Leetha kind of ran the house out there on the lake [Old Hickory Lake] when John and June were gone. Leetha cooked and cleaned, and Sonny took care of the cars and boats, kept everything running. So I called—this was before Rosanne and I actually got married.

So you were going together.

We were going steady, we were living together, and that wasn't going over real well. So anyway, we were in Nashville, and I needed to go to Muscle Shoals to meet with this guy down there about my second record—I already had one record out. So I called Johnny. He and June were out of town. And I said, "John, can I borrow your Cadillac to go to Muscle Shoals?" And he said, "Yeah, go ahead. Get Sonny to gas it up for you." So I had to go through the gauntlet of Sonny.

Was it black?

Oh yeah. It was one of those two-door black Cadillacs. A fine automobile.

Black-black on black?
Black-black on black. Plus it was Johnny Cash's . . .
the Man in Black's black-black on black.

What year?
This was 1979, so it was probably a '77 model. And so . . . *(long pause)*
I was not paying attention. I had just left the house at the lake, and I
. . . *(tape runs out and is quickly turned over)* I wasn't two blocks from
the house. I was looking down at the seat, trying to get something.
I wasn't paying attention—and there was a pick-up truck coming at
me, so I ran off the road, barely missing a head-on collision with that
truck. But I crashed into the back-left wheel well of that pick-up,
and took out—it didn't really hurt the pick-up, just scraped it a little
bit, put a little dent in the back—but it took out, just *peeled back*
the left bumper and the headlight on John's car. And so I was stuck
there. I hadn't gotten two blocks from the house. So I told the guy,
"Your truck's not hurt too bad, I'll write you a check right now to
cover repairs." And he said, "I don't want your check. You get me cash
money and we'll be all right." So we . . . I got the guy's phone number
and got him the cash to fix up his truck. But then I had to go back . . .
I had to walk back to the house on the lake.

So Cash wasn't home.
Cash wasn't home. He was on the road. So I went in and said, "Ah,
Sonny, we've got to get John's car back here. I've had a little . . ." and
Sonny goes, "Oh, Mister Cash ain't gon' like that . . . Mister Cash ain't
gon' like that." So I'm thinking, "Oh, shit . . . all right . . ."

**So you wreck Johnny Cash's car . . . and then he lets you marry
his daughter?**
Well, here's what . . . Okay. I wrecked his car. And so I called him and
said, "Well, John, damn it, I wrecked your car." And I said, "But I'm
going to go ahead and get it fixed for you." I said, "I'll get your car
fixed. I'll take care of it." So, I got his car fixed and paid . . . I think it
was two thousand dollars' damage on that car.

What did he say when you told him you'd wrecked his car?
He said, "Well . . . I wrecked a-many of them." But then he said, "I've seen a lot of them come and go around here, but didn't anybody ever offer to pay for anything." So, you know, I think I got his respect.

So he was understanding.
Yeah, he was understanding. He kind of thought it was funny. But he was surprised that I actually took responsibility and paid to get his car fixed, because he was usually the one left paying for everything. *But . . .* dig this. It wasn't two weeks later, there was a bunch of us all out on the lake one night, and Bee Spears, who was Willie's bass player, and Rosie Nix and Carlene and Rosanne, and all of us, we were having a big—John and June were gone, and we were having a big party. So the drunks got the idea, "Let's take the boat out!" So Bee and Rosie took the boat out—they were skiing at night, doing something out there crazy, and they ran over . . . they knocked a big hole in the bottom of John's boat. So they came back in, and everybody's going, "Oh, no . . ." So I called John wherever he was on the road and said, "Hey, man, we took your boat out," I said. "And we knocked a big hole in it. But . . . *(clears his throat)* . . . but I'm not going to pay for this one." And John said, "You weren't driving the boat, were you."

That's great. So he *knew*.
He knew. He said, "You weren't driving the boat, were you." And I said, "Nah, I wasn't driving the boat, and I'm not going to tell you who was. If they ever want to come clean, they can." And so we were cool. Forever after. But the next day, Sonny comes in. *(starts laughing)* And I said, "Sonny, let me show you what happened." 'Cause Sonny had to get the boat out of there and get it fixed. So . . .

Sonny stayed busy!
Sonny stayed busy. Anyway, so Sonny pulls the boat out, sees the big hole, and says, "Oh, Mister Cash . . . Mister Cash . . .
(in unison) Mister Cash ain't gon' like this!"

Where is Sonny? Somebody needs to ghostwrite *his* autobiography. I can see the title on the bestseller list now—*Mister Cash Ain't Gon' Like This! (laughter)*

So from those two little things, I got John's respect, and we became really good friends. But I never won over Sonny. And I tried every way I could to win him over. I tried talking to him, I tried, you know, like, "I have a hit record," and everything like that. But Sonny would have nothing of it. He shut me down. In Sonny's eyes, I was just a gold-digging, car/boat-wrecking . . . I was just out there destroying Mister Cash's property.

Emmylou Harris

My earliest memories of Emmylou are sketchy at best. Let's see. At one point—it may have been 1972—Emmy was waiting tables at a Polynesian restaurant out on White Bridge Road at about the same time Rodney Crowell and I were working at T.G.I. Friday's. I can't remember if I met Emmylou then or not. But I distinctly remember the first time I heard her singing voice.

My friend Danny Flowers (writer of "Tulsa Time") was living in a big old rambling house on Blair Boulevard, sharing rent with two other musicians, one of whom was Crowell. My most vivid memory of that house revolves around the afternoon Danny turned me on to the legendary James Burton. For hours, I sat and listened while Danny played song after song from different albums featuring Burton on guitar. I'd never heard of Burton, but I was familiar with his licks, having heard them coming out of the radio on songs like "Suzie Q" by Dale Hawkins and the Merle Haggard classic "Mama Tried." To Danny, James Burton was like a god.

At first we listened to some Ricky Nelson albums. Like everybody, I knew Nelson from the *Ozzie and Harriet* TV show and from radio hits like "I'm Walking" and "Hello Mary Lou." Early in his career, Nelson had been labeled a "teen idol" due to his incredible good looks. But the label didn't do him justice. That afternoon with Danny, I discovered that Ricky Nelson was an artist in the truest sense. Not only could Ricky Nelson sing and write songs, but he knew how to make records, and a large part of that was surrounding himself with great musicians like James Burton.

Another album we listened to was *Grievous Angel* by Gram Parsons. I'd never heard of Parsons either. Nor had I heard of his singing partner, whose voice sounded like an angel. Emmylou Harris was her name, and the sound of them singing together was like a universe unto itself—Gram's voice brimming with confidence, even if he didn't always hit the notes, and Emmylou's right on pitch, that beautiful vibrato never wavering. To this day, *Grievous Angel* remains one of my all-time favorite albums.

That same afternoon, Danny played me a song he'd written called "Before Believing." Emmylou had just recorded it for her first album. I'd never known anybody—much less an actual friend—to have a song they'd written on a real honest-to-God record, so I was beside myself with excitement. When Emmylou's album came out, I was first in line to buy it and was thrilled to see Danny's name listed among the songwriter credits. In addition, a phrase from Danny's song—"pieces of the sky"—was chosen for the album's title.

THE FIRST TIME I ACTUALLY MET EMMYLOU was probably at a party at Beth and Chuck Flood's house during DJ week 1976. I'd just finished recording my first album for Epic and was riding high that night. I'd arrived at the party with an entourage that included Ben Tallent, Bonnie Garner, Ian Tyson, Raeanne Rubenstein, Melva Matthews, and Canadian journalist Roy MacGregor, who was in town doing a piece on Tyson. Earlier that afternoon, I'd done a photo shoot with Raeanne; Ben had produced my album; Bonnie had signed me to the label, and Melva was managing both me and Tyson. Naturally, I had a crush on Ian. And who wouldn't? He was one good-looking dude—a real cowboy, unlike the "hat acts" that have saturated country music since 1990. Ian was also a hell of a songwriter, having penned the classics "Four Strong Winds" and "Someday Soon." The crush may have been mutual, but I don't want to sound like I'm flattering myself.

As it turned out, Emmylou Harris was at the party, along with Jerry Jeff Walker, Guy and Susanna Clark, Ray Benson, and a host of others. At some point, Emmylou and I were introduced. But whatever memory I have of that moment was mostly obliterated by what happened shortly after our crowd left the party.

We had all piled into my 1961 Ford Galaxie—which everybody called "Whitetrash"—to head downtown to the Old Time Pickin' Parlor where Asleep at the Wheel, Emmylou, and Jerry Jeff were scheduled to play later that evening. I was driving. At least I *thought* I was driving.

Beth Nielsen Chapman, Marshall, and Emmylou Harris
at the release party for Marshall's album *Love Slave*, Sept. 1996

A case could be made that I was *sort of* driving as I was sitting in Tyson's lap while he was in the driver's seat.

As we pulled away from the party, Ian worked the accelerator while I worked the steering wheel. Since Ian couldn't see the road, due to the fact that a woman six feet tall was sitting in his lap, it was left for me to navigate. "Okay, here's a stop sign," I'd say, and Ian would apply the brakes. "Okay, all clear. Let's go," and Ian would press the accelerator. This arrangement seemed to work just fine. That is, until we approached that sharp curve on Belmont Boulevard—the one just past where the Curb Center and Bongo Java are today, the one that's graded the wrong way. At that point, our signals somehow got crossed and instead of slowing down, we suddenly sped up. I'm not really sure what all happened next. But I distinctly remember hearing screams and the screeching of tires as Whitetrash careened uncontrollably around the curve, barely missing a police car going the other way.

The following is an excerpt from MacGregor's article that ran in the December 12, 1976, *Canadian*. Like *Family Weekly* and *Parade*, the *Canadian* was a Sunday-supplement magazine that serviced every city in Canada.

Two years ago, I lost the end of a finger on my right hand, and for a minute I thought it had happened to someone else. But that's the way it is in a crisis, you tend to become detached to what's really going on. Take what happened in Nashville a few weeks back. The car was about to crash and for all I cared, I could have been casually thumbing through a series of photographs, one of the speedometer at 80, another pasted across the windshield showing a CAUTION sign and a curve like a fishhook, another of the car up on two wheels. Not that all things were quite so clear that night—much of it was like trying to read through an ice cube—but I distinctly remember sitting in the death seat of a white 1961 Ford Galaxie. I recall sailing along the city back streets with all windows down, the night air fresh from the Cumberland River, the crickets steady above the radio. And I know there were others in the front seat; some of them were driving.

I know, too, that someone screamed as we went into a two-wheel drift, not loud, but long, the sound floating like a lariat in the car and finally falling about us too late. A police car swerved to avoid the Ford.

After we came to a stop, a mobile Breathalyzer unit was summoned, and the next thing any of us knew, the police had Tyson and me up against the unit with our arms outstretched. I later learned that just before we had come to a complete stop, one of our passengers—and I won't name names—had taken off running with a briefcase down a nearby alley. Evidently, there was something in the briefcase the passenger did not want to share with the police.

While Tyson and I were splayed up against the mobile Breathalyzer unit, a car carrying Emmylou, Jerry Jeff, Guy and Susanna, and Ray Benson happened to pass by. I can still see their faces, wide-eyed with bemusement and surprise. Somebody—it may have been Jerry Jeff—yelled "Lock 'em up!" amidst giggles and a wolf whistle. Amazingly, no one was arrested. Mainly because the police could never determine *who* was actually driving. Plus, our Breathalyzer tests registered way under the limit, which seemed to surprise the officer in charge. I guess there's no way to measure being high on life.

AS FOR EMMYLOU AND ME, our paths have crossed many times since that crisp fall night in 1976. I've sung on one of her albums, and she's sung on one of mine. I've ridden on her bus and once sang on stage with her at the Peace Center in Greenville, South Carolina. We've played countless benefits together in Nashville. For years, the two of us and Ashley Cleveland would raise the roof (Ashley would hit that high note) at Vanderbilt's Memorial Gym, singing the national anthem for the Vanderbilt women's basketball team's last home game of the season. We've been to parties and had dinner in each other's homes. There's probably more, but I'll close with two stories that will tell you everything you need to know about Emmylou Harris.

Christmas Eve, 1977

MY BAND AND I HAD BEEN in Los Angeles for a week, rehearsing at Al Kooper's house as we prepared to record *Jaded Virgin,* my second album for Epic. On Christmas Eve, we went to hear Rick Danko play the Roxy, a rock club on Sunset Boulevard. After the show, the guys all bolted for the Rainbow Bar just up the street, leaving me standing alone on the sidewalk in front of the Roxy. They'd invited me to join them, but I just wasn't up for going to a bar on Christmas Eve. I didn't know what I was going to do. And I wasn't ready to walk back to the Tropicana, which is where we were all staying.

As I stood there gazing at the silver Christmas trees with pink lights along the concrete median on the Sunset Strip, I suddenly became homesick. Homesick for what, I wasn't sure. Just anything but this artificial display of yuletide cheer. *What about snow? I want some goddamned snow! Fir trees, boughs of holly, a partridge in a pear tree,* anything *but these fucking tinsel town trees with their pink lights. Give me something* real*, for chrissakes!* I'd been in Los Angeles so long, I was beginning to wonder what real was. I was on the verge of tears, when I heard a voice ring out:

"Marshall Chapman, what are you doing in Los Angeles?"

It was a beautiful, strong voice. Perhaps the voice of an angel. I turned around to see Emmylou Harris standing on the corner with her husband, Brian Ahern.

"I'm not really sure," I answered.

"Well, what are you doing tomorrow? Do you have plans?"

"No, not really."

"Well, I'm cooking my very first turkey. A real one. I'm getting ready to go home and put it in the oven. Why don't you come over tomorrow and have Christmas dinner with us?"

Sounded good to me. But then I thought about the guys in the band. They didn't have anywhere to go either. I can't remember what all was said after that. All I know is, as I walked back to the Tropicana, I had an address and phone number scribbled on a piece of paper, and an invitation for Christmas dinner that included the guys in the band.

January 1996

AN OVERDUB SESSION HAD BEEN scheduled at 16th Avenue Sound, one of the many recording studios located on 16th Avenue South, one of the two one-way streets that make up Nashville's venerable Music Row. The studio was on the second floor of an old house that had been converted to commercial space to accommodate the music industry. Producer Michael Utley and I were putting the final touches on my second album for Margaritaville/Island. I was especially looking forward to this session because Emmylou Harris was booked to sing harmony with me on "I'm a Dreamer" and "Better to Let Her Go"—two songs that ended up on the album. The session was set for ten o'clock in the morning.

As fate would have it, a winter storm had raged across Middle Tennessee the night before. The snow was still coming down when my phone rang.

"Hey, it's Mike. Have you looked outside?"

"Yeah, it's like a blizzard out there."

"Well, Jim [Jim DeMain, the engineer] just called. He lives way out and says it's pretty bad. It's bad out here, too." (Mike lived about twenty miles toward Franklin on Big East Fork Road.)

"Yeah? Well, it's bad here and we're just a few blocks from the studio."

"We should probably reschedule. Will you call Emmylou?"

"Sure."

"Okay. We'll talk tomorrow."

"All right then." *Click.*

When I called Emmy's house, whoever answered said she was out warming up her Jeep. As soon as we hung up, I called Mike.

"Hey, Mike. Emmy's planning on coming in."

"You're kidding!"

"She was out warming up her Jeep. She may have left by now."

"Wow. Okay, well, I'll call Jim and we'll see you there."

"Sounds good." *Click.*

At the studio, I'm standing at a picture window, looking out over the drifts of snow covering 16th Avenue South. Suddenly I see a red Jeep flying through the snow like a runaway snowplow. At the wheel is Emmylou Harris in a red plaid lumber jacket. I'll never forget this image as long as I live. In fact, every time I hear her voice on "I'm a Dreamer" or "Better to Let Her Go," I still see her driving that red Jeep through the snow. How can you not love a woman like that?

Nashville
December 1, 2008

I AM AT EMMY'S HOUSE near Green Hills. It's cold and gray outside with occasional snow flurries. Like Shotgun Willie, Emmy's "got all her family there." Plus twenty or so dogs she has rescued from the animal shelter. Two of the dogs are named Henry. The bigger Henry has a pronounced underbite and looks so much like former Pittsburgh Steelers coach Bill Cowher, I suggest his name be changed to Coach to avoid confusion with the other Henry.

We go inside and sit down on a sofa in the living room for the interview.

So Emmy, is it true you were a waitress at that Polynesian restaurant, or did I make that up?
Oh, yes. It was called the Mahi Mahi. It later became the Golden Dragon. It was out on White Bridge Road.

This was the *first* time you lived in Nashville, right?
Yes. The first time I came to Nashville was in 1970. Hallie was a baby. She was born in March of 1970 in New York City. But shortly after that, New York seemed like a scary place. It had never seemed scary before. But once I had Hallie, I felt vulnerable with her. All of a sudden, the city seemed dirty and dangerous. *(laughs)* So we went to Nashville.

Was that your first time ever in Nashville?
Yes.

Your parents had never taken you as a child?
No. I'd never been there. So I guess, because I was doing a few country songs almost as a joke in my show, I somehow thought I could make it as a country singer in Nashville. *(laughs)* You know, you don't think things through. You're so young. And also, when things get hard—we didn't have much money, I hadn't been able to make it in New York, and the marriage was not in the greatest shape at that point—so my philosophy for many years [when times got tough] was . . . "Let's move!"

The old geographic cure.
Exactly. Somehow you think that's going to solve everything. It's a form of running away . . . only it requires more packing. *(laughs)*

So how did you get to Nashville? Did you come by car?
I believe at that point we had—I don't remember the model—but it was one of those small Fords, not a Fairlane exactly, but a small version of it, do you remember? They were always that beige color. You know that flesh color? Anyway, the car had belonged to my uncle. He sold it to me for four hundred dollars. It was a great little car. I suppose we must have gone down there in that.

Did somebody drive you? Did you drive yourself?
I'm sure that . . . let's see . . . I was still married to Hallie's father [Tom Slocum]. We split up in Nashville once we'd been there for a while.

So he drove you down?
Probably . . . or the two of us. And I'm sure . . . yes, what we probably did was drive to Birmingham first—where my aunt and uncle were living—to get kind of situated. I think I do remember this. *(laughs)* I could be making this all up. I remember we bought a used baby bed, and I remember my uncle painting it.

What color?
White. And so we were getting ready to go to Nashville—I don't remember if we had already rented a place or what. Surely we must've scouted it out. Anyway, we just kind of took some rope and stuck it [the baby bed] on top of the car, and then just wrapped the whole car with rope. Of course, we hadn't gotten very far outside of Birmingham before it all came crashing down on the hood. I'm surprised we didn't have an accident. This was before cell phones and we were out in the middle of nowhere. I don't know how we got to a phone and called . . . I think my mother was visiting her sister down there, my aunt. So they got into a huge DeSoto that had belonged to my grandfather, who had died a few years earlier. You remember those huge DeSotos that had trunks that you could put . . . that you could live in? And so they drove and picked us up. The baby bed was cracked, so we went back to Birmingham, and my uncle—God bless him—fixed it. He could fix anything. He glued it and secured it properly, and then we went on to Nashville.

So did you end up going in the DeSoto?
Oh, no. No, our car was okay. It was just the baby bed. *(laughs)*

Did you go in a caravan? Did they go with you?
No, it was just me and Tommy and Hallie. We just drove on to Nashville, as I recall . . . or as I don't recall. Somehow we ended up in Nashville.

So you came to Nashville through Birmingham . . .
Through Birmingham, because that's where I was born, and my aunt and uncle were living there at the time. So we *did* have family.

Do you remember where you first lived in Nashville?
We lived in that little area near Hillsboro Village, off Natchez Trace. We had an attic apartment there for a short period of time. At that point, I was working at a gay bar across from the Trailways bus station downtown. I can't remember . . . was it the Hi-Hat? I believe that was the name. And so I did that, but I was nursing Hallie. It was very painful because my breasts would fill up with milk during my shift.

So your first Nashville gig, you're breast-feeding and working in a gay bar.
Yes. That's pretty good, isn't it?

That'll work. *(laughs)*
And after that, I can't remember, but we ended up living in a house on Blakemore [Avenue]. And we had a roommate, a guy who helped us with the rent.

Were you singing then? Any gigs?
After Tommy and I broke up, I remember singing in some place out on Murfreesboro Road, in a lounge for happy hour. I don't even remember the name of the place. Or was it on some pike?

Elm Hill Pike?
No, that wasn't it. Was there such a road called Albert Pike? Anyway, who knows what it was. It was some motel lounge, a chain motel

probably. But in Nashville [in 1970] I really didn't do much singing. I waited tables. First at the gay bar, then the Mahi Mahi. Somewhere along in there, the problems Hallie's father and I were having kind of came to a head, so he just decided to go on back to New York. He hitched back to New York and I kept the car. After he left I couldn't keep the rent up, so I moved in with some friends—actually this gal who was best friends with one of my cousins from Birmingham. I'd only met her briefly when we were teenagers, when I was visiting my cousins down there. She and her husband had a little cinderblock house out on Charlotte [Pike] way before it got all built up out there. I had no money. I was broke. So I moved into their attic. They had a little boy they called Hambone who was about Hallie's age. I was on food stamps at that point, still working at the Mahi Mahi. I remember they wouldn't let the waitstaff eat the food, so I was living on fortune cookies and food stamps. It's hard for me to remember what all happened after that. But at a certain point, I realized I just had to go home.

What was your impression of Nashville during that time? I know you were struggling to make ends meet, but did you make any connections with your music?
I didn't make any connections in music, but you have to realize I'd just come from New York, where I met Paul Siebel [wrote "Spanish Johnny"], Jerry Jeff Walker, David Bromberg . . . I mean, there was just music happening, even though it was a down period, there was still a little bit of a music scene [in New York], although once I got pregnant and had to deal with that, I was taken out of music. I really didn't think I would ever do music again. I don't even know if I missed it. I was just trying to figure out how I was going to survive. Even though—and it sounds a little dramatic—but I always knew that I had my parents. My parents had always stood by me, no matter how many mistakes or crazy things it seemed like I was doing. I always knew I could go home. But for a while there, I was thinking, "This is my life, this is my bed, I've made it, and now I have to lie in it." I don't think it was because I was too proud, but I just thought, "I've *got* to make this work. I can make this work." Then finally I realized it was not just about me, it was about me and my daughter. But then it *was* about

me. I just thought, "This is a place where I can go and we can be safe until I can figure out what I'm going to do."

How old were you at this point?
Let's see . . . 1970, so I was . . . twenty-three? I should have known better. So I was twenty-three and I pretty much felt my life was over. I thought I was never going to have any fun anymore. And I worked a few jobs . . . I got a job as a hostess for model homes. But I would take my guitar.

So this was when you were . . . ?
Back at my parents'.

. . . who were living in . . . was it Virginia?
They were living in Maryland, and they had a little, it wasn't exactly a farm . . .

What town?
Clarksville.

Clarksville, Maryland.
Yes. And so I had a job in Columbia, Maryland, which was one of those first communities to have neighborhoods with names like "Hobbit's Glen." *(laughs)* Everything had to be a little charming.

Sort of a bedroom community for D.C.?
Yes. And so I would take my guitar and hide it in the closet. Nobody ever came. All I had to do was just hand people an application if they walked through the hall. I was in the office, and there were about three versions of the houses they were selling . . . *(Emmy's cell rings)* . . . oh, I'm sorry . . .

It's okay. We'll take a break.

(Later)
When did you come back to Nashville? I realize you came back here to live for good in 1982. But after 1970 . . .
The next time I came [to Nashville] was in triumph. *(At this point, some dogs go running through the living room as Emmy's mother walks by on a walker. She announces she's going to get something cold to drink in the kitchen because she's thirsty.)*

So in a hundred words or less, how did you go from food stamps to triumph?
A hundred words or less . . . *(we both laugh)* . . . well, let's see . . . *(a small dog can be heard yapping in the background)* . . . in moving back to my parents' . . . *(yapping continues)* . . . there was a neat little music scene in D.C. So eventually I went from being a hostess in model homes to actually playing in clubs through the help of—I have to mention Bill and Taffy Danoff [Fat City, Starland Vocal Band]. They were kind of like local stars in the club system, and they were aware of me from when I used to play the hootenannies when I was in high school. So they just took me under their wing and said, "Come here. You've *got* to start singing again." And they single-handedly got me back into music.

And their names are?
Bill and Taffy Danoff.

Taffy?
Taffy, like the candy.

T-A-F-F-Y?
Yes. Bill and Taffy Danoff. They're no longer a couple, but they're still friends.

It happens.
Boy, does it happen. *(laughter)* And so while singing in the clubs, that's where I hooked up with Gram [Parsons].

Of course, this is all documented. You go to L.A. and record with him and the rest . . .

Yes. So after Gram's death, I go to L.A. to make a record, and all of a sudden, "If I Could Only Win Your Love" is on the charts. So when I come back to Nashville, the first day I'm there I meet Dolly Parton and George Jones and I throw up. Not because I was drinking or anything, it was just so overwhelming. I met Dolly in her studio, and then we went to his [Jones's] club, Possum Holler.

So when you come back to Nashville in triumph, you fly in from L.A. So this is in the mid-'70s?

Yeah. The album [*Pieces of the Sky*] came out in January of 1975.

I remember meeting you at Chuck Flood's house. I think that was the first time we actually met.

I'm so glad you remember all that.

It's crazy. I have this incredible memory, at least about some things.

Was it at his Christmas party?

It was at a party, but it was during DJ week. I recently heard from Beth [Beth Flood]. It was some anti-music-establishment party. Jerry Jeff was there. And you were there.

Wow. That must have been '75.

It may have been. Was that the first time you had come back to Nashville?

Yeah. Because the record came out in January. For some reason, my albums always came out in January. We recorded it in '74, and it came out in early '75.

This would have been that fall.

I think I did the CMAs [Country Music Association Awards]. Was it '75 when I sang "If I Could Only Win Your Love" with Charlie [Louvin]?

It may have been. But now that I think about it, that party at Chuck's was in '76. For sure, because I had gone to Boston for this disastrous relationship-thing and come back in shame *(laughs)* to retrieve my two-hundred-dollar car.
Oh, well, at least I had a *four*-hundred-dollar car! *(We both laugh)*

(We take a break)
So after that first album, you would come back to Nashville . . .
Yeah, we started coming back pretty regularly for different things.

Did you come back to record?
Never to record. It was always CMAs or things like that.

What was it like meeting Dolly [Parton]?
It was a big deal. Here I was this hippie girl with a hit record . . .

A country hit record, right?
It was a country hit record, and the album was doing really well. People from the rock world and the country world were buying it because . . . obviously the association with Gram. There was a curiosity thing to it probably. So somebody had arranged for me to meet Dolly because I had recorded [her] "Coat of Many Colors." In my interviews, all I ever talked about was Dolly Parton and George Jones because I was such a convert to country music. I was trying to carry on Gram's legacy kind of, because I was a fairly new, obnoxious convert to country music. I *thrilled* at turning people who had never heard Dolly Parton onto Dolly Parton, making them listen, and then watching their reaction when I showed them her picture. I remember one guy, he literally just fell over.

I talked to Dave Hickey recently and he said, "Hugging Dolly Parton is like being run into by a soft Buick."
Oh, how funny. *(laughter)* So how is Dave Hickey?

He's good.
I love Dave Hickey.

Yeah, me, too. He's one of those people who just . . . He's the last person you'd expect to still be alive.
I'm glad he's still around. He's still one of the best interviewers I ever had. He loves music.

Yeah, and he wrote that great article about Hank Williams—I think I sent you a copy. He wrote it on the very day that Hank Williams had been dead longer than he'd been alive.
Wow.

It was called "Hank Williams and the Glass Bottomed Cadillac." Somebody's doing a documentary based on it.
Really?

Yeah. Okay. So one more question and I think we've got it. Why did you come back to Nashville to live?
Ah . . . I think, once again, when things get bad . . . *(wild scratching sound. A dog jumps up on the sofa and sits on the voice-recorder between us.)* Ernie! Ernie! Mother! Can you take Er— . . . Mother! . . . She can't hear me. Ernie, get down! *(Ernie settles down)* . . . Sorry.

Interruptions are good. They break it up.
Well, once again it was another relationship thing. Brian and I . . . our marriage was kind of ending.

You and Brian had that house out in . . . what was the name?
Oh, you mean Camp Pretentious? *(laughs)*

No, no, the one where I went for Christmas dinner. It was a little ranch-style . . .
Oh, now *that* was a nice house.

It was in a little valley.
Yeah, it was in Studio City. On a street called Oakdell. I loved that house.

I remember it was in a canyon. I can't remember the name. Laurel?

Laurel. Yes, that's it!
Yeah, it was off Laurel [Canyon Boulevard]. It was great. *(Emmy's mother's voice rings from the kitchen: "I left some coffee in here. I had to get it." Emmy calls out, "Okay!")*

So you and Brian moved into a bigger house after that?
Yeah. Camp Pretentious. That's what Phil Kaufman called it. It was an early McMansion. One of those starter castles . . . with an elevator. *(laughs)* It was on sale.

Where was it?
It had been Clark Gable's estate and then they built these ridiculous houses. Anyway, moving to Nashville was part of moving away from that, and the marriage, and trying to make a new start. Rodney and Rose [Rodney Crowell and Rosanne Cash] had moved here. And through Rodney, I'd met Guy and Susanna and gotten to know them. They had become really good friends of mine. So I kind of felt like I had people I knew here. I also rationalized that even though it was still nine hundred miles away, I was closer to my parents in Virginia, where Hallie was spending a lot of time because I was spending so much time in the studio and on the road. So she was actually kind of being raised by them. Eventually, once I got things a little more together down here, she came back and lived with me.

I remember one time running into you and Meghann [Emmy's second daughter] at the Dragon Park. Meghann was five. I was with my sister and niece who were visiting from South Carolina. I remember Meghann and my niece were the same age.
Oh, the Dragon Park! We had the Nashville Saturday Mothers Club. It was Holly Tashian and Rosanne and me. We all had kids about the same age. Rain or shine. Sometimes we'd just picnic in the back of Holly's Volkswagen station wagon if it was raining. *(laughs)* That was really great. I found Nashville . . . you know, the first time [in 1970]

I wasn't impressed with Nashville because I was going through so much trauma and so many changes, and trying to figure out, you know, food stamps. No music. I didn't really have any friends— well, other than the friend of my [Birmingham] cousin that took me in, who was terrific. But ultimately, I needed to go home. It wasn't a Nashville experience for me. But when I came back to *live* here, it took me a while but I tell you, I am *so* in love with this town! It's like when I first came, I was on my way to someplace else. Because . . . *(nasal accent)* Nashville? You know, I'd lived in New York, in Boston, in L.A., traveled all around the world. At first I thought, "Well, I'm certainly not going to stay *here*." And gradually, you start putting down roots. Nashville, for me, has been like some guy you've known all your life and he's a friend, but you never really thought romantically about him. Then all of a sudden, you wake up one morning and you realize this is the person you want to spend the rest of your life with.

There's the places and all the things it has, but mainly, it's the people I fell in love with. The people and the friendships and the memories. And also, a big part of it is my mother coming to live with me. I'd only been in this house two or three years when my father died and my mother came to live with me. Before, it was always, "Okay, how long am I going to be here in *this* house," in the back of my mind. So there's that. You get attached to the people.

Also, there's something wonderful about familiarity. Knowing the shortcuts. Knowing the little places you would take somebody. I have friends from out of town and the first thing they want to do is go to Pangaea. Because there's not a store like it anywhere as far as I know. And I love going to baseball games at Greer Stadium, and I hope that's not going to become a thing of the past. I just love knowing my way around and having most of my friends really close by. I can even bike some of the places.

Like Lola and Jamie [mutual friends Lola White and singer-songwriter Jamie O'Hara].
Lola and Jamie and, you know, Buddy and Julie [Miller]. But I'm sorry, *(laughs)* I can't bike to Lola and Jamie's. It's too far and too

many hills! But Buddy and Julie and Nanci Griffith, they all live close by. And another wonderful thing that has happened, all these years when I was traveling, I would only see my family on holidays and if I played in the town they were living in—northern Virginia and Maryland, Birmingham, whatever. But now my mother is here, and my brother is actually living with us right now. Two of his children have moved to Nashville and have houses. One of my nieces works for me; she brings her baby who was born on my birthday. And I've got three grandnieces and nephews who live in Nashville, and we are always having these spontaneous family gatherings.

So now, you're *here*!
I'm here for good. All my pets are buried in the backyard, which is where I'm going to end up. At least my ashes. I've got my pet cemetery back there. The house is paid for. It took me . . . I was on the road for *years*, but then it took *one tour*—the Down from the Mountain tour—and the house was paid for. Because I didn't have to take a band. *(laughs)* That's where all my money goes.

Having a band is like having a drug habit.
It is. I've got a very small band now—just three pieces. I could probably go out by myself now, but it's not much fun. I had a rhythm section this past year because I put out a new record. We did the whole promotion thing. But now I've stripped down. I had to let my drummer and lead guitar player go. Now I've got an accordion player, a bass player, and a fiddle/mandolin player. And they all sing, and we're doing the Opry this week.

The Carter Family with instruments!
That's it.

Is there anything else, something special about Nashville, something that could only have happened in Nashville, a special Nashville memory?
Well, right after I moved back here for good, Paul [Paul Kennerley, English songwriter-producer] and I were out driving around and for

some reason, we decided to check out the Bluebird [Café]. There was a little handwritten sign in the window that said STEVE EARLE & THE DUKES. I had no idea who Steve Earle was. I'm thinking, "That has to be a made-up name."

Steve Earle & the Dukes?
Yeah.

Oh, yeah. I just got it!
And so we walk in and there's Steve with a drummer and a bass player. And one of the first songs he did was "The Devil's Right Hand." And so I turned to Paul and said, "This was the right move . . . moving to Nashville."

Bobby Bare

I FIRST MET BOBBY BARE at Monument Recording Studio in Nashville in 1971. Harold Bradley, who was playing guitar on the session, had invited me to drop by. I was fresh out of Vanderbilt, and this was my first time in a recording studio with a session in progress.

I'd met Harold at the annual BMI Awards dinner, which was held at the Belle Meade Country Club in those days. Some mutual friends had arranged for us to sit together, since they knew how much I loved playing guitar. My family had always made light of my passion, but not Harold Bradley. He asked me all sorts of questions about my guitar and my plans for the future, and didn't laugh when I answered. At one point he mentioned his brother, Owen. I had no idea who Owen was, but I later found out. To this day, Harold and I remain good friends.

My most vivid memory from that evening was seeing Audrey Williams walk up to accept an award on behalf of her late husband Hank. She was wearing a long, shimmering gown, and as she strolled by our table, the bright spotlight following her movements revealed everything she was wearing underneath her gown, which was pretty much nothing. People gasped. Some snickered. I didn't know what to think. This was my first experience with Hillbilly Glamour. Where I come from, a lady always wore a full slip under her gown. This Audrey Williams didn't seem to give a rat's ass what anybody thought. Deep down inside I felt a sort of admiration for her. She looked like a woman who'd seen some things.

But back to Monument Studio. When Harold asked if I'd like to meet Bobby Bare, I was so excited I couldn't speak. For years, I'd heard Bobby Bare singing on the radio, songs like "Shame on Me" and "Detroit City." This was a real star! My heart was beating wildly, but I tried to remain cool as I managed a "nice to meet you."

**Marshall and Bobby Bare at the Opryland Hotel Ballroom,
March 1993**

I didn't see Bare again until 1976 in Gonzalez, Texas. I was standing in the wings onstage at Willie Nelson's Fourth of July Picnic, looking out over the crowd of 120,000, when a long, lanky singer wearing
a cowboy hat came up behind me and said, "You wouldn't happen to
have a guitar strap on you, would you?" It was Bare. They were already announcing him, so I scurried around and quickly found one.
As he calmly fastened it to his guitar, he looked at me again and said,
"You got a pick?" Fortunately, I had one in my pocket. Then, just as he
was about to stride out in front of the massive crowd, he turned and
said, "You wouldn't happen to have the lyrics to '500 Miles Away from
Home,' would you?" Then he flashed that thousand-watt grin and was
gone. All I could think was, *Goddamn! That's got to be the coolest som-
bitch on the planet!*

We later became friends. I was sitting with Bobby and his wife Jeannie at the Exit/In the night the Anderson sisters and I jumped on stage with Fats Domino. I've had the pleasure of opening some shows for him, and once was a guest on his TV show, *Bobby Bare & Friends*. I've visited his house on Old Hickory Lake—a couple of times with a boyfriend high on speed. I was hoping the cool lake waters and the Bares' warm hospitality would somehow calm him down. Who knows *what* the Bares were thinking. Whatever it was, they never said anything about it. This was back when I thought if you loved somebody enough, they'd stop doing drugs.

When it came time to do my second album for Epic in 1978, I was hoping to record with my touring band. Naturally, Epic wanted to hear what they sounded like, so Bare ended up producing some sides on us at Glaser Sound Studios (aka Hillbilly Central or Outlaw World Headquarters). I was moving so fast in those days, I probably never thanked him, other than a mention in the album's liner notes: "Thanks to Bobby Bare for being so goddamned cool."

I still think Bobby Bare is the coolest guy I ever met in the business, but Bobby swears he's just shy.

Hendersonville, Tennessee
May 14, 2008

I'M AT BARE'S HOUSE ON Old Hickory Lake just outside Nashville. Bobby's saying goodbye to his granddaughter who's been visiting for the morning.

"What's my name?" he asks the three-year-old.

"Pushover!" she replies, laughing. A few minutes later, we sit down for the interview.

So Bobby, I know you were born in Ironton, Ohio—right there across the river from Ashland [Kentucky], and then you went to California before coming to Nashville, right?
Yeah. I left home when I was sixteen years old, looking for a job.

Where'd you go?
Stayed with different relatives around. I had an uncle and some aunts and my grandmother who lived in Springfield, Ohio. So a couple of months after I left Ironton, I loaded up my uncle's car and went to Springfield, which is just west of Columbus. I got a job in a garment factory there. Then I got me a little gig playing. I put a little band together, and we got to playing around, and we got to making a little money—well, actually more money than I was making in that garment factory I was working in. So . . . I haven't worked since. *(laughs)* That was the last job I had.

So we got pretty good, started going down on weekends to Wellston [Ohio], and then we'd play in Washington Court House [Ohio]. At one point, me and the band would drive down on Fridays and do Wellston on Friday and Saturday night. Then they would come back to Springfield, and I'd go on down to Portsmouth [Ohio] where I had a Sunday night gig. I'd ride a Greyhound bus to Portsmouth, which was only about forty miles away, do that gig, and then hitchhike back to Springfield.

You played solo on Sunday nights?
Well, they had a little band.

Pick-up band?
A pick-up band, yeah . . . with an old fiddle player. But sometimes it'd get tough hitchhiking. Because if you were driving—it's a couple of hours to drive from Portsmouth to Springfield. I remember one time I got *almost* to Springfield . . . to South Solon. I'll never forget it, because it was raining and I just *could not* get a ride from South Solon to Springfield—it was only about fifteen more miles. And so there was a bar right across the street, so I went across the street, got a beer, and watched the Academy Awards. This was 1951, maybe 1952, because it was the year Gary Cooper won for *High Noon*. *(laughs)*

Black and white [TV], right?
Yeah. Black and white.

So you banged around Ohio for a while, then went to Los Angeles.
Well, yeah. I banged around Ohio and got real popular. I had this huge following in this little area, and they were all young people. I didn't know it at the time, but America was *really ready* for Elvis. They were so ready. Because all my fans, you know—I was what, seventeen, eighteen years old . . . same age as Elvis—and all my fans were in that age group. Fourteen, fifteen years old . . . teenagers.

You were born the same year [1935] as Elvis?
Yeah. So *anyway*, I knew I wanted to make records. And the only way to do it was out of Cincinnati. So I went to Cincinnati and made all the rounds there with King Records and Queen City Records, did all of them. And the only response I got was from Queen City Records. Chuck . . . ah . . . I forget his last name now. He wound up an engineer at RCA later on. But he wanted me to do cover records on Webb Pierce, and I said, "Well, I can't sing that high." I even auditioned at King Records with the same engineer who, four or five years later, engineered that "All American Boy" record that I cut that was a great rock & roll hit. And so I had exhausted all my intents there, and I thought, "Well, I've got to go somewhere. There's nothing going on here." I thought about going to Nashville, but the more I thought about it, the more scared I got. I put that [moving to Nashville] off forever. I kept putting it off, because all my heroes lived here. I couldn't imagine going to Nashville and competing with all my heroes.

Like . . .
Well, there was Carl Smith, there was Webb Pierce, there was Ray Price . . . all of them. They were all here. George Jones didn't live here then, but he was recording here. And then one night, I was working in this club in Portsmouth, Ohio, and a guy had been coming in for about a week or two. He had on a Nudie suit—first one I ever saw. And he had a red Dodge convertible with the back plastic window half ripped out. And he had a PALOMINO CLUB bumper sticker on it. This was in '54, I believe. It was November of '54. November or the first of December. It was coming up on Christmas. I remember it was cold

and snowing out. This guy was always telling us how we could get a lot of work in California: "There's just all kinds of work out there, you'd have jobs left and right." So one night he came in, and he said, "You guys want to go to California with me? I'm leaving in the morning." I said, "I'll go!" And my steel player, he said, "Yeah, I'll go, too!" But my bass player—he had a wife and two or three kids—he said, "I can't go." So then I said to the guy, "If you'll let me borrow your car so I can take this girl home, I'll go with you." He said, "Okay."

So he let you borrow the red Dodge convertible?
Right. So I took the girl home, then we left the next morning. After my steel player went to pay his bar bill, he still owed 'em five bucks. *(laughs)* So he didn't have any money. I think I had fifty dollars. And away we went.

That's a great story.
You don't think about that shit when you're young. You know? You just go.

Right.
. . . you just go.

So how long did you live in L.A.?
Ten years. Anyway, so away we went. And when we got to L.A., the guy, sure enough, knew Jimmy Bryant [session guitarist] and Speedy West [steel guitarist]. He really did. And he introduced me to Speedy West, and Speedy loved me from the very beginning. I was trying to write songs and he loved that, loved my singing, and he wound up promoting me. And eventually, he got me a record deal there at Capitol.

So you had a deal with Capitol in L.A. . . .
. . . in 1955.

Were they [Capitol] in that tall round building? Was it built then?
I cut the first session in that building.

Really? The one on Hollywood and Vine?
In that studio, yeah, I cut the first session. So I was there [L.A.] until
'58 when I got drafted. So I'd been there, what, three years?

Yeah.
And then it didn't take very long until something—I don't know
what—drew us together, but all of a sudden one day, there was me,
there was Harlan Howard, there was Wynn Stewart, Buck Owens . . .
Wynn and I were working clubs about a half mile apart. Wynn was the
first one of that California sound thing to really make a move. He was
having semi-hits back then, and then Harlan—we didn't even know
Harlan wrote songs. He was just some guy who hung out in clubs and
drank.

I guess you can do both.
Yeah. *(laughs)* Anyway, that's where Harlan met Jan, his wife—Jan
Howard [country singer]. She was a friend of Wynn's girlfriend.
Harlan met her, and then somehow me and Harlan wound up staying
at Wynn's house. Then there was Hank Cochran ["Make the World
Go Away"]—he was always hanging around with us. And then little
by little . . . Hank didn't have anything going, so he went back to
Nashville and got him a gig plugging songs at Pamper Music. And
then Harlan, he had a big hit by Charlie Walker and a big hit by Ray
Price—"Pick Me Up on Your Way Down" and "Heartaches by the
Number." And then, all of a sudden, Harlan moved to Nashville.
Meantime, I was too chickenshit to move there. Same reason—all my
heroes were there. Then I got drafted in '58 . . . got out in '60.

Drafted into?
The army. I spent two years in the army.

Where were you stationed?
I did basic training in Fort Knox [Kentucky]. But right before I went
in—maybe two days before—I went in King's [King Records] studio
and recorded "The All American Boy"—a takeoff on a guitar picker
getting drafted that everybody thought was about Elvis. It became a

huge rock & roll hit, it was like #2 in the pop charts. And of course, everybody knew it was me, but it had Bill Parsons's name on it—my buddy who was actually singing on the back side of the 45.

So they put his name on both sides by mistake?
Put his name on both sides by mistake. But I didn't care. I was in the army. I couldn't do anything. I told Bill, I said, "Just run with it. Buy you a car or something." I remember he lip-synched it on *American Bandstand*.

To your voice?
Yeah. So when I got out of the army, the record company in Cincinnati [Fraternity]—they knew that it was me singing it, so they wanted me to do some more records for them. So I said, "Sure." So after the army, I did a little record for Fraternity, and it got popular, then I did it on *American Bandstand*. So I would come back here [Nashville] to promote. I got with this promotion guy who took me around to different towns to all the radio stations. He broke the Patsy Cline record—"I Fall to Pieces."

So the very first time you came to Nashville was to promote a record?
No. The *very* first time I came to Nashville was in 1952. Might have been '53. Bill Parsons was a friend of mine—the guy whose name ended up on that record.

Right. So you and Parsons are about seventeen or eighteen?
Yeah. Bill was originally from Crossville [Tennessee], and one time we decided to go down there to Crossville and see his folks and then go to the Grand Ole Opry in Nashville. So away we went.

How'd you get there?
We took a Greyhound bus. And so we hit Crossville—me and Bill— and I met all his folks and all his relatives and everything. And we went over to one of his cousins' house—she took a liking to me—and we were all sitting around there drinking moonshine. I'd never drunk moonshine before. I remember somebody was frying chicken. And

when it came time to eat the chicken, that moonshine was *kicking . . . my . . . ass.* So I set that glass of moonshine down there beside that chicken, and when I started eating that chicken, I forgot there was moonshine in that glass—it looked like water. So I just up and drank it, and as soon as it hit my stomach, I was up like a shot. I ran to the bathroom and everything came up. *(clears throat)* That moonshine can do it to you.

When the weekend came, we got in the car—me and Parsons's sister, him and his other sister—and drove to Nashville. It was about a hundred miles across bad roads, on old [Highway] 70.

What kind of car were you in?
I think it was a '49 Ford.

You remember what color it was?
Black . . . a black '49 Ford. And we drove without a heater, I might add. And this was wintertime.

I sense a theme developing here. *(laughs)*
And so we drove straight to the Ryman [Auditorium], pulled right up, looked at it, our mouths gaping wide open, and then we went inside. And the Opry was going on. I ended up sitting behind a pole, but it didn't bother me at all. I was just glad to be there—thrilled to death, taking it all in. It was the very first time I had ever heard an honest-to-god PA system. And I was a huge fan of Carl Smith at that time.

So Carl Smith was on that night?
Oh, yes. He was on that night. And he came sliding out, looking like a movie star. He was a sex symbol before Elvis. Girls would scream for him.

Yeah, I saw him in the mid-'60s in Greenville, South Carolina, and I still remember it. He sang "Take My Ring off Your Finger," and he had those blue eyes that could cut across a coliseum.
You should have seen him in the '50s. Anyway, we just watched it

all. I had never seen a big show like that before. I went to see Hank Williams twice, but he never showed up either time. It was across the river from Ironton in Ashland. He was booked there, and I went to see him twice, but he never showed.

So you never got to see him live?
I never did, which is too bad, because I was eat up with him.

I can imagine.
I went to see Little Jimmy Dickens when I was seventeen, eighteen years old, and he treated us like a million dollars. Me and my little band, he took us backstage and introduced us to Del Wood and Walter Haynes, Spider Wilson, and the rest of his band—great band. But we didn't get to meet anybody when we came to the Opry. When the show was over, we got in that car and drove on back to Crossville.

So your very first night in Nashville, you go to the Grand Ole Opry, you don't spend the night, then you go on back to Crossville.
Back to Crossville with no heater in the car, freezing to death. I'm sitting in the back seat with Parsons's sister . . . cute little girl. And she kept my hands warm. It's a good thing 'cause we were freezing. And then we got back to Crossville, and come time to go home, I realized I was broke. So I had to call my stepsister, and she sent me enough money to buy a bus ticket back to Ironton.

Can you remember the next time you came to Nashville?
Yeah. The next time I came to Nashville . . . by then, Harlan and Jan had moved back.

Right. So it was from California?
Well, no. It was after California. I was back here doing all the radio stations, promoting. And the record company was in Cincinnati. So the next time I came to Nashville was to record. I came down a couple of weeks early and stayed at Harlan and Jan's house, which is where I met Roger Miller. Eventually, Roger and I became friends and we started running around.

What label were you on then?

Fraternity Records. I recorded one of Harlan's songs that became a pretty big hit.

You remember the name?

It was called "Sailor Man": "I'm a sailor, that's all that I am . . ." And then the next time I came down after that, I hooked up with Hank Cochran, and went to . . .

So you're coming down from Ohio during these trips?

Yeah. I was just wandering around, staying first one place then another—with my sister, mostly . . . in Dayton, Ohio. My sister always took care of me. And so, I came down and Hank Cochran took me to a Willie Nelson demo session. I met Willie and just instantly fell in love—with Willie, his singing, the whole package . . . just like all of America has nowadays. I bought the whole package.

I had the same experience. This was just before he took off. He was at a party [in Nashville], and nobody was listening to him. This guy with long, red hair—people were shooting pool and stuff—and I just sat at his feet, and I just followed him around like a puppy dog.

Yeah. Everybody did. It was not unusual at all. He didn't have a record deal at the time, but I was just blown away. So I became really close with Willie, and there was Roger, and there was Harlan, and there was all these guys, and we started ganging up.

And then somewhere in there—about the fourth time I came to Nashville—by then Harlan and Hank and all of them had become really established, friends with Chet Atkins and those people. Chet had heard some of my stuff because he'd cut one of my songs with Jim Reeves. He liked "The All American Boy" . . . he liked the way that I talked. So I got word that Chet wanted to meet me. And a guy by the name of Troy Martin, who was an old-time publisher–song plugger. Troy took me over to meet Chet.

At RCA?

Yeah, RCA. And Chet said, "I like what you do." And I said, "Well, I *know* I'm gonna cut some hit records. And I honestly believe that I could do it with you." And Chet said, "I think so, too." Then he said, "Let's get some songs together, and you come back down in a couple of weeks, and we'll get the contracts here, and we'll make some records." And I said, "Great!"

What year is this?

'61, I believe. Probably late '61.

Were you married then? Were you and Jeannie together?

No, no. We didn't get married until '64. [Marriage] was the farthest thing from my mind. I was just wandering around . . . mulling around, really.

So I came back down [to Nashville] in two weeks. But first, I went back up and told—by then I had become really good friends with Harry Carlson, who owned Fraternity in Cincinnati. He'd just had another hit by Lonnie Mack ["Memphis"]. So I went up and told Harry and Louise [Harry's wife] that I had a chance to be on a major label, and so he wished me well and we remained friends.

So they let you go.

Well, I was never even under contract. But he understood. They loved me enough that they just wanted what was best for me. So I came back down. Chet had the contracts, he had some songs, I had some songs, and I had a horn sound in my mind that I wanted. Then he played me a song called "Shame on Me" that Lawton Williams had written. So that was the first thing I cut and it sold a million records. So then I got a publishing gig with Cliffie Stone—I was tired of wandering around—so I took a gig writing for Central Songs out in Hollywood.

So when did you actually *move* to Nashville?

1964. That's when I moved to Nashville for good.

So before that, you're just going back and forth, from your sister's house in Dayton mostly, to record with Chet . . .
Just wandering around.

. . . and then things started happening, and then you're traveling around, promoting . . .
Yeah, I spent one whole summer up in Iowa, working ballrooms and that kind of stuff. As a matter of fact, that's where I was when I got word that Chet wanted to work with me.

So how did you come to move to Nashville for good? What caused that decision?
I wanted to get married.

So you'd met Jeannie.
I had met Jeannie, and we . . .

Where'd you meet Jeannie?
I took a show into Reno, Nevada. I was putting a show together and needed a girl singer, and I hired her.

Was there an audition?
Well, we considered two or three. We didn't audition. Somebody knew how good they were.

So she came highly recommended.
Yeah. Then we kind of hit it off.

Was it love at first sight?
Kind of. Two days, I guess. We hung out for about a year. Then in '64 we decided to get married. I didn't want to raise kids in L.A.—I knew too many crazy people out there. A marriage can't possibly last in L.A. if you're in show business. There's no way.

. . . unless you're Steve Lawrence and Eydie Gormé.
Oh, well. That's a different ball game. They're Jewish. *(laughs)*

So whose decision was it to move to Nashville? Was it something you and Jeannie decided together?

Actually I didn't give her much choice. I knew I had her hooked. I had her hooked real good. *(laughs)* No, we talked about it.

You had me thinking you drove her kicking and screaming to Nashville.

No, she was eager. She wanted to do it. We both did. We wanted to come back here and have babies and live.

Where was the first place you lived?

We came back and Jan [Howard] took Jeannie around—and then us—to look at houses, and we found one over on Broadmoor Drive in Madison. Jan and Harlan lived over there then. June Carter lived over there, pretty close. And Kitty Wells. And so we got us a house over there. Then Willie was living out at Ridgetop. And we'd go out there.

Ridgetop? Out beyond Goodlettsville?

Yeah, it's past Goodlettsville. You just keep going on out to Ridgetop.

Wasn't he raising pigs then?

Yeah, he was raising pigs and chickens. He was farming. Had on overalls and a big, black beard and a big belly. He was just a farmer.

A *black* beard?

Well, reddish-black. It was dark.

No gray yet. *(laughs)*

Oh, no . . . but his beard was darker than his hair.

Well, I think we've 'bout got it. So when was the first time you ever heard the word "Nashville"?

I can't remember when I did *not* hear the word "Nashville." Like everybody in the whole world, we listened to WSM . . . Nashville, Tennessee . . . the Grand Ole Opry. I'd listen to the Opry, and when the batteries would go down on our radio, I would sneak around the hill on Saturday night, until I heard it coming in on somebody else's radio. Then I'd go down and get as close to their house as I could, and sit there behind a tree and listen.

So, Bobby, tell me one thing that could only have happened in Nashville . . . a Nashville memory . . . just a Nashville anything.
Well, when I was living in L.A., I was flying in here to record, and the one thing I distinctly remember was getting off that plane—usually Hank Cochran would pick me up at the airport. I would get off that plane and immediately feel the vibe. It was like electricity in the air. There was so much going on. It was like electricity. And I would join up with it, you know?

It'd get on you.
Yeah. It would get on you. You couldn't help but get caught up in it. You'd get very creative and want to *do* something. It was magic.

Miranda Lambert

"WE'RE PLANNING TO FEATURE HER on the cover."

That's what *Garden & Gun* editor Sid Evans said after he asked me to interview Miranda Lambert for the magazine's September/October 2008 issue. For the uninitiated, *Garden & Gun* is a magazine that spotlights southern culture. Often described as a cross between *Oxford American, Southern Living,* and *Field & Stream,* it was launched in early 2007 out of Charleston, South Carolina.

In all honesty, I had only vaguely heard of Miranda Lambert. She could've been the hottest thing in country music for all I knew. And even if she *was,* I was wondering if Evans had lost his mind. A country singer on the cover of *Garden & Gun?* The idea seemed far-fetched. Like Mother Teresa on the cover of *Playboy.* Or Paris Hilton on the cover of *Mother Jones.*

"She's from Texas," Evans said.

"Texas?" I replied. "Is that the South?"

"Well, she's from *East* Texas," he continued. "She writes some pretty interesting songs. I think you'll like her. Merle Haggard is her favorite singer. And . . . ah . . . she has a concealed handgun license. I'll overnight you some of her press. Look it over and we'll talk." *Click.*

The next morning, a FedEx box arrived at my doorstep. The box was noticeably heavy. Inside were articles featuring Miranda from every publication imaginable—*Rolling Stone, Texas Monthly, People, Entertainment Weekly, USA Today,* the *Village Voice, No Depression,* the *New York Times, L.A. Times, Washington Post . . .* you name it. The kid was hot.

As I read the articles, I found myself silently rooting for this Miranda Lambert. Her first album had sold over a million copies *without* a radio hit, which is almost unheard of these days. The girl had moxie,

The New Queen of Country

Marshall Chapman sits down with
singer-songwriter Miranda Lambert

Lighting It Up:
Lambert at the Nashville
home of Marshall
Chapman.

Miranda Lambert at Marshall's house, June 25, 2008

no doubt about it. She seemed to be single-handedly shaking up the country music establishment in a way that hadn't been done since Loretta Lynn sang "Don't Come Home a-Drinkin' (with Lovin' on Your Mind)."

That evening, my husband and I sat down and listened to Lambert's first two CDs—*Kerosene* and *Crazy Ex-girlfriend*.

"She sounds like Dolly Parton backed by Lynyrd Skynyrd," I said. "I'll bet she knocks 'em dead when she plays live." One line in particular caught my attention: "His fist is big, but my gun's bigger / He'll find out when I pull the trigger."

The next morning, the phone rang.

"Well, what do you think?" Evans said.

"Count me in," I replied.

WHEN I HEARD THE PHOTO SHOOT would be in Nashville, I offered my house and garden as a location. I was thinking Miranda and her people could make themselves at home, and—best of all—I wouldn't have to leave the house.

Two days later, a photographer and his assistant flew to Nashville. After all was said and done, it was decided the shoot would, indeed, take place at my house.

The day of the shoot was like a circus come-to-town. At one point, there were twenty people running around the house and yard—photographers, assistants, hair and make-up specialists, managers, road managers, publicists, assistant publicists, caterers, gofers . . . you name it. Racks of clothes were wheeled into our dining room, which ended up being a makeshift beauty salon and dressing room for Miss Lambert. My husband, who was working for the city government at the time, even arranged for a retired policeman to drop by for additional security. All the activity was a welcome break from my usual monastic routine. Plus, I learned a new word.

"Would it be okay if we used the dining room for Miranda's glam?"

"Her what?"

"Glam . . . you know . . . hair and make-up."

I immediately filed *glam* away with another favorite showbiz word—*gherm*. *Gherm* is a verb that means "to gush excessively when around a famous person." I love turning my literary friends on to these words. I mean, how can you have an MFA and not know about getting ghermed? *Man, you wouldn't be-LIEVE how I got ghermed at the mall yesterday!* I like to imagine that *getting ghermed* somehow derived from *getting slimed*, from the movie *Ghostbusters*.

I spent most of the day of the photo shoot working in my writing room. But every now and then I'd venture out to watch the circus. After the shoot, as things started winding down, Miranda and I sat down for the interview.

I found her refreshingly open and *sane* as she talked about her love of Merle Haggard, her fear of snakes, playing Gruene Hall in New

Braunfels [Texas] and hearing herself sing on the radio that first time, while touring stations with her mom—"just like Loretta and Doo." When she mentioned that her mom used to babysit David Allan Coe's kids, that's when it hit me: *My God, she's only twenty-four years old! She's a baby!* With her petite stature (5 feet 4 inches), lustrous blond hair, and dimples to die for, she seemed more girl-next-door, cheerleader at the local high school than country music star. But there was no doubt that inside that cheerleader body lived an old soul.

When Miranda mentioned she had once lived in Nashville, the thought crossed my mind to interview her again for this book.

NOW FIVE MONTHS LATER, here we are. Meanwhile, Miranda has charted her first Top Ten single ("Gunpowder & Lead") and—just four days ago—performed at the annual CMA Awards show, where she was nominated for Female Vocalist of the Year and Single of the Year (for "Gunpowder & Lead").

We meet for coffee just before noon at the downtown Hilton on a bright and blustery November Sunday. With Nashville's churches still in session and the Titans in Jacksonville, we have the lobby bar all to ourselves.

Downtown Nashville
November 16, 2008

I know we touched on this briefly when we talked before, how you came to live in Nashville when you were nineteen years old. Was that the first time you had ever been to Nashville? Did you ever come with your parents, like when you were a child?
Yeah, I did. I came the first time when I was fourteen. I came for Fan Fair.

And that was the *very* first time?
Very first time.

What was it like?
Well, I was *so* excited to come because I love country music, and I

was a huge fan. So to come during the week that . . . you know, now I realize *(laughs)* it's probably the last week anyone *else* would want to come, but as a fan I was just so excited.

Did you wait in line to meet any of the stars?
I didn't, because I didn't want to miss the shows. You know, because people were performing while people were signing autographs.

What year was that?
I was fourteen then and I'm twenty-five now, so . . . I don't know. Can't do the math yet. Haven't had enough caffeine. *(laughs)* I just remember I had my best friend Laci with me and my mom and dad.

Did the four of you drive up from Lindale [Texas]?
Yes. And after we got here, I remember we were walking down Broadway and some guy comes up and says, "Are y'all from Texas?" And I guess you could just tell, you know? *(laughs)* And so, I just remember walking by every door, and there was country music blasting out of every door on Broadway, and I was like, "This is heaven!"

Did you get up and sing or anything?
I sang, like, at a karaoke place. And then I came again when I was sixteen.

Do you remember what you sang?
Not then, but when I was sixteen, I came and I did this little showcase thing that I'd gotten invited to do.

When you came back at age sixteen, were you again with your parents?
Um-hm. I came to Nashville at age fourteen, fifteen, and sixteen—all for Fan Fair. And at sixteen I came for a showcase I was invited to, because by then I had gotten into singing, but I wasn't sure it was, like, what I wanted to do, but I knew I was good at it. So Mom and Dad drove me up here to a showcase. And I sang at Lonnie's Western Room.

Lonnie's . . . ?
You know where that is? Down on Printer's Alley?

Oh, okay.
I sang "Blue" by LeAnn Rimes and "Something to Talk About" by Bonnie Raitt.

Was there a house band?
No, it was karaoke. That was one of the last times I sang to tracks. *(laughs)*

Were you well received?
Yeah, I think so. They were like, "You're good!" But I was a kid, you know . . . sixteen.

So the next time you came [to Nashville], you were nineteen, right?
I came a few other times. I can't remember for what reason. Just back and forth. But when I was nineteen, I flew to Nashville for *Nashville Star* [the TV show that helped launch Miranda's career]. It was the first time I had ever flown by myself. And the first time I had ever left home without my parents. It was like going off to college. I remember I cried at the security gate.

Who took you to the airport?
My mom and dad.

Did you fly out of DFW [Dallas–Fort Worth]?
Um-hm.

So they're telling you goodbye at the security gate, and . . . I imagine your mom's crying like a baby.
I'm crying, she's crying, I'm like, "I can't do it. I don't want to leave home!" Because I'd had a band for two years in Texas at that point, two and a half years, you know? Just traveling around in a motor home, and my parents were always right there by my side, so this was sort of my first step out. And so I flew to Nashville and the *Nashville Star* people picked me up. All the cast flew in.

Did they pick you up in a van? A limo?
It was a van. They had a van pick me up with all the *Nashville Star* cast, and I knew no one. I got in the van with a bunch of total strangers. It was a very different experience.

Where did you spend that first night?
I spent that first night at the . . . let's see, where did we stay? I think we stayed at the Opryland Hotel . . . which was perfect. *(laughs)*

Did you have your apartment secured by then?
When I did *Nashville Star*, we all lived in a house on 18th [Avenue South]—the Nashville Star House. It was for all the contestants.

So Mom and Dad are back in Lindale.
Yes. And I'm by myself. But it was a really good experience. It was one of those things where, if I hadn't been forced to do it, I probably never would have left Lindale, you know? I've always been kind of a homebody, family person. So when I was forced to leave and go be on *Nashville Star*, it was good for me. I never went to college, but *Nashville Star* was my college experience in that it separated me from my family. It forced me to grow up a little.

What happened after *Nashville Star*?
My mom came up and helped me find an apartment. I had nothing. I didn't have a straw—zero. Forks, spoons . . . literally, I had nothing. We went to Goodwill and garage sales and got whatever we could get—dishes, old furniture, whatever we could find. We filled up my apartment for really cheap.

Where was your apartment?
It was off Briley Parkway, out near the airport.

Do you remember the name?
It was called . . . I can't really remember the name of it. It was kind of in the ghetto.

If you think of it, let me know.
Okay. My mom probably remembers.

**I'm trying to get these little details. Like when you first drove
to Nashville with your parents when you were fourteen, what
kind of car were you in?**
It was a Ford Expedition.

**Oh, yeah. The one you and your mom drove around Texas in? With
your guitar and a cooler full of baloney sandwiches in the back seat?**
Yes. *(laughs)* That's right! It was that same car.

Like Doo and Loretta touring radio stations?
Like Doo and Loretta, yeah. *(laughs)*

Did you have a car when you later lived in Nashville?
Yes. It was a Toyota Celica.

What was it like, living in that apartment?
Well, I remember the first night I stayed there by myself. I was scared
to death. I was like, Okay, I'm living here in this strange city and . . .

Did you have a TV?
I did.

Did you watch TV that first night?
Yeah.

Do you remember what you watched?
God, no . . . just anything to try to get my mind off being alone. I
cried a lot that year, just because I was so lonely. I loved Nashville,
but I loved it better when my friends and family were up. But when
they were home, I felt all alone again. I kept thinking during those
times in my apartment, just sitting there by myself, that . . . this is
what a songwriter, a struggling artist, is supposed to go through.
To get where I'm going, hopefully. While I was sitting there crying,

wanting to go to Texas, I kept telling myself I was paying my dues. I learned a lot about myself living in that apartment.

Did you write any songs then?
I did. I wrote a lot.

Any that you later recorded?
I wrote one called "Guilty Sunday," but I haven't recorded it yet.

Were you hung over? What's it about?
It's about being with some guy the night before, some guy I had no business being with, and knowing I was gonna be with him again. *(laughs)*

Been there, done that. *(laughter)* Okay. So how long did you live in that apartment by yourself?
Six months. Then I got another apartment with one of my best friends from Texas. She moved up here and we found another roommate—just a random roommate. We had a three-bedroom. And that was when I started making my record.

Kerosene?
Um-hm. And that apartment was off of Stewart's Ferry [Pike]. It was a better situation because I wasn't living by myself. I had my friend from Texas.

So you had the apartment off Briley Parkway for six months by yourself, and then you got the one on Stewart's Ferry Pike.
Yes.

Both of those places are way out.
Yeah, looking back on it, I probably should have lived closer to town.

Out there, it's like Anywhere, USA.
Exactly. My only friends were my producer and my booking agent, and they had families. So they'd have to go home at night, and I'm

like, "But wait! Don't go home!" I got used to it after a while. But I just felt like my home is where my family is. Wherever they end up, that's where I'm going to be.

So you lived in Nashville totally for how long?
A year. Not including *Nashville Star.* Probably a year and a half in all.

I'm just going to shoot you one last, crazy question: can you remember the first time you ever heard the word "Nashville"?
Hmm . . . *(barely audible)* heard the word "Nashville" . . .

"No" is a perfectly acceptable answer. *(laughs)*
I can't remember the first time I heard the *word.* Nashville was just one of those places I was always hearing about. It was where the dreams came true.

Your father had the dream, right?
Yeah. He had a band, like, before I was born. He was a singer-songwriter.

Do you feel that, in a way, you're living out his dream?
He never knew I would be doing this, but he was excited when I decided to. But growing up, I don't remember the first time I *heard* it [the word "Nashville"], but every time somebody would say "Nashville," I always got a little flutter in my stomach.

Bobby Braddock

I FIRST SAW BOBBY BRADDOCK at a "guitar pull" at Harlan Howard's house on Otter Creek Road in Nashville. A "guitar pull" is what you call a Nashville party with lots of songwriters, but only one guitar. The liquor starts flowing, spirits rise, normally shy songwriters become emboldened, a guitar materializes, and next thing you know, everybody's pulling at it. Well, not really, but you get the idea.

My favorite "guitar pull" story is the one about Roger Miller. As the guitar was going around, it seemed like every songwriter was prefacing his or her song with a pitiful introduction like, "This is a song I wrote after my girlfriend left me . . ." or "This is a song I wrote after my dog died . . ." or "This is a song I wrote after my truck broke down . . ." and so on. Just real downer kind of stuff. When the guitar finally got to Roger, the room suddenly got quiet. Everybody was looking at Roger as he fiddled around with the guitar. Then he looked up and said, "This is a song I wrote while that guy was singing that last one."

I don't remember meeting Braddock that night at Harlan's. But I remember him and a gal sitting at an upright piano singing "Golden Ring," a song Bobby had written with Rafe Van Hoy that was a huge hit for George Jones and Tammy Wynette.

It was quite a gathering. I can still see Leon Russell sitting cross-legged on the floor singing "A Song for You." I had gone to the party with Joe South, but at some point, Joe had bolted, so I ended up leaving with John and Susan Loudermilk. There's a lot more to the story, but we'll just leave it at that.

Not long after that, I finally met Braddock somewhere, I can't quite remember. It might have been Ciraco's, an Italian restaurant between Vanderbilt and Music Row. But what I clearly remember is Bobby telling me how much he loved my song about Hank Williams, even going

John D. Loudermilk, John Egerton, Bobby Braddock, Marshall, and Michael Gray
at the Country Music Hall of Fame and Museum, Sept. 15, 2007

so far as to quote some of the lyrics. I was completely blown away. Bobby was about the hottest songwriter in Nashville at the time. "He Stopped Loving Her Today," a song he wrote with Curly Putman, had just won CMA Song of the Year.

For a while, Bobby would show up—usually with an entourage that included his daughter, Lauren—at the Bluebird Café whenever I played there with my band. Once, after a show, I ended up following Bobby and his cronies back to his girlfriend's apartment off Thompson Lane, where we played Scrabble until well after sunup. My most vivid memory from that night is of the dictionary we used to look up challenged words. It was called *The Official Scrabble Players Dictionary*. I had one just like it at home, only mine wasn't covered with phrases that looked like somebody had tried to carve them into the dictionary with a ballpoint pen. Each phrase was punctuated with multiple exclamation points, as in *This book sucks!!*, *This book's a lying son of a bitch!!*, *Whoever published this piece-of-shit dictionary ought to be hanged!!!*, and so on.

Evidently, whenever Braddock and the dictionary would disagree, instead of throwing the dictionary against the wall, Braddock would vent his frustration in true songwriter fashion by throwing words on the dictionary.

For years, whenever I'd stop by Kroger on my way home after a late night at the Bluebird, I inevitably would run into Bobby Braddock. It was uncanny. We'd laugh as we'd be the only two people there. Lately I've been running into Buddy Miller, but for a while—like ten years running—it was Braddock every damn time. You could set your watch by it. Two o'clock in the morning? Book it. Bobby Braddock is Krogering in Green Hills. I think it's safe to say that Braddock, besides being one of the most successful songwriters ever to hit Nashville, is a night owl.

My house in Nashville
November 18, 2008

So, Bobby, I've read your wonderful book [*Down in Orburndale: A Songwriter's Youth in Old Florida*, LSU Press, 2007] about growing up in pre–Disney World Florida. As I recall, you just up and drove to Nashville with your new wife. Would you talk about that for a minute? Was that your first trip to Nashville?
Well, I had *passed through* Nashville when I was a kid going somewhere with my parents, but I first *came* to Nashville in, like, the later part of '58, the early part of '59, because I was hooked up with a con artist / rock & roll singer out of Atlanta, and actually got to sit in on some recording sessions . . . Red Foley and Lefty Frizzell.

As a keyboard player?
No, not as a keyboard player. I was part of a band that this guy had—a rockabilly act called Chuck & Betty—and he came up to see Owen Bradley, and we went in and got to sit in as visitors on a Red Foley session. Not in the control room, but out where the musicians were. We could've sneezed or farted and just blown the whole take, you know? *(laughs)* They wouldn't let you do that now.

How long were you guys in Nashville?
Just a couple of days. I didn't really seriously come . . . well, I came here to scope it out, maybe a few months, before I finally moved here.

So how long have you lived in Nashville?
I came here for good in September of 1964.

Wow.
Yep. I was seven years old! *(laughs)*

Right . . . and Cotton's a monkey. *(more laughs)* So, where did you come here from?
Well, I came here from Florida. Small town called Auburndale. But I came here more directly, I guess, from Orlando, which was more my base because of a rock & roll band I was playing in.

Okay, so you drove up with your wife in . . .
Drove up with my wife in September of 1964, and that was to move to Nashville and *stay*. Nobody I knew thought that I should come. The only person that supported me in coming was my wife, and that's because she wanted to get away from Florida . . . and my ex-fiancée. *(laughs)* It wasn't that my wife believed in me and thought that I would do great things, she just wanted to get the hell out of Florida. And my family and friends, they had no idea what I was doing or why I was doing it. I had friends tell me later, "We thought you'd go up there and stay, you know, a few months and then come back."

I feel like my whole career has been that way. I'll be on a roll and do really well, and then I'll have some dry years and everybody, you know, starts writing my musical career obituary. And then I'll come back, and then cool off, and then I'll come . . . my whole career's been that way—peaks and valleys. First and foremost, you've got to believe in yourself. You do, or nobody else will. Then sometimes, nobody else will *anyway*. *(laughs)* You just have to show 'em. Then when you show 'em, that's when they finally believe it. Seems like you have to show 'em over and over again.

Well, you get that first hit, then some doors open.
Yeah, well, maybe for a while.

What's that saying? "You're only as good as your last gig"?
Yeah. That's it.

First time I ever saw that was on a T-shirt. John Stewart was in town recording *Cannons in the Rain*. His bass player had that on his T-shirt.
It's a business of quick turnovers.

Like being a football coach in the SEC.
Yeah . . . a very fluid business.

Like when was the last time you won a game?
Right! *(laughs)* History recedes fast. It does.

Okay, so when did you first hear the word "Nashville"? Or hear about Nashville?
I remember Tennessee was the third state I ever heard of, after Florida and Georgia. And Wisconsin was the last! *(laughs)* I remember when I was seven years old, I asked my mother, I said, "What's Wisconsin?" She said, "That's a state." I said, "Hmm, never heard of it." But Nashville? Probably when I was a kid, hearing the Grand Ole Opry on the radio. I remember some times we'd hear the Opry when it was broadcast over the networks on Saturday night. So I was probably six, seven years old when I first heard of Nashville, yeah.

Okay, so what made you move here?
I wanted to be a songwriter. Plus I thought I could get gigs as a piano player. I had confidence in my musicianship. I thought I was pretty decent with that, but I wasn't sure about the songwriting part. It was something I aspired to, but I didn't know if I really had the ability or not, at least not until I got here. And after I was here for a few months, I got a gig playing piano with Marty Robbins and he recorded a couple of my songs, and I thought, "Hey, I guess I really am a songwriter!"

So I asked him if I could quit the road, and I went to one publishing company—it was then called Tree—and I called Buddy Killen up. Buddy had heard my Marty Robbins song, the one Marty had recorded. It was called "While You're Dancing." It was an absolute rip-off of "Save the Last Dance for Me." If it'd been a big, big hit, I probably would have been sued. *(laughs)* But Buddy had heard it, and so he met with me, and he let me know that he didn't usually personally meet with new writers. And I played him some songs, and he liked them, and he signed me up, and that was it. I've been there, in some form or the other, ever since.

Which is how many years?
Oh, I've been with Sony/Tree—now known as Sony/ATV Music Publishing—since May of 1966. Forty-one and a half years. *(laughs)* I started getting songs cut left and right, between Buddy Killen who owned the place, and Curly Putman—the great Curly Putman—who was Buddy's chief song plugger. Curly was a great song plugger. He was good pitching other people's songs.

And he was a writer, too.
That's what I'm saying.

And y'all wrote . . .
Um, "He Stopped Loving Her Today" . . . Curly did the melody change on "D-I-V-O-R-C-E" that made it a big hit. And between Buddy and Curly, I was getting songs cut left and right, man. I mean, it was every few days I'd get a cut. I thought it'd be that way for the rest of my life, which of course, it wasn't. I thought, "Hey, man, this is a great gig!" Every few days, I'd get a new cut.

Okay, I got another question. What mode of transportation brought you to Nashville? Your car, right?
Yeah.

Did you own it?
Yeah . . . I'm just trying to think . . . I had an Oldsmobile, and my bride had a Volkswagen.

So y'all were a two-car family when you left Florida?
We *were* a two-car family. But somehow, that seemed to mesh into one car. I'm not exactly sure how that happened. *(laughs)*

She probably gave hers to her little sister or something.
Yeah, something like that. Anyway, after I'd been in Nashville for—I don't know, maybe for less than a year, because my folks subsidized my career a little bit—we were able to buy a house. And after "D-I-V-O-R-C-E" became a big hit—I was probably twenty-six, twenty-seven years old—I went totally hillbilly and got a swimming pool. *(laughs)* The only swimming pool I ever had.

You were probably the only songwriter in Nashville that had one. Where was this swimming pool?
On Whispering Hills Drive.

That's poetic.
And when I got this swimming pool, this contractor came out there, and it took *months*, I mean, it just . . . there was a *hole* in the ground forever and ever. I mean it just would not go away, and it never turned into a swimming pool. So finally, I went up to the guy, and . . . he was a little guy, and I won't take any crap from a little guy, I'll tell you! *(laughs)* And so I went up to him and said, "If this thing's not finished in six weeks, I'm gon' whip your ass! You understand that?" And he said, "Okay. I promise you. It'll be finished." And it was. Six weeks to the day.

Okay. So that first night in Nashville with your wife . . .
Actually I came up *before* my wife. She stayed with her sister in Alabama while I came up and got a place.

So you dropped her off in Alabama, then drove on in by yourself?
Yeah. I had a contact in Nashville—a former rockabilly star from Tampa named Benny Joy, who was enjoying a somewhat successful career as a songwriter. And he managed to get me a place to stay while I was looking around. It was . . . Hank Snow's guitar player was on the road, so I got to sleep in Hank Snow's guitar player's room in a

rooming house for two or three nights while I looked around for a place. I ended up getting us a place near the fairgrounds on Rains Avenue.

Any early experiences that stand out in your mind?
Okay. How 'bout my first job in Nashville?

Another job besides writing songs?
Oh, yeah! My first job was . . . I got a job as a trumpet polisher at Hewgley's Music Store on Commerce Street. The store was about a block long. It was just a music store, but kids came from all over Tennessee. That's where you came to get your band instruments, and to get your band instruments repaired. And so I polished trumpets. Then I got fired for getting my apron caught in the trumpet-polishing machine. It nearly choked me to death. *(laughs)*

How many days had you been on the job?
Two or three.

Man, it's a good thing you didn't die, or some songwriter might've had to write "He Stopped Writing Songs Today." *(laughs)* **Anything else you remember? Something that stands out in your mind? Like maybe the first time you came through here with your parents as a child, or that time you came up with the rockabilly band . . . just anything that happened, something you saw on the street?**
Yes, I've got . . .

. . . something that happened in the middle of the night?
All right. In the summer of . . . it must've been around the first of July in 1954. I was thirteen years old. My mother had a brother who worked in a steel mill in Hammond, Indiana, and we were driving from Florida to Hammond, Indiana, driving through the middle of Nashville. And I remember seeing a black man and a white man walking down the street talking to each other, and I thought that was kind of unusual. It wasn't something I was used to seeing in my little small town in Florida. I didn't think of it as being bad or good, I just thought of it as being significant and unusual.

Terri Clark

UNTIL RECENTLY I DIDN'T PERSONALLY know Terri Clark. But I knew her house. In 2006, Terri bought a house a few doors down from mine. I figured I'd run into her eventually. But I never laid eyes on her. All I knew was that her house was adorable—a renovated bungalow with beautiful stonework and a Swiss chalet feel—and somebody sure did a nice job keeping up her yard.

Terri is a bona fide country music star, which means she's out of town a lot. But even country music stars occasionally have to come in for a landing. I was beginning to wonder if she existed.

Then about a year later, I was raking leaves near the sidewalk in front of my house, when a tall, slender brunette jogging down the sidewalk pulled up and took off her headphones.

"Hi, Marshall. I'm Terri Clark."

"Oh, hi! I was beginning to wonder if anybody lived in your house."

We had a nice visit. I told her that Matraca Berg and I had knocked on her door only days before, and that I loved her recording of "Nashville Girls," a song Matraca wrote with Gretchen Peters. We talked about the neighborhood, mutual friends, and, briefly, the dismal state of the music business. I mentioned that I was writing a book and that I'd like to interview her at some point. And now, almost a year later, here we are.

So Terri, I've googled you. I know you moved here from Canada in 1987. You were eighteen years old. Was that your very first time in Nashville?
Well, actually, when I was about seventeen, I was living in Michigan with my dad for a few months, and we drove down to Nashville for a little weekend trip.

Where did your dad live in Michigan?
The Port Huron area. He was living up there with his wife at the time, and I went to stay with them for a while, because I was trying to find a way into the country.

As in United States of America?
Yeah. *(laughs)* Because I was Canadian, you know? And I was trying to get my native Indian band number, because there's a way for Indians to get across the border. If you have a band number and have enough of that in your bloodline, they'll let you in. Of course, as it turned out, I didn't have enough. So my dad says, "We'll go to Nashville." 'Course I grew up just *dreaming* about Nashville! I was fascinated with it. I was raised in Alberta, which is way the hell on the other side of the moon from here. But I had watched shows about Nashville on television growing up.

So when did you first hear the word "Nashville"?
Oh, gosh, probably my grandparents. My grandparents were a club act in Montreal.

What were they called?
Her name was Betty Gauthier [pronounced "Go-*shay*"], and my grandpa's name was Ray.

What was their stage name?
Betty & Ray. Anyway, they supported five kids playing country music in clubs. They opened shows for Little Jimmy Dickens, Johnny Cash . . .

Were you a toddler when they were playing?
They had pretty much wound down by the time I was born [1968]. But we sat around and jammed. My grandparents and I had a very special connection.

What did Ray play?
Fiddle and guitar . . . some bass.

And Betty?
She played guitar and sang. Anyway, so Nashville was always discussed. I really didn't get serious about playing and singing until I was about twelve or thirteen, and then I *really* got into it. By the time I was fourteen, all my ambitions to be a cop went out the window, and I decided I was going to be a singer and move to Nashville. My mom and I were big believers, we just had the dream, and she was like, "*You can do it!*" Everyone thought we were *nuts*. But the very first time I came to Nashville was when my dad brought me down on that little weekend trip.

Did you guys drive?
Yep. Both times I came to Nashville, it was by car.

What kind of car?
I can't remember what he drove at the time.

Was it a sedan or a truck?
I think it might have been a truck. A pick-up truck or something like that. But later, when I actually *moved* to Nashville, my mom and I made the trek in a Honda Civic.

That was when you were eighteen?
When I was eighteen, right.

Marshall and Terri Clark on Marshall's front porch, March 10, 2010

So when you came down the year before with your dad, where did you stay?
We stayed at the Days Inn off I-65 just north of town. And when I came the second time with my mom, we stayed at the Motel 6 off of Trinity Lane, and it was, you know, *(laughs)* pretty basic.

How long were you and your dad here?
Only two days. It was more of a touristy thing.

Were you writing songs then?
Yes.

So that first time wasn't a career move.
No, I was a tourist, just visiting, getting a feel for it. I never will forget looking out the window at the Days Inn, seeing the skyline

of Nashville, thinking, "Oh, my God, I've got to conquer that?" A little prairie girl from Canada, standing there looking at the skyline going, "Oh, my God, it's a city!" *(laughs)* You know, like, "What am I *doing*?!" So then my dad took me to the Nashville Palace. After we'd been there a little while, I asked to get up, and so they put me on a waiting list. I ended up going on last. We sat there until after midnight. I sang "Mule Skinner Blues" and "Singing the Blues" (the Gail Davies version of the old Guy Mitchell hit) with the house band. The guitar player—he also played with Randy Travis—told me I belonged in Nashville and that I had more raw talent than he had heard in there in ages.

So your first night in town and you're singing at the Nashville Palace. Sounds like your dad was supportive.
Yeah. I'm not as close to my dad as I am to my mom. My parents divorced when I was young, so I didn't get to spend a lot of time with my dad.

How old were you when they divorced?
Eight. So I think he wanted to do something nice for me, and he knew how much music meant to me.

Did he play music?
No, no . . . never. Mostly my mom's side of the family played.

Did your mom play?
Yep. She played guitar and sang songs to me instead of reading bedtime stories. My lullabies were country, soft folk . . . Janis Joplin, Joan Baez . . .

What songs did she sing while you were falling asleep?
Oh, "Bobby McGee" . . .

That's a good one.
"I Got a Brand New Pair of Roller Skates" ["Brand New Key"] *(laughs)* . . .

Oh, yeah . . . Melanie.
And she would sing "Daddy Frank," "Blowin' in the Wind," "Piney Wood Hills" by Buffy Sainte-Marie . . .

I have a feeling your mother and I are about the same age.
She's fifty-eight.

I'm right there. *(laughs)* **When you mentioned those songs, I'm thinking, "Those sound familiar!" Okay. So tell me about coming down with your mom. It's a year later, and you've decided you are moving to Nashville.**
Yeah, well, my mom flew to Toronto, where I was staying with a longtime family friend of ours named Pat, who was a character. She and my mom were like Thelma & Louise. So we got in Pat's Honda Civic . . .

So it's Thelma & Louise and Terri taking off for Nashville.
Um-hm. With my guitar in the back seat with everything I owned.

Were you living in Toronto then?
No, I had gone to visit Pat, and then my mom flew down and then we all drove down.

In Pat's Honda Civic?
In Pat's Honda Civic.

What year?
Oh . . . it was an early to mid-'80s two-door hatchback.

What color?
Silver.

Okay, so what happened?
Well, we had to cross the border. I remember the border official saying, "Where you guys going?" And Pat rolled down the window and said, "We're going to Nashville!" Little did he know I wasn't

planning on coming back. You always tell them you're just going for a visit. And he goes, "You going to the Grand Ole Opry?" And I said, "Yep!" Then he looked at my guitar and went, "Okay! Off you go!" And little did *I* know that I would be inducted into the Grand Ole Opry as its first Canadian female member [seventeen] years later.

Did you listen to the Opry growing up?
No, not on the radio. I heard it, well, saw it on TNN [The Nashville Network]. But still, it was very, very important. To me, it's just where we all came from.

Were you an Ian & Sylvia fan?
My mom definitely was. She used to sing their songs to me, too. *(starts singing)* "There's a young man that I know . . . "

"Someday Soon"—what a great song. Okay. So you and your mom and . . . what's her name . . . Pat?
(laughs) If you met Pat, you would die laughing. She is a *character!*

So you and your mom and Pat drive to Nashville, then check into the Motel 6 on Trinity Lane. Anything in particular you remember?
Just that it was a really cheap hotel! *(laughs)* I just remember, the first few days we did some tourist-trap things that I didn't get to do when I came with my dad, because we didn't have enough time. Let's see, we went to the Hall of Fame . . .

Do you remember what you did that first night?
I think that night we basically went to sleep because we had been driving and driving and driving. And then we got up the next day. The first order of business was to find me a place to live, and then to find me some kind of job that would pay cash, because I didn't have a green card. So we decided to put an ad in the paper for babysitting work. That I would babysit for cash. *(laughs)* And so we were getting the ad all ready to go, before starting out on our day. We went to the Hall of Fame, and we took a little tour of the Ryman [Auditorium] before they did the whole renovation . . .

Was the Hall of Fame on Music Row then?
Um-hm.

Anything in particular you remember about it [the Hall of Fame]?
I remember seeing Patsy Cline's dress, and some stuff the Judds had
in there—I was, like, a big Judds freak, too. It was all just fascinating
to me. The whole . . . I love stuff like that. Just the history. *(laughs)*
I've got pictures of me in my Judds T-shirt posing in front of all this
memorabilia in the Hall of Fame.

I might want a copy of that [for this book].
I've got them somewhere, yeah. Anyway, so in our journeys, our little
traipsing around town to see what we were going to see, we ventured
into Tootsie's Orchid Lounge one afternoon. The place was empty, and
this guy let me get up and sit in. This was about one in the afternoon.
So I started singing, and after about twenty or thirty minutes, people
started filtering in, 'cause they used to leave the door open. Pretty
soon, the place was packed. So they offered me a job. So out went the
babysitting job and in came the Tootsie's job. *(laughs)* I'm like, "Well,
of course, this is what I'm here for!" Of course, Lower Broadway was a
war zone back then, if you can remember.

Oh, yes.
Peep shows, dope, transients all over the place . . .

. . . the Demon's Den. *(laughs)*
Plus, I didn't have a car, and I didn't know what I was . . .

So how long did Pat and your mom stay down with you?
They stayed about a week.

So they left you down here . . . ?
Yeah, I found a place to live at the end of Nolensville Road, in this
condo with a woman who was separated from her husband. She had
a two-year-old son, and she was looking for somebody to rent a room
out to. We had found it in the paper. So that's where I lived. And then

later, when her husband came back, I had to leave because all they did was fight. It was really wicked.

So your first apartment was out Nolensville Road?
Yeah, out by the Wal-Mart.

You remember the name?
It was called McMurray Place. And so, I just had to figure out how to get to Tootsie's and back every day.

So when Pat and your mom left, you didn't have a car?
That's right. So I took the city bus. There was a bus stop on Nolensville Road, and I'd carry my guitar there everyday—in my cowgirl outfit. *(laughs)* And I didn't know where I *was*, I didn't know *anybody*, I mean . . . my mom and I would laugh. Everyone thought we were *nuts*. And I don't know if I would do it again.

How long did you have the gig at Tootsie's?
On and off for probably two or three years. I had the 10 a.m. to 2 p.m. shift. I still go down there and play sometimes. *(laughs)* It was not then what it is now. There were hardly any people. I scraped to make thirty dollars a day playing in there. I lived on a hundred bucks a week. But when you have no credit cards, no gas to pay for, you can do it. And I did it. I lived on four or five hundred bucks a month. I lost a lot of weight, *(laughs)* but I played there. I would tie my guitar to my wrist with a shoelace walking down Lower Broadway—even in broad daylight. I mean, I was afraid someone would grab it. I had a [Martin] D-28.

Did you ever consider going to Los Angeles or New York?
It was always Nashville. I might consider living in Los Angeles *now*, because it's a whole different ball game. But no, I never considered anything else.

So you moved to Nashville because . . .
I wanted to be Reba McEntire! *(laughs)*

Before you came here, who were your favorite country music singers?
The Judds, Reba, Patsy Cline, Loretta Lynn, Ricky Skaggs . . .

Okay. So tell me one thing that's happened since you came here, that could only have happened in Nashville.
Well, I was shopping for a bra in Macy's two weeks ago, because I was hosting the Canadian Country Music Awards. So I'm looking for undergarments for that, and I'm on the phone doing an interview with the *Winnipeg Free Press* about the show, and I look up, and I run smack into Reba McEntire in the middle of the underwear section! *(laughs)*

Who saw who first?
We saw each other right about the same time. We were kind of walking toward each other, and I'm like, "Hey!"

So you guys had met before?
Yeah, we're pretty good friends, and she's one of the nicest people in the world. But this isn't the end of the story. And so I go down the escalator to the jewelry department, and I run into Michelle Wright [Canadian country singer] in the jewelry department. Only in Nashville, right? I mean, that couldn't happen anywhere else. You wouldn't be at a bar watching somebody play and be standing next to Emmylou Harris anywhere else, you know? And that's what I love about this town. The energy here is so . . . everybody came here for the same reason. That excitement just hangs over the city. You don't get that anywhere else.

So tell me, in all honesty, how did you feel that first night here, after Pat and your mom left?
I was scared shitless. Scared but excited at the same time. I didn't have a green card, I didn't have a car, I couldn't get a real job even if I had wanted to, I didn't know anybody, I was eighteen . . . it was just such a naïve, blind leap of faith. Something you would only do when you're eighteen.

Eddie Angel

"I'D LIKE TO BREAK BOTH his damned arms!"

That's what Scotty Moore said after hearing Eddie Angel play guitar for the first time. I'd given Scotty an advance cassette of my album *Dirty Linen* (Tall Girl/Line, 1987), which featured Eddie on lead guitar, along with a cassette of some of Eddie's own recordings.

"There've been a lot of Scotty Moore imitators," Moore went on to say. "But Eddie Angel *is* Scotty Moore. And more importantly, he's Eddie Angel."

Scotty Moore played guitar with Elvis Presley. He's often called the father of rock & roll lead guitar. For him to say, "I'd like to break both his damned arms" . . . well, that's like Carl Sandburg saying he'd like to take your poetic license away if you're an aspiring poet.

These days, Eddie plays in a band called Los Straitjackets, a rock instrumental group he founded in 1994. The original members were all based in Nashville. Eddie is the only current member still living here. The band is sort of a modern-day Ventures served up with a sartorial twist, in that Eddie and his bandmates wear Mexican wrestling masks while performing.

Los Straitjackets have been nominated for a Grammy, appeared on *Late Night with Conan O'Brien* (seven times), toured Russia, starred in a movie called *Psycho Beach Party* (where they play themselves), and opened for Tom Petty & the Heartbreakers. Petty called them his "favorite American band." They have a huge following in Spain and in Mexico, where they once played to an audience of seventy thousand and have achieved a sort of superhero status. Today, kids all over Mexico bang out the band's surf instrumentals while wearing the trademark masks.

Marshall, Harlan Howard, and Eddie Angel at Bogey's, 1987

The band's marketing strategy has always been about overstatement, beginning with the title of their first album, *The Utterly Fantastic and Totally Unbelievable Sound of Los Straitjackets*. The blistering lead guitars of Eddie Angel and Danny Amis do most of the talking. But on the rare occasion anyone speaks, it's usually Amis (whose stage name is Daddy-O Grande) spewing out some sort of Spanish-derivative psycho-babble while introducing a song.

Los Straitjackets is my favorite band ever to come out of Nashville. And just for the record, Eddie Angel is my favorite guitar player. Whenever I hear Eddie play, I feel the same excitement I felt as a seven-year-old hearing the early recordings of Elvis Presley. The mere fact that a band like Los Straitjackets could even *exist* in Nashville—a band that goes against all convention, a band that is arguably the most unself-conscious band ever assembled—makes me glad I live here.

I FIRST MET EDDIE ON Tuesday, April 8, 1986. My friend Diana
Haig had taken me to the Exit/In to hear a group called Jeannie & the
Hurricanes that had just moved to town. "Wait 'til you hear their lead
guitar player!" she said. "His name's Eddie Angel." I remember thinking, *That's a hell of a name for a lead guitar player.*

As it turned out, I was blown away the minute I heard Eddie play
the first note. I loved his style, his look, his name, everything. I was
working on my *Dirty Linen* album at the time. After we were introduced, I asked Eddie if he would be interested in playing on my record.
So we ended up working together.

Eddie was unlike any guitar player I'd ever known. Besides his talent and good looks, he was kind and humble and articulate. And just
plain fun to be around. Being around Eddie was like being around
Elvis.

Soon Eddie was playing in my band. My band in those days (1986
to 1988) consisted of Eddie on lead guitar, Nick DiStefano on drums,
Rick Bedrosian on bass, and Dwight Scott or James Hooker on keyboards. We mostly gigged around town at places like the Bluebird Café
and the Ace of Clubs. One notable gig was New Year's Eve at the Bluebird. It was the venue's first smoke-free show, which had owner Amy
Kurland concerned that people wouldn't show up. "Hell, let's just *ad-
vertise* that it's going to be smoke free," I said. So that's what she did. As
it turned out, the place was packed.

Another notable gig took place at the Orpheum Theater in Memphis, where we played on a bill with Lonnie Mack and Stevie Ray
Vaughan.

TOWARD THE END OF 1988, I took a year off from performing to
deal with some personal matters. That next winter and spring, I opened
some shows (solo) for John Prine. Two were in California—one at the
Coach House in San Juan Capistrano and the other at the old Ventura
Theater up the coast. I had just bought a new car—a black BMW with
tan interior. So I'm thinking, *What better way to break in a new car than
drive it to California?* So that's what I did. As I was leaving Nashville, I
stopped by Tower Records, where I ran into Emmylou Harris.

"Hey, Marshall Chapman, what are you up to?"

"Well, I'm fixing to drive to California. Want to go?"

"I don't think so," she said, laughing.

After our brief conversation, she wrote down the names of three CDs I should buy for the trip—*Acadie* by Daniel Lanois, *Yellow Moon* by the Neville Brothers, and *Oh Mercy* by Bob Dylan—all produced by Lanois. As it turned out, those were the only CDs I listened to all the way to California. Lanois's production had a seductive, dark quality unlike anything I had ever heard.

I remember driving across New Mexico while listening to a song on the Dylan CD. Suddenly it hit me: *Oh, my God! That's it! That's the sound I've been looking for!* The sound was from the track "Everything Is Broken," which featured intertwining guitars driven by a mesmerizing bass line. No keyboards. Just guitars. The more I listened to it, the more I began envisioning a band with two lead guitar players.

After I returned to Nashville, I went in the studio to lay down final tracks for *Inside Job*. Eddie Angel and James Hollihan played lead guitars. Jackie Street played bass. And by then, Lynn Williams had joined us on drums. The chemistry and sound were so good that we decided to play some live shows, calling ourselves Marshall Chapman & the Love Slaves. We even had T-shirts made up with our motto printed on the back: "We're all slaves to something . . . might as well be love!"

Our first four gigs were Monday nights at the Bluebird Café in January 1991. Meanwhile, *Inside Job* was receiving heavy airplay on WRLT in Nashville. One day I came home to find a message on my answering machine from a man claiming to be Duane Eddy. He said he'd heard us on the radio and really liked our sound. When I first heard the message, I thought one of my friends was playing a joke. But then the truth dawned. *Shit! This really is Duane Eddy! Kiss my ass, I'll never smile again!*

These kinds of things often happen in Nashville. It's why I live here. For an artist, one experience like that can keep you plowing another five years.

When the Love Slaves and I arrived for our next gig at the Bluebird, the first thing we noticed was this tall, lanky man in a cowboy hat sitting directly in front of Eddie's amp. Sure enough, it was Duane Eddy. We were beside ourselves. As I recall, Eddie worked the vibrato bar on his Telecaster a little more than usual that night.

In 1993, the Love Slaves (including Eddie on lead guitar) and I recorded a live concert at the Tennessee State Prison for Women. When Jimmy Buffett heard the tape, he signed me to his label. *It's About Time . . .* was my first live album and the first release for Margaritaville/ Island Records. It received rave reviews, including a write-up in *Time* magazine.

After the album came out, the Love Slaves and I hit the road, opening every show for Buffett that spring, summer, and fall. About halfway through the tour, though, it became obvious that Eddie needed to be with Los Straitjackets full time, as their popularity was on the rise. So Eddie split and Kenny Vaughan came in to play his spot for the rest of the tour.

While Eddie was with us, his wife Melanie would often come out and join us on the road. We were traveling in style in a customized bus, and Melanie was a good soul to have on board. It's not every day you get to ride on a rock & roll tour bus with a bona fide Mafia princess. Melanie's stepfather was a New York mobster named Tony. To help pass time on some of the longer runs, I often encouraged Melanie and Eddie to tell "Tony stories." I've always been a sucker for a good story, and the ones about Tony had us all rolling in the aisles. Like the one where Tony comes to visit Melanie and Eddie in Nashville, only he thinks he's in Memphis the entire time. No amount of correction could convince him otherwise. He had it in his head he was in Memphis, so by God, that's where he was! Then there's the one where Eddie goes to Tony to ask for Melanie's hand in marriage, and they end up going to the racetrack. I could go on, but I'll stop for now.

My house in Nashville
May 6, 2008

So Eddie, how long have you lived in Memphis—I mean, Nashville?
Let's see. '86. February of '86, so twenty-two years. I thought I'd only be here six months to a year. That I'd come get my big record deal and, you know, live happily ever after. *(laughs)*

So when did you first hear the word "Nashville"?

I don't recall. I mean, "Nashville Cats" [the 1967 hit by the Lovin' Spoonful]—I remember hearing that on the radio. But I probably heard something before then. I mean, I always liked country music growing up. That's what my mother liked—country music. I asked her once, you know, I was curious about what she liked when she was younger. So I said, "Frank Sinatra, was that around?" And she said, "Nah, I liked Hank Williams." So that was there.

So you knew that music was coming out of Nashville.

Yeah. And I remember in high school talking to a friend of mine about going to Nashville—I don't know why. We both liked country music. He played guitar, we both were into country guitar playing. And I remember bringing some friends to my house one time—this was in high school, right?—and playing Red Foley's "Smoke on the Water." You know that song? And I'm thinking, "Listen! You guys have *got* to listen to this! This is *great*! Listen!" And now when I think back on that, they must've thought I was retarded or something. *(laughs)* I mean, high school kids listening to Red Foley?

What were most high school kids listening to at that time?

Oh, Jimi Hendrix, probably . . . Cream, Led Zeppelin, that kind of stuff.

And you're listening to Red Foley's "Smoke on the Water."

That's 'cause I had the record, you know? *(laughs)*

Where did you live before Nashville?

I grew up in Albany [New York], in that general area. I lived in D.C. for a couple of years in the early '80s when I played with Tex Rubinowitz. But other than that, I was in Albany, in upstate New York. My life was like a William Kennedy novel.

Oh, yeah . . . *Ironweed*.

Yeah. I feel like I fit his demographic—Irish Catholic, working class, you know.

So when was the first time you came to Nashville? Was it with Jeannie & the Hurricanes?

No, the *very* first time was actually in the mid-'70s. I was in a band called the Star-Spangled Washboard Band. We toured quite a bit, mostly along the Eastern Seaboard, but we got on some tour—I guess opening for somebody—and wound up playing the Exit/In in '75. We opened for Don Everly. We weren't on tour with him, though. It was a one-off.

So your first time in Nashville, you open for Don Everly?

My very first time, yeah.

Did you guys spend the night?

Yeah.

Where'd you stay?

Hmm . . . it was on West End Avenue.

The Anchor Motel?

I think that was it, yeah. Right by that church?

Everything in Nashville's by a church. *(laughs)* But yeah, the Anchor was next to an old Catholic church [Cathedral of the Incarnation] that had beautiful Florentine architecture. Most of the bands that played the Exit in those days stayed at the Anchor.

Yeah, that's where we stayed. Our van got broken into. I remember that. *(laughs)*

Tell me about that.

All I remember is that I had this nice leather jacket. I think it was, like, white or something. I just remember that it got stolen.

Out of the van?

Yeah.

So that first night, it's like—BAM! You get robbed. So when was the next time you came to Nashville?

Let's see. The next time we came to Nashville, we opened for Sha Na Na at the [Municipal] Auditorium. We toured with Sha Na Na in the mid-'70s.

Oh, that's perfect! *(laughs)*

Yeah, I know, right? I wanted to be in that band so bad. *(laughs)* In fact, on one of the shows we played with them in Chicago—after the show, they were going out to a nightclub, so they invited me and a couple of the other guys along. So we went with them and wound up in this club on the north side of Chicago. So we walked in, and there's this big buzz—"Hey! There's Sha Na Na," right? So they ask Sha Na Na to sit in, and their guitar player wasn't there, so I got asked to play guitar. So I'm up there onstage with Sha Na Na at this little club, and the audience was, like, blown away, right? And I remember looking out at the faces of the people there, and I thought, "This is what I want to do. I want to see that look on people's faces every night." It was just . . . they were *thrilled*, you know?

Oh, that's great. So . . .

So, yeah—a couple of times at the Exit/In . . . Don Everly . . . and I think we opened for Sonny Terry and Brownie McGhee once. If we didn't open for them, I saw them there.

At the [Old Time] Pickin' Parlor?

No, no, it was definitely the Exit/In. We played there twice.

I might have been in the audience that night.

You saw Sonny Terry and Brownie McGhee?

I *know* I saw them at the Pickin' Parlor, and I may have seen them at the Exit/In, too.

Yeah, I remember the Pickin' Parlor. I remember going by there.

That was the other happenin' place. Okay. So you first came through town as a touring musician. Anything in particular you remember about Nashville?

I just remember thinking it was smaller than I thought it was going to be. It had loomed larger in my mind or something, you know? And then I remember on that tour, at that time, I had a tape of some songs I'd written, and I actually went to some publishers and somehow got in the door and played it for them. It was like, Wow! I mean, you couldn't do that today. I just, like, called somebody or knocked on the door.

Yeah, they'd let you in back then. You could just walk in off the street.

Of course, I thought I'd written some great songs.

They were probably crap.

Any titles?

Oh, man, let me think of one . . . "Too Many Nights in a Gin Mill." That was one.

Most people think of you as a guitar player, but you've written some great songs—both instrumentals and ones with lyrics. And, of course, we've written a few together. "Who's Gonna Be My Santa Claus This Year?" Were you in on that one?

I don't think so.

Oh, yeah. That was me and Diana [Haig]. But you, Diana, and I wrote one called "Too Cool for Christmas."

Yeah? "Too Cool for School" or . . . ?

Nah, it was "Too Cool for Christmas": "Black leather jacket / Black duck tail / A black Cadillac that he bought on sale / My baby's too cool for Christmas / Too cool for Tennessee . . . too cool for Christmas / Too cool for anybody but me."

I remember that. And "Ready to Go Steady" . . . did we ever finish that?

Oh, yeah. "Ready to Go Steady with You." Those were our two hits. *(laughs)* But back to your songs. You had one that was on an album that was nominated for a Grammy, right?

Yeah. "Stuck in Lonesometown." Eddy "The Chief" Clearwater recorded it. I wrote it right after I moved to Nashville, after about six months. I was working at the Sheraton Hotel, parking cars and bussing tables.

I remember.

The first line is "There's no music, there's no fun." That was sort of where I was at, at the time. I wasn't having any fun. *(laughs)*

So Nashville was the inspiration.

Well, obviously there was a lot of music here, but not for me. I was used to playing, like, three or four times a week, and when I got to Nashville, it seemed like I stopped playing.

Nashville wasn't much of a live performance town then. I mean, in the early '80s, Cantrell's was pretty much it. Then about that time, the Exit/In got renovated and was never the same. It was a weird time.

Well, and also it seemed like we [Jeannie & the Hurricanes] were just talking to lawyers and managers and music business people. We were going through *that* phase. 'Cause that's what we were here for. We wanted to get a record deal. So that was my brush with the music business. So I think it was the music *business* that inspired "There's no music, there's no fun." It wasn't particularly Nashville. In Albany, I was a big fish in a small pond. Everywhere I went, people knew me. Then I get here, and I'm parking cars at the Sheraton. *(laughs)*

So when you moved here to stay, that was in '86 with Jeannie & the Hurricanes, right?

Yeah.

So how did you get here? How did you arrive?

We drove down in Dave's [Dave Durocher, drummer for the Hurricanes] car—a Ford station wagon with a U-Haul.

So the four of you were in a station wagon?
Well, actually three. Ricky [Rick Bedrosian, Hurricanes bass player] came later.

Oh, so it was you, Dave, and Jeannie. What color was the station wagon?
It was white, probably a 1979. Jeannie had her cat in a travel box sedated with catnip or something. We were pulling a U-Haul with all our belongings in it.

Were you and Melanie together yet?
We were. We weren't married yet, but we were together. I'd met her the year before.

Did she come down then?
She was still in college when I moved here, so she finished college, then came down that summer.

But I remember Dave picking me up, the day we left. It was, like, February in New York. My driveway was all ice and snow. We had to push the U-Haul trailer *and* the car out of the snow. I think that's the last time I pushed a car out of the snow. *(laughs)* But that, to me . . . that's what winter was.

So the further you drove, the warmer it got.
Yeah. It took us two days to get here. I remember we stopped and spent a night in Staunton, Virginia. When we got to Nashville, we stayed at the Shoney's Inn on Demonbreun.

Oh, yeah. That was brand new then.
Everything seemed brand new to me, man. I mean, like our first apartment out on Elm Hill Pike? I thought I was in the lap of luxury, because I was used to living in old, drafty houses. Run-down, hundred-year-old houses. So now I'm living in this brand-new apartment, and I'm thinking, *Wow! This is pretty neat! (laughs)*
We even went out and bought new furniture.

How long did you guys stay at Shoney's?

Couple of days, you know. We had started apartment hunting. We only knew two people. Well, we didn't know *anybody*, but we had the *names* of two people we should go see—Garry Velletri at Bug Music, and Jim Rooney. We had the contact at Bug Music through John Tichy, who was in Commander Cody and His Lost Planet Airmen. He was a good friend of ours. He's still one of my best friends. He lives up in the Albany area.

So you and Tichy grew up together?

No, no. He moved to Albany later. He grew up in Michigan somewhere. But then he got this job as a professor at a college in upstate New York, and we became good friends. So we told him, "You know, we're thinking we're going to move to Nashville." And he said, "Well, you know I'm with Bug Music, and they've got an office there, so look up this guy—Garry Velletri." So we had an appointment to go see Garry, and—as it turned out—Garry had a copy of the very first 45 that I had put out in 1981. An instrumental called "Rampage." He was probably one of five hundred people—I don't know, maybe a hundred—that had it.

In the whole world.

Yeah, right! *(laughs)* It was, like, one of his favorite records. You know, it was one of those things, like, who is this guy, how can I find his office? And then . . .

Serendipity kicks in.

Yeah. So we were "in like Flynn" at Bug Music.

Did you sign a publishing contract with Bug?

Yeah.

You're still with them, right?

Yeah. Still with Bug.

Me, too. We're probably the oldest horses in the stable. *(laughs)* The Strom Thurmonds of the songwriting world. The George Blandas of Bug.

Man, I know. *(laughs)*

Okay. So where are we? Oh, yeah. Garry Velletri and Jim Rooney.
Right. So we went to see Jim Rooney, and that was more of a sobering experience. He wasn't encouraging. He'd probably seen guys like us come and go. But I remember one thing he said. He said, "Nashville will be good to you, if you commit to it."

Sounds like good advice.
Yeah.

Now here you are, twenty-two years later. I'd say you're committed.
I know. *(laughs)* Jim Rooney's not even here anymore!

Jim Rooney moved? I didn't know that. Okay. So you moved here for the chance to play in a bigger pond.
Well, yeah. I knew it was kind of Palookaville staying around Albany, playing in bars.

Palookaville?
(laughs) That's my term for any kind of dead-end situation. I mean, Albany's great, but it's not a music center like Nashville, L.A., or New York. But I think I made the move because . . . number one, I had nothing to lose. And number two, I'd fallen in love with Melanie, you know? So I'm thinking I've got to make something of myself. I can't keep goofing around in bars up here.

Did you ever consider moving to Los Angeles or New York?
No, not really. Certainly not Los Angeles. Actually, I went to Los Angeles when I was twenty. But New York? One of the reasons we came here was because we'd gone through a period where we had a manager in New York, who managed Marshall Crenshaw. So it was big-time management because Marshall Crenshaw was happening at the time. It was big stuff for me, because I was a big fan of his.

So we had his management and there was some guy, some record label that was interested, but the guy turned out to be a cokehead or something, like with a rap label or something. It was something goofy, but it was a big-time kind of thing at the time. Then, when that fell apart, we thought . . . and people were saying, "You know, you guys just don't fit in New York, you know? I mean, you guys sound country." Because Jeannie kind of had—at least to our ears, to people up there—like, a country sort of twang. We were sort of like, you know, a rockabilly band. Sort of a hybrid.

Jeannie always sounded Jersey-girl-group to me.
That's funny, 'cause to me, she sounded kind of country. But when I think about it, we were like a hybrid of country, rockabilly, and Phil Spector girl group.

Phil Spector country.
Yeah, why not? *(laughs)* Plus, in New York at the time, all the records—there were no *guitars* on them, you know? It was all electronic synthesizers. So we were thinking, "We've got to go to Nashville, man!" It seemed like the best option. And I remember Dave Durocher—he was the one who had the idea to come here. And I'm thinking, "Yeah!" It just resonated. It just struck me that Nashville was where we should go. And you know, within a year, we had a record contract with CBS and Steve Buckingham. Little did I know. *(laughs)*

So you move to Nashville in 1986. Anything in particular you remember? Something just totally Nashville?
Well, after I moved here, I noticed everything had "Music City" on it, like Music City Window Cleaning, Music City Loan Company. Then I got a job at the Sheraton Music City. Music City Taxi even had musical notation painted all over their cars. I loved it! It made me feel like I was in the right place.

That's great. So tell me one thing that's happened to you, that could only have happened in Nashville.
Well, I once got to spend a day with Bob Moore, the A-team bass player who played on everything from Patsy Cline to Elvis. The Everly

Brothers, Roy Orbison, I mean, just about every hit record that came out of Nashville, he played on it. A friend of mine, Mark Neill, was in town, and he took me to Bob Moore's house. And he [Bob Moore] got out his date book and showed us all the dates, all the Elvis dates that he played, you know, the songs he played on, what he got paid, everything. Then he took us down to RCA Studio B, and he was telling us one story after the next. I remember he said, "When Elvis would come in, he'd ask us, 'Where does Roy like to stand? I want to stand where Roy stands when I sing.'" 'Cause he [Elvis] was such a big fan of Roy Orbison's singing. And then he [Bob Moore] told us how, in one day, they cut two #1 records in the same day. They cut "Don't Worry" with Marty Robbins at the old Quonset Hut [Columbia Studios], then they came over to Studio B and cut "Last Date" with Floyd Cramer. Nice day's work, huh?

I'd say so.
So that, to me, is Nashville. Those guys. The session guys. They just blow my mind. Buddy Harman, you know? I mean, they just could play such a variety of styles. Just great musicians. Reggie Young, Buddy Emmons . . . it's like, they don't seem human to me, you know? Like a great athlete that doesn't seem human. I think there is something to that. I think there are some people that have some kind of extra chromosome or something.

Don Henry

DON HENRY IS ONE OF THE MOST ORIGINAL and remarkable songwriters I've ever known. We first met while playing an in-the-round at the Bluebird Café. According to a journal I was keeping at the time, the date was Saturday, May 21, 1988.

Gary Nicholson had been telling me about Don for months. "Man, you've got to hear Don Henry," he said. "You guys will love each other!" So when Gary invited me to join him, Don, and Kevin Welch for an in-the-round, I accepted even though I'd never played one.

"So let me get this straight," I said. "You sit in a circle in the middle of the audience?"

"Yeah, man, it's cool. Like being in somebody's living room."

"Okay. So what if I have to go to the bathroom?"

"Well, I guess you just get up and go," Gary said, laughing.

I'd always played solo or with a band. This in-the-round business had me feeling a little apprehensive. Plus, I was already feeling fragile, having just returned from a co-dependency workshop out in the middle of nowhere in the North Georgia mountains. The idea of rubbing elbows with the audience while playing music seemed too bizarre.

I CLEARLY REMEMBER THE NIGHT, and not just because it was my first in-the-round and my first time to hear Don Henry. It was just everything and everybody. Across the board, the quality of the songs just knocked me out. Kevin sang "Sam's Place," then Gary played "Brilliant Conversationalist." But when Don Henry sang "Harley," I knew I was listening to something totally original. A few days later, I tried describing Don to a friend. "He's like a cross between Randy Newman, the Beatles, and Walt Disney!" I exclaimed.

"Harley" tells the story of a hippie biker couple—a man and his "motorcycle mama" who's in the latter stages of a pregnancy. One day, they're roaring through Bakersfield, when suddenly her water breaks. So they go to a nearby hospital, where she gives birth to a child they name "Harley." To maintain family unity, they have a sidecar welded onto their motorcycle. Then off they go. At some point, they visit a tattoo parlor and get matching tattoos.

The family that gets tattoos together, stays together, right? Wrong!

One day, they're cruising up the coast, when suddenly, the sidecar comes undone. Only the couple doesn't notice. They cruise on, while the sidecar and child go bouncing across a field, finally coming to rest at the feet of a childless farmer's wife. Sensing a miracle, the farmer and his wife take Harley in. Years go by. Adolescence sets in. Harley runs off and becomes a sort of Evel Knievel figure on the fairground circuit. As fate would have it, the hippie biker couple happens to be in the audience one night. They see this daredevil guy jumping his motorcycle over fifty trucks. They hear the crowd yell, "Har-*ley*! Har-*ley*!" They put two and two together. "Could this be our long lost child?" they wonder. After the show, they introduce themselves. Harley is skeptical. They compare tattoos. Hugs and tears abound. I mean, who needs DNA when your tattoos match?

Only Don Henry could spin such a tale. And only Don Henry could do it in under four minutes. Plus—and correct me if I'm wrong—I'm laying bets "Harley" is the only song ever written where someone's water breaks.

I've never trusted witty songs. Shakespeare said, "Brevity is the soul of wit." I say, "Wit is brevity of the soul." That is, unless Don Henry's the one creating the wit. I don't know how he does it, but Don's wit has soul.

Of course, Don has a serious side. "Beautiful Fool," a song he wrote to commemorate Dr. Martin Luther King, rips my heart out every time I hear it. Then there's "Where've You Been," a song he co-wrote with Jon Vezner that won the Grammy for Best Country Song in 1991. Again, only Don Henry could write a song set in a nursing home and win a Grammy.

Don and Gary Nicholson wrote a song called "Motel, Motel, Motel" that gets my vote for best in-the-round song ever written. Unless Clear Channel goes bankrupt, you'll never hear it on country radio. But

Don Henry, Gary Nicholson, Marshall, and Kevin Welch
at the Cockeyed Camel, 1989

you can hear it on Don's second CD, *Flowers and Rockets*. Another song on that CD is one Don and I wrote called "What Kind of Girl." As in, what kind of girl could fall in love with a guy who seems to be a complete jerk. The answer?

A girl without a brain
A girl without a clue
A girl who does the things
A girl in love'll do

More recently, Don and I wrote a song about overpopulation called "The Earth Is a Dog." We were thinking, *Okay, let's pretend the earth is a dog. If so, then we humans are the fleas. And we all know what happens when a dog has too many fleas. She starts to itch and twitch and shake!* Not long after we finished it, the huge tsunami that killed over 150,000 struck Southeast Asia. It was eerie. Now, every time a tornado tears through Tennessee—which seems to be happening with greater and greater frequency—I'll email Don: *Looks like she's starting to shake!* For three nights in January 2007, we sang "The Earth Is a Dog" to an appreciative audience of environmentalists as part of Al Gore's initiative to teach others about climate change. Gore was there and introduced us each night.

Don and I have shared some good times over the years. Other highlights include that gig in West Chester, Pennsylvania, and the time we played a private, after-dinner concert at the Vanderbilt chancellor's residence. It was me, Don, Pat McLaughlin, and Cowboy Jack Clement. I'll never forget Cowboy, dressed in a bright red Hawaiian shirt, waltzing into the main ballroom, brandishing an unlit Virginia Slim, asking anyone within earshot—including Vanderbilt Board of Trust chair Martha Ingram—"Where might an alien go to have a smoke?"

I HAVE HEARD THAT DON and his father dropped by Pete Drake's recording studio one night while I was working on my third album for Epic. This was in April 1979, and apparently it was Don's first night in town. By the time they showed up, the session had pretty much turned into a party with all kinds of folks dropping by, including Willie Nelson. I remember Pete saying, "Marshall, you and Willie go out there and sing something." So we did. I still have a little reel-to-reel tape of us singing "It's Not Supposed to Be That Way." My overall memory of that night is a bit hazy. As I recall, there was a lot of smoke hanging in the air.

My house in Nashville
March 3, 2008

So, Don, was that [i.e., the night in April 1979] your first night in Nashville?
Yes, it was.

How'd you get here?
Well, my dad hauled my car. I had a little Opel car. My dad had this old beat-up Chevy station wagon. He and my mom were going

through some tough things, and they were on the verge of splitting up. So he wanted to help me out, but he was also happy to get away. So we hauled that car all the way across from the Bay Area.

So you and your dad are in his station wagon, pulling your Opel. Tell me about the car.
It was a little sporty Opel. It was like, uh . . . how would you say . . . a bronze, turd color. Yeah, that was the color.

What year?
I couldn't tell you what year it was. I know it was a four-cylinder, basic car that I could actually work on—my dad and I would work on it. It was that simple. It was like a lawn mower. *(laughs)*

Two-door?
Yeah. Two-door. It was a sporty little thing. And it sounded cool, man. But you know, eventually some holes wore through in the back, and the fumes would come in, and I realized at some point—this was after I'd started running tape copies at Tree—that I'd have to get rid of it.

So you and your dad drive here from . . .
California. Morgan Hill, California.

How old were you?
I was nineteen. It was 1979—April.

Did you stop anywhere to spend the night?
We stayed a night in Barstow—I'll never forget that. And then probably Oklahoma City. And then all the way over. But we did it pretty quick. I took a lot of photographs of road signs along the way, mostly mileage signs showing how close I was getting to Nashville.

Oh, that's great!
Of course, when I got to Nashville, I had no money to develop the pictures. I didn't develop them for years.

About what time did you guys arrive in town?
Man, I wish I could remember.

Was it dark?
It was dark.

Did you go straight to Pete's Place [Pete Drake's studio]?
Yes. Well, come to think of it, we might have arrived while it was light. I can't remember exactly. We may have driven around and maybe hooked up with [Sonny] Throckmorton or something like that, because my dad was old friends with Sonny. But that's a blur. All I really remember is that night. My dad called Pete and said, "Look, we're out and about. We just got in town and just wanted to say hi." And Pete said, "Well, we're kind of taking a break here, if you want to drop by."

How did your dad know Pete?
He played in a group . . .

So your dad was a musician?
Yeah. He played bass and saxophone in a group with Larry Black and Bobby Black, the steel guitar player—you probably know those guys. Larry played guitar in Linda Hargrove's band for a while. Bobby's the steel guitar player that played with Commander Cody. So my dad had been in a band with those guys for years. They grew up playing music together in the Bay Area. Hoyet Henry & the Black Brothers—that was the name of the band.

So your dad's the lead guy?
Yeah.

Did he write songs?
Not that much. And that's probably why they didn't . . . they were always looking for material. None of them really wrote their own material.

They should have waited for you!
That would have been great, because they had the coolest sound.
Actually, they got approached by Fantasy Records just before Fantasy
signed Creedence [Clearwater Revival]. They were looking for a Bay
Area band they could turn into a country rock band to be the next big
thing, right? And my dad's band—they played everywhere in the Bay
Area—they were *the* hot band. When Fantasy approached them, my
dad said, "Nah . . . you guys are a jazz label. What could you do with
our band? Besides, we don't write our own songs." He goes, "Man, it
wasn't a year later, Creedence was all over the radio. I just didn't think
they were that serious about putting a band out, you know?"

But then he's got this son who's writing songs.
Oh, yeah.

**How many songs had you written by the time you guys were driving
to Nashville?**
Not that many. Twenty or so. Maybe two or three that were worth
anything. When I was fourteen, I had written about three songs, and
my mom said, "You ought to play those for your dad." Daddy never
was one to push me into the music thing. So one day he says, "Your
mom told me about some of these songs you've been writing. You
want to play me a couple?" He was putting on his clothes, getting
ready for work, 'cause he played in a nightclub every night to make
a living. And I said, "Okay." I was kind of shy as far as playing for
anybody. So I played him the three songs. He didn't really say much.
He just said, "I have a friend that has a four-track studio if you want
to go demo some of these. Would you be up for doing that?" I said,
"Yeah."

So the following weekend, he arranged for us to go to our old
friend Barry Blackwood's house in San Jose. There was this drummer
there, Roy McMeans, who played in my dad's band. My dad played
bass, Barry played rhythm guitar, and I just stood up to a microphone
and sang with headphones on. And you know what it's like . . . when
they count it off, and your song—that little song you were playing in
your room to yourself—is suddenly inside your head, in headphones

with a full band playing. I was transported! The minute I heard that sound, I remember thinking, *this* is what I'm going to do for the rest of my life. There was no more question about it. Of course, sticking with high school for the next three years became a challenge, because I didn't want to be there anymore. So that was my first experience.

Then a few years later, my dad says, "Well, my old friend Sonny Throckmorton is kind of hot in Nashville. I haven't talked to him in a while." Sonny used to write in Los Angeles and the Bay Area, when he lived out there. He was in several R&B bands and stuff with my dad. They all knew each other back then.

So Sonny was from California?
He's not *from* California, but he worked out there a lot. And my dad played on his demos and stuff.

So your dad and you drive to Nashville, and he knows Sonny Throckmorton and he knows Pete Drake. How did he know Pete?
He knew Pete because of that band I was telling you about earlier with Larry and Bobby Black, and they had actually had some kind of deal with, like, United Artists or somebody like that.

All steel guitar players know each other. They're like a secret society.
Hey, you're right! *(laughs)* Anyway, they had come to Nashville and cut some things, and so Pete had suggested even then, "You know, you should be living here being a studio musician, because that's what you're best at." My dad was a pretty good player.

What all did he play?
Bass, but anything really. In fact, Pete used him on piano and trumpet, and bass and guitar. My dad could play anything. He was a utility guy. Anyway, so that's how he knew Pete. And my mom just wasn't up for moving out to Nashville.

So you and your dad walk into Pete's Place. What happened then?
Well, we walked in the door, and Pete says to my dad, "Hey, how are you? Good to see you, man." And I walk in there, and I don't know who—I knew who Pete was because I'd seen his pictures and heard

about him. But right away, he said, "This here's Marshall Chapman. We're working on a project together," and you were like, "How you doin'?" "And this is Pam Rose . . . Mary Ann Kennedy . . . and Hoyet, what's your son's name? Don . . . and of course, you probably know Willie Nelson here," or "Willie," or whatever he said. It was a quick introduction to everybody, because you guys were in the middle of singing and playing.

Oh, yeah! That must have been when Mary Ann and Pam were overdubbing vocals on my third album for Epic.
Yeah. You guys were obviously taking some sort of break, because you were in the control room, probably working out harmony parts, but had been sidetracked by playing songs.

Yeah, whenever Willie drops by, those things tend to happen. (laughs)
It was great, man!

Were you sitting in those chairs behind the console when the guitar was being passed around?
Yeah, I think so.

Did you play a song?
No, no, of course not. The only people that played songs, I think, were you and Willie. The girls sang harmony. They would join in on songs that they hadn't heard before, and that blew me away—that people could sing harmonies on songs they're hearing for the first time.

It's funny. I just barely remember a man from California coming by with his teenaged son. I don't remember being introduced, but it's like I *knew* you were there. It's like this peripheral kind of memory. My most vivid memory from that night is Pete saying, "Hey Marshall, you and Willie go out there and sing something." And of course, I remember the engineer, Al Pachucki, because he engineered a lot of Elvis stuff and I'd get him to tell me stories.
I want that tape of you and Willie singing.

Well, it's so weird. I had saved that tape for *years* in a box with all my reel-to-reels. Then the other day, I was looking for it, and I couldn't find it. I either took it somewhere to have it transferred to disc, then forgot where I took it, or it's somewhere in the house. You've got to find it.

I know.
I couldn't tell you what the song was even . . .

It was "It's Not Supposed to Be That Way."
Oh, okay.

I had the tape for years—like a *year* ago, I had it.
Wow.

And then something . . . I think I took it somewhere to get it transferred. I've got to find it. [Note: I had a dream the night after this interview in which the whereabouts of a metal cassette copy of the reel-to-reel were revealed to me.]
Well, what I love about that moment in retrospect is that those people came to mean so much to me. I mean, Pam and Mary Ann, and you—you guys have crossed my path so many times since then, as writers and as friends, and it just shows how this town works. I mean, there's no reason why this little nineteen-year-old kid would have any connection with you guys unless he became a songwriter, you know? A songwriter in today's situation might be different, 'cause there's so many of them. But back then, there were lots of them, too, but we all just—the ones that stuck around all kind of knew each other.

Well, that's ironic because the first time I remember meeting you . . .
. . . was at the Bluebird.

. . . was at the Bluebird nine years later.

(After a break)
Okay. So you've lived in Nashville how long?
Twenty-nine years this April.

So when did you first hear the word "Nashville"?
I had just always heard it. Here I was, living all the way across the country, and that word was just a part of my life. Everything that was talked about. There was always that connection.

So when you heard the word "Nashville," what would you be thinking?
Music. It was all about music.

Were you thinking, as a child, Well, I've got to get there?
No, not until I became a songwriter.

That first time in the studio?
Yeah. I knew then I wanted to go to Nashville. But, up until that point, I had bought records of everyone from Bob Dylan to Neil Young to Tom T. Hall to, you know, Dolly Parton, and I knew who all the musicians were on the credits. And I knew those records were made in Nashville, and I knew they were mastered in Nashville.

Did you learn the names of the songwriters?
Yeah. I knew all the songwriters before I even moved here. But you know what? I knew all the engineers, and I knew *all* the musicians. The musicians were my heroes. And the songwriters, of course, because that's what I wanted to be. But I knew every credit and who played what on every record.

Wow. Okay, so I guess you've answered "What made you move here?"
Yeah. That was it. The desire to be a songwriter. All my friends made fun of me in high school. *(talks through nose)* "Well, you gonna go to Nash-veel?" They're in California, so they're thinking *Hee Haw*, you know? But see, I grew up around the business. I knew a little bit about it. I knew the realities of it, to an extent.

Because of your father.

Yeah. So I knew I had to go to Nashville. Because, let's face it, in 1979, if you wanted to take an acoustic guitar somewhere, you weren't going to L.A. or New York. There's no way. Because with disco and metal and pop music, there was no room for acoustic singer-songwriters anymore. At that point, I had already bought *Old No. 1*, the Guy Clark record—my dad bought it for me. He said, "Listen to this. Take the Elton John record off and listen to this!" *(laughs)* And I remember going, "Whoa!" And I knew Dave Loggins had recorded all his really cool stuff here. I knew a lot of the pop stuff that had been recorded here, as well as all the country stuff that I loved. Whether it was Charlie Rich or . . .

Who were your favorite country artists?

Well, I was just a kid, so I'll tell you . . . *(lowers voice)* I had a real thing for Tanya Tucker, man. I thought she was so-o-o . . .

So you had the hots for Tanya?

Oh, God! I thought she was . . . and she sang so great. Of course, I liked the early, early hits she had. "Jamestown Ferry" just blew me away.

Yeah. I always loved "Blood Red and Going Down."

Oh, God! But it was not so much a matter of my favorite singer as my favorite production. I bought that album . . . and *David Allan Coe Rides Again*. Oh, man, I *loved* that album! I wore it out. I wore it out as much as I wore out my Elton John records.

Could David Allan Coe have been the precursor to "Harley"?

Could have been, man. I never really thought about it.

Did that album have "Would You Lay with Me in a Field of Stone"?

No, that was one or two albums later.

"Take This Job and Shove It"?

No, but I did have those. My dad bought those albums in advance. I became a David Allan Coe fan early on, because I'd heard his version of "Desperados Waiting for a Train." Hey, you want to hear the weirdest thing?

Yeah.
My dad was at Pete's one day on a trip to Nashville. And so he meets this guy. It was David Allan Coe. And David says, "Hey, man, you want to hear a song?" And my dad says, "Sure." So David Allan sits and plays "Desperados Waiting for a Train," just him singing with a guitar. And my dad goes, "Shit! That's the greatest fucking song I've ever heard!" And this is what David Allan Coe said: "Well, thank you."

He didn't say Guy [Clark] wrote it?!
HE DIDN'T EVEN SAY GUY WROTE IT!

That's our David!
My dad said he never knew Guy wrote it, until he bought Coe's *The Mysterious Rhinestone Cowboy* a year or so later. He brought it home and said, "Man, I can't believe this guy."

That is so funny! And I believe every word.
Yeah, man. He stood right there . . .

I believe you.
He didn't tell him he wrote it, he just didn't say he *didn't* write it, you know? So for years my dad thought he wrote the song. Then, when he saw Guy's name listed as the songwriter, he went right out and bought Guy's *Old No. 1*, which of course blew us all away.

That's such a great story. Okay, so Don, let's go back to your first twenty-four hours in Nashville. Where did you and your dad spend the night? You know, after you came by Pete's that night.
We stayed at that place on West End. It was that old Holiday Inn. It's not a Holiday Inn anymore, it's something else.

The Shel Silverstein Holiday Inn?
Yeah, it might have been that one.

The Shel Silverstein Holiday Inn had an all-night restaurant out front, next to a little swimming pool. The Pancake Man, I believe it was called. Pete Drake used to hang out there a lot.
Oh, you're kidding?

Yeah, it'd be packed after the bars closed. Occasionally, someone would end up in the pool.
That must've been the place. So there's the bank on the corner, then Mrs. Winner's, the chicken place, is there, the gas station, and then right up there, it looked like a Holiday Inn.

On the north side, right?
Yeah.

Then you were at the Shel Silverstein Holiday Inn. That's where Shel always stayed when he came to town to hang out with Bobby Bare and pitch songs.
Then that's where we stayed. I'm positive now we stayed there.

Probably on a recommendation from Pete.
Well, we'd been there before. Because, you know, my dad had connections with Nashville through his music, and he would come out from time to time. When I was a thirteen-year-old kid, we actually moved to Nashville for about three months.

Oh, so you had been to Nashville before?
Yes, I had. And we would've stayed here, but my mom couldn't take it. And my mother, you know, they butted heads, so we moved back to California after three months.

So when was that? What year?
I believe it was '73, like, fall of '73.

Were you an only child?
Yeah. So anyway, my dad played on sessions. He played . . . do you remember Steve Baron?

I don't think so.
Pete produced this really great pop singer-songwriter named
Steve Baron. My dad played on that album.

**I think Linda Hargrove's first album [*Blue Jean Country Queen*]
came out right about then.**
Yeah, my dad might have played on that one, too. I don't know. There
was also a guy named Randy Lee that Pete produced. You remember
him?

No.
There were all these singer-songwriters, because it was
the thing at the time.

**Well, Pete was the champion of the underground scene. I mean,
he would take chances on people like George & the Arizona Star—
do you remember them?**
Oh, yeah!

And David Allan. I mean, and me *(laughs)* . . .
Yeah. Because he *knew.*

**Pete was sort of the link between the mainstream and the under-
ground, having played steel guitar on everything from "Stand by
Your Man" to Bob Dylan's "Lay Lady Lay." Pete was . . . Pete
was cool.**
Yeah. He *was* cool. He was putting out the stuff, man. It was a magical
time. It really was very cool. And even though I was too young then
to play in the game, I got to be around it for a short while. I went to
St. Edward's, if you can believe it—a Catholic school—for about three
months.

Is that here in Nashville?
Yeah, over on Thompson Lane. But it was all of three months, and
then we moved back to California. So it was just a very small splash.
I was totally into music at the time, but I hadn't really learned to play
the guitar, and I hadn't written any songs.

So what was your impression of Nashville at that time?
I thought it was interesting, but it was a real tough time, because I was making the transition from seventh to eighth grade, my mom and dad were butting heads. We moved out here for his job. It wasn't this thing where I could have planned to come out here yet. So I didn't know what to think, except that I was very lonely.

(barely a whisper) . . . yeah.
You know.

So when you came back in '79, is there anything that happened in that first twenty-four hours that stands out in your mind, besides meeting Willie Nelson, Marshall Chapman, and Mary Ann and Pam? *(laughs)*
No. Because that was such a huge memory. To be able to be treated to that kind of introduction to Nashville, you know, you couldn't buy that. I thank my father for these kinds of things again and again, because who gets to do that their first night in Nashville? Nobody. You might get to experience something like that after you've been here a while.

So you had an inside track.
Uh-huh.

Okay. One more question. In your twenty-nine years living here, is there anything that's happened, that could *only* have happened in Nashville?
Hmm, let's see . . .

Just anything.
Well, I wrote a song with my friend Craig Carothers called "Open Mic" that's kind of about this. It's not *one* thing happening—it's something that *continues* to happen. I can remember several times, since coming here to learn how to do this, seeing people come into town that really wanted to do this, but they just didn't have it, you know? And you couldn't tell them no, but they kept at it. They were persistent. They just wanted it so bad. And I don't know how many

times it's happened that, not a few years later, I'd see their name on a #1 song, or having great success, and I'd think to myself, You know, you shouldn't judge this whole thing, because I heard Johnny Cash once say—and I don't know verbatim what it was, but it was all about perseverance, this whole Nashville thing.

Is there anything else, just a crazy something that happened?
Well, one night I was at 328 Performance Hall watching somebody play, and it was packed. So I'm standing there. There was no place to sit. It was standing room only. I'm standing there with a friend, and I look over and there's Jon Bon Jovi standing right next to me. So I lean over to my friend and go, "Hey man, Jon Bon Jovi's right next to me." Then I watched the band, and then leaned back over and said, "I can't stand Jon Bon Jovi!" *(laughs)* But that's Nashville, too. You see a whole lot of sparkle here—people that you wouldn't really buy their records, or know, or want to know. On the other hand, you see just as many that you idolize, that you've revered and listened to everything they've ever written.

Like?
Well, Guy Clark, John Prine. But they're always the same guys, aren't they? Seems to me like we name the same guys. Bobby Braddock is my hero. He would be embarrassed to hear me say this, but if I had to pick a mentor it would be Braddock. And not because he went out of his way. Just because through osmosis, or by being my friend, or showing me how a really great, superior songwriter can be so humble and kind, give you the time of day, help you out. Braddock, and Bobby Bare . . . the list goes on. Shel Silverstein? An absolute hero. When I used to make tape copies at Tree, it wasn't unusual for Shel to just come in and sit down with a guitar and play one song after the other.

Did you ever play him your songs? I would think he would *love* your songs.
Oh, he might have, but there were always girls around. And when there're girls around, with Shel—he was *on*. He wasn't going to give up that kind of attention for anything, because he *loved* women,

man. *(laughter)* He'd sit there and play one song after another, and the girls would laugh and giggle, the girls that worked in the office. And so you'd never get a chance. But only in Nashville can you work at a place like Tree—where I worked as a tape copy guy for, like, four years—and see on a daily basis Waylon, Roger, Harlan, Willie . . . they all came in every day.

Mary Gauthier said she came to Nashville because she "wanted to be uplifted by greatness."
Oh, that's great. That's it, exactly.

All right. So Don, just tell me anything Nashville. Just anything that comes to mind.
Okay. Well, when I was first learning to play guitar out in California, I used these guitar strings called "Nashville Straights." They were packaged straight out, not curled up in a little baggie like most strings.

Were they made in Nashville?
I don't know. Could be. But here's the deal—I would buy them at this music store in California where I worked for a while. They claimed not curling up the strings improved their tone, right? That was the sales pitch. Now, I don't know if that was true or false. But because it said "Nashville" on it, I bought those, man. They were the only guitar strings I bought until they went out of business. I'd bring home those long, thin boxes, and put those guitar strings on. Plus, they came with a sticker that said "Nashville Straights." I had one on my guitar case. I learned about them from my dad. He said, "Why don't you try these new Nashville strings, and see if you can tell any difference?" So I did. And you know what? They didn't sound any better than the other ones. They were total bullshit. But anything Nashville, man, I had to check it out.

John Hiatt

"**WHY DON'T YOU JUST COME OUT** and say it, Marshall. I was fat."

Hiatt says that every time I try to describe what it was like seeing him for the first time, when he was performing at the Exit/In in 1972. I don't know why he tries to put those words in my mouth. The truth is, he was *not* fat. Being nineteen years old, however, he had the full face of a young adolescent, which made him look, well . . . cherubic. It was an interesting contrast. That angelic face housing those smoldering, haunted eyes. I was intrigued but not yet a fan. Not back then. Hiatt was writing songs with titles like "We Are Hungry for the Magic Christ," "I Killed an Ant with My Guitar," and "Since His Penis Came Between Us," and quite frankly, I didn't know what to make of him.

A few years later, I briefly hung out with a guy named Travis Rivers, who was managing both Hiatt and blues singer Tracy Nelson. Rivers had an attic apartment/office on 19th Avenue South. I remember it had concert posters covering the walls and ceiling and four or five desk phones scattered about, some of which were plugged in.

Travis was known in music circles as the guy responsible for getting Janis Joplin from Texas to San Francisco, where she teamed up with Big Brother and the Holding Company. Before meeting Travis, I had read *Buried Alive*, the Janis Joplin biography (by Myra Friedman). In one passage, Joplin credits Travis's sexual prowess with inspiring her to make the move. I won't quote here exactly what Joplin said, but her comments had every chick singer in Nashville slipping Rivers a phone number. I can't exactly recall how Travis and I got together, but I'd like to think it had nothing to do with Joplin's comments. But I could be deluding myself.

I remember I was reading *Buried Alive* while visiting my parents in Spartanburg. When my mother saw the book, she frowned with disapproval: "Marshall, why on *earth* would you read something like that? Don't you realize we *are* what we read?"

"Oh Mother, that's ridiculous! If I read a biography about Hitler, does that make me Hitler? Maybe I'm reading this so history won't repeat itself."

"But that poor girl was a *drug addict!*" Mother protested. "Why would you read something like that?"

"So I won't overdose on drugs?" I replied.

ONE TIME TRAVIS TOOK ME to a concert at Southwestern College (now Rhodes College) in Memphis. The concert featured Tracy Nelson and her band, with John Hiatt opening solo. Travis had picked me up in a 1970 Subaru station wagon that belonged to Nelson. Before leaving Nashville, we swung by an apartment complex to pick up Hiatt, who was living with a woman named Linda who had a twin sister named Brenda. It somehow seems perfect to me now that Hiatt would be living with a woman whose name rhymed with her twin sister's.

Hiatt opened the show singing songs he had written, including the aforementioned "I Killed an Ant with My Guitar." Later, he joined Nelson's band to play some blues guitar, which is when I sat up and took notice. In those days, I was more into John's guitar playing than his songwriting.

John Hiatt's not the first artist I was slow to catch on to. I wasn't that enamored with the Beatles when they first came out either. In early 1964, my cousin Alice Means brought a 45 of "I Want to Hold Your Hand" over to the basement playroom at my parents' house, where we listened to it on a little RCA record player that only played 45s. My older sister Mary was crazy about the Beatles, but quite frankly, I thought they were kind of silly. Maybe it was that picture on the record sleeve—the one of them wearing those matching suits and ties, grinning those goofy grins underneath those goofy mod haircuts. In those days, I was totally into James Brown, Bobby Blue Bland, and Big Joe Turner. I had no time for these limey upstarts.

But all would change in December of 1969. I was living in Aix-

John Hiatt and White Duck at the Exit/In, ca. 1971

en-Provence, spending my junior year abroad with the Vanderbilt-in-France program. For Christmas, my sister Dorothy sent me an LP of *Abbey Road*. When I first listened to it, I liked it well enough. But when I got stoned and listened to it, well . . . it's kind of hard to put into words. I was grooving along to that mesmerizing riff at the end of "I Want You (She's So Heavy)," and when it abruptly stopped, it was like someone had pulled the plug on my psyche, which then went into a free fall into the abyss of the unknown. From that moment on, I was a goner.

MY MOST VIVID MEMORY OF that Memphis trip with Hiatt and Rivers involves something that happened after the show. Actually, something that happened *twice* after the show. It was well after midnight. Travis was driving us back to Nashville along I-40 when suddenly, one of the tires blew. After pulling over, he and John unloaded a couple of amplifiers from the back so they could get to the spare and tools stored underneath the Subaru's floorboard. As they changed the tire and reloaded the amps, I could hear them back there huffing and puffing. John seemed a little grumpy, while Travis was his usual good-natured self. It was all I could do to just stay quiet and out of the way.

Forty miles later, we were cruising merrily along when suddenly, *another* tire blew. I couldn't believe it. I've had one, maybe two flats in my entire life, but never two in succession like that. When that second tire blew, it was beyond real—like being in a twilight zone. John was rolling his eyes while I tried not to laugh. We somehow made it back to Nashville after one of the guys from Nelson's crew brought us another tire.

Later that summer, I bought my first electric guitar—a sunburst Fender Telecaster that belonged to Hiatt. I'd seen it lying around Travis's office and was always picking it up and playing it. When Travis told me John wanted to sell it, I promptly wrote out a check. That guitar marked the beginning of a rock & roll odyssey that would last . . . well, it could still be going on for all I know.

In the decade that followed, Hiatt left Nashville to embark on a rock & roll odyssey of his own. Every now and then I would hear or read something about him. I knew he was making waves, recording albums for Geffen Records on the West Coast, but I wasn't really paying that much attention.

One time—in late 1984 or early 1985—I ran into Hiatt and photographer Jim McGuire at a bar in Nashville called Close Quarters (where the Bound'ry is today). I had written a bunch of new songs and was looking for a publisher. At that time, Hiatt was writing for an L.A. outfit called Bug Music that was revolutionizing the song-publishing world. Founding brothers Dan and Fred Bourgoise believed songwriters should own their copyrights (i.e., songs), which was a novel idea at the time—usually publishers owned copyrights. So they started Bug to protect and promote those copyrights, and also to collect royalties once the songs got recorded. They got the idea after helping their buddy Del Shannon collect "missing" royalties from his 1961 smash hit "Runaway."

They were so successful they thought, *If we can do this for Del, why not other songwriters?* Thus, Bug Music was born.

That night at Close Quarters, Hiatt piqued my interest in the "Bug Brothers." "Dan and Fred would love you, Marshall! You should meet with them." Sounded good to me. I liked the idea of owning my own copyrights. Plus Bug had some cool writers on their roster. Besides John Hiatt and Del Shannon, there was Willie Dixon, Muddy Waters, T-Bone Burnett, Los Lobos, and Dave Alvin. A part of me was thinking, *Hmm . . . maybe some of that cool will rub off on me!* Another part was thinking, *Man, these guys need a cool* gal *on their roster, and I know just who would fit the bill!* My one concern was their location—Los Angeles.

A month or so later, I heard Bug was opening an office in Nashville, which I took as a good omen. Then I heard they had hired my buddy Garry Velletri to run it, which I took as a double good omen. So that summer, I signed with Bug.

Today, Bug handles thousands of writers worldwide. But when the Nashville office first opened in 1986, there were only five—Hiatt and four newly signed: me, Fred Koller, Nanci Griffith, and John Prine.

In August 1984, Hiatt checked himself into a treatment center. Most recovering addicts are advised to take it easy during those first few fragile months of sobriety, but John was never allowed the luxury. In early 1985, his estranged wife committed suicide. Their daughter, Lilly, was just shy of her first birthday. After a European tour, John moved back to Nashville with Lilly, hoping to make a fresh start.

The songs John wrote in the aftermath of this tragedy were hard to ignore. In early 1987, he recorded *Bring the Family*, an album many consider his masterpiece. It was his eighth album—and his first to chart on the *Billboard* 200.

Bring the Family hit me like *Abbey Road*. The songs, the musicianship, John's voice . . . everything just seemed to come together on that album. "Memphis in the Meantime," "Thing Called Love" (later a hit for Bonnie Raitt), and the now-classic "Have a Little Faith in Me" (later recorded by Joe Cocker, Delbert McClinton, Chaka Khan, and others) were but three of the album's ten songs, all of which resonated with me in a powerful way. And John sang them like a man who'd been thrown a lifeline. To this day, *Bring the Family* is one of my all-time favorite albums.

The following year, John played a series of Thursday-night shows at a Nashville club called 12th & Porter. The shows were word-of-mouth affairs whose purpose was to tighten up the band before going into the studio to record *Slow Turning*. The band was a group from Louisiana called the Goners that featured Sonny Landreth on slide guitar.

I was in the audience for every one of those shows. I just sat there riveted while John sang one new song after another. Songs like "Drive South" (later a country hit for Suzy Bogguss), "Tennessee Plates" (later recorded by Mark Collie), "Georgia Rae" (about his newborn daughter), and "Feels Like Rain" (later recorded by Buddy Guy). By then John was becoming not only a respected artist worldwide but a hit factory as a songwriter. There aren't many artists who can say they've had a song recorded by Bob Dylan, much less one recorded by Bob Dylan, Willie Nelson, *and* Bruce Springsteen. "Across the Borderline," which John co-wrote with Ry Cooder and Jim Dickinson, may be the only song holding that distinction.

OVER THE YEARS, I'VE PLAYED a few gigs with John—mostly benefits and a Bug showcase or two. And every now and then, I'll run into him at the grocery store or an industry soiree. John and his wife Nancy and their daughters came to one of my Christmas parties at the "Sky Palace," which is what my friends called the high-rise condominium where I used to live. I'm also listed as John's co-writer on "Old Habits," a song he recorded for *Perfectly Good Guitar*. I use the term *co-writer* loosely here. Truth is, we never sat down and wrote the song together. I'd run into John in the hallway at Bug Music. Through conversation, I mentioned a song idea I had—"Old Habits Are Hard to Break." John said it sounded "like somebody doing the same thing over and over, expecting different results." Then I proceeded to tell him this wild story I'd heard as a child in South Carolina. Our maid Cora Jeter was always telling us stories about her childhood in Union County. In this one, she was picking cotton in a cotton field where "there wasn't a tree for miles around"—except for this one tree. Her father had warned her to stay away from it "lest a tree frog jump out and attach itself" to her. Cora was always warning us about tree frogs. It got to the point I wouldn't ride my bicycle down a street with overhanging branches lest a tree frog jump out and attach itself to *me*.

As it turned out, Cora defied her father's warning, and sure enough, when she walked under that one tree, a tree frog jumped out and affixed itself to her, wrapping itself around her waist until she was "blue in the face." When Cora's father saw the snakelike tourniquet around his daughter's waist, he shouted, "Cora, that tree frog won't let go 'til it thunders!" At that point, Cora would look us in the eye and say, "And child, there wasn't a cloud in the sky!" I don't know why I told John that story. One of those southern impulses, I guess.

Months later, I ran into John at a recovery group meeting. Afterward, he said, "Ah, Marshall, you remember that song idea you were telling me about? Well, I went home and finished it, and Ronnie Milsap just recorded it." So my name ended up on the song. And even though she died in 1983, I imagine Cora Jeter could have been credited as well, since images from the tree frog story run throughout the first verse. But the truth is, John pretty much wrote the entire thing.

OKAY. BEFORE WE GET TO the interview, I have a confession to make. I used to have a *major* crush on John Hiatt. This was right after he had moved back to Nashville. It got so bad that every time I'd see him, I couldn't speak. I don't mind admitting it now, but back then, I tell you . . . I had it *bad*. Then I heard he was seeing this cute girl named Nancy, and I hate to say it, but I was jealous. I remember one time he was performing at a club called Music Row. After the show, I was hanging around, probably hoping he would notice me or some fool thing—who knows? Then suddenly, there he was! Standing just a few feet away. My heart was pounding wildly. But just as I was about to get up the nerve to approach him, to tell him how much I'd enjoyed the show, I saw him walk over to this woman who was sitting in a chair. *Oh, that must be Nancy*, I thought. So I'm standing there watching as he walks up and kisses this woman right on the mouth! It was a long, hard, passionate kiss that was reciprocated. It was Nancy all right. She was sitting with a bunch of her girlfriends, and John just sauntered over there and laid one on her, right there in front of God, her girlfriends, a few straggling fans, me . . . everybody. He didn't give a shit. He was sober and he was in love, by God. Of course, my heart sank, but on some higher level, I knew I was witnessing something very real.

It took a while, but I got over my crush.

Of course, John ended up marrying Nancy, and I ended up in treatment, but that's a whole 'nother story.

John's farm outside Nashville
March 10, 2009

IT'S AN UNSEASONABLY WARM and breezy afternoon as I drive out to the Hiatt homestead beyond Big East Fork Creek. After I pull up in the gravel drive, I knock softly on a side door. When no one answers, I turn the knob. The door is unlocked and cracks open.

"Anybody home?" I call out.

Nancy comes to the door, and we exchange greetings. Then she takes me on a tour of the house, which was originally two separate buildings: a log cabin built in 1820 and a Federal-style farmhouse built in 1910. Since the Hiatts came on board, they've added a spacious light-filled kitchen and a comfortable living area that serves as a TV room. Nancy has overseen all renovations, and it's obvious she has an artist's eye. Of particular interest are several large wooden beams in the living area that were salvaged from the old train shed behind Union Station.

After the tour, John and I sit down on the porch outside his studio. He lights a cigar as I turn on the tape.

So John, you came to Nashville from Indianapolis?
That's right.

Just out of high school?
Well, I quit high school when I was sixteen. I went until I was fifteen, then sort of skipped a year. Then I'd show up every once in a while. I faked night school the second semester, then never went back.

Were you playing in bands around town?
I was mostly playing in people's basements. But there was this one place on Indiana Avenue run by this black dude—sort of a hippie folk club kind of place with cushions everywhere, against the walls and stuff. I'd play there every once in a while. I've always had a little band together ever since I was about twelve.

Did you always play guitar?
Yeah. Well, in this one band, I played bass.

What made you decide to go to Nashville?
I think the main thing that got me here was the band Area Code 615. They were recording all this off-the-wall stuff like "Lady Madonna" with banjos. *(laughs)* David Briggs played piano, they had steel guitars . . .

Didn't Russ Hicks play steel?
Hicks played later with Barefoot Jerry, which was sort of a 615 spin-off band.

Mac Gayden?
Yeah, and Wayne Moss on guitar. Norbert Putnam played bass.

I used to go hear those guys at the Exit/In. They were *the* cool band. So they got your attention?
Well, they were doing pop songs . . . rock & roll songs . . . but with this whole other interpretation, and I'm like, What the hell's going on down there? *(laughs)* They just piqued my interest. And then the second reason was, I was looking to go somewhere to try and get something going musically, and L.A. and New York were just too intimidating, too far away. Nashville was only three hundred miles south.

So you drive south, and you're how old?
Eighteen. I was eighteen.

Was that your very first time in Nashville? Did you ever come down to scout things out?
Well, I came through when I was seventeen.

Who were you with when you came through?
I came through with a couple of friends. We were just, you know . . . it was one of my attempts to get out of Dodge.

Did you spend the night?
Yeah. In fact, I befriended a guy who was from Memphis named Bob Frank. You know Bob Frank?

The name sounds familiar.
Fantastic singer-songwriter. Still makes records.

So you meet Bob Frank that first time while passing through with your buddies.
Yeah. He was actually writing for Tree [now Sony/ATV Music Publishing]. But he was a folk singer. He had a deal with Vanguard Records, and also a songwriting deal with Tree. He said, "They pay me twenty-five dollars a week!" So I made note, and we headed west, ostensibly to California, but we wound up sleeping in a rice field in Arkansas somewhere, and waking up just *bit to death*.

Bugs?
Oh, God! *(laughs)* Yeah, mosquitoes.

So you were just sleeping on the ground next to your car?
Yeah, we had no idea.

No motels?
No motels. I was traveling with a friend who had an old hearse. That was a cool way to get around back in the day. And so we're in his hearse . . .

One of those old Cadillacs?
Yeah.

With the thing on the back?
Yeah, you know, for the casket. We used to all just ride around in that. Smoke dope, you know, talk about how we were never gonna be straight. *(laughs)*

So it's you and, what, two guys?
Yeah, two other guys.

Were they musicians?
No. It was my friend Mark Albert, and this guy . . . his name escapes me now. He was kind of a charismatic guy, kind of an oddball. Much older than we were. A former minister of some denomination.

Defrocked?
Oh, I'm sure.

So this first trip, you're just out exploring, seeing what's out there. You go through Nashville, but now you're waylaid in Arkansas, after thinking you were going to California.
Yeah, after I got et up in that rice field, I said, "Boys, I'm going home!" So I hitchhiked back to my family in Indianapolis.

(Wind kicks up. Wind chimes tinkle nearby.)
So the guys went on?
Yeah, the guy in the hearse . . . Bob . . . Bob Hicks, I think was his name. Not the Robert Hicks we know, but I believe that was his name.

So you're seventeen, and then a year goes by . . .
Well, so I go back home and I get a job. Because I figure I've got to have some money if I'm going to relocate. I'd always had jobs. My mother had always insisted I work when I wasn't going to school. I

John Hiatt   165

flipped burgers for a while. But this time I actually went and got a job at an insurance company—in the main office stock room, filling orders for the other offices. Minimum-wage stuff.

So you're living at home, saving money. Did you have a car?
Well, I bought a car from this guy who was friends with the guy who wound up riding down with me. It was a 1963 Corvair. It had no floorboard. He'd put two pieces of tin over what was left of the frame, just so you wouldn't Fred Flintstone away. I mean, you had to have some place to set your feet! *(laughter)* That car burned oil like you wouldn't believe. It took five quarts to get down here. We were buying bulk oil at twenty cents a quart.

So you buy this car, then you and your buddy drive down. Or did you drive down by yourself?
No. My buddy Mark Albert came with me. He and I were traveling buddies. We used to hitchhike all over. I think he later became a sheriff. Anyway, that Corvair cost me thirty-five dollars.

Wow. What year did you say it was?
A '63 . . . white . . . convertible.

So you're eighteen. It's 1971. You're heading for Nashville. Your suitcase is packed. You're with your buddy. You and Mark are in the Corvair . . .
We're in the Corvair. And he knows I'm going [to Nashville] to stay. He doesn't know what he's going to do. He said, "Yeah, I'll ride down with you." And so we spent that first night in Centennial Park, sleeping under a picnic table.

That's so funny, because Rodney [Crowell] spent one of his first nights sleeping *on top of* a picnic table.
Well, Rodney's from Texas so that makes sense.

Must be that Texas sky. They're not used to sleeping under trees down there.
Yeah, well, I wanted coverage.

So was the picnic table back near the Parthenon?
It could have been. I want to think we slept right there in front of it.

Near West End [Avenue]? That's where all the hippies hung out.
Well, then that's where it was, because my buddy met a Peabody gal pretty much right away, and she fed us for a couple of days.

So she took pity?
Yeah, she took pity and took us in.

Where did she live?
I don't remember. But she was of Spanish descent. Jeannie Helguera was her name. A lovely young girl.

I'm thinking Peabody wasn't part of Vanderbilt back then. It was a teacher's college.
No, this was the high school.

Oh! The Peabody Demonstration School [now University School of Nashville].
Yeah, that was it.

So she was a student there.
Yeah.

Did y'all go out to any music places?
No, we didn't. I spent my days going around to the publishing companies.

So you had sort of a plan!
Well, I'd made these tapes. Sort of my opus, you know. I had a friend who had a couple of two-track tape machines back home. I had about

six or eight songs, and I'd made these demos where he and I played everything . . . you know, drums and bass, piano, guitars, and all that shit. We'd ping-pong everything back and forth between those two tape machines. I thought this was my ultimate brilliant rock record . . . or whatever. *(laughs)*

Did you hook up with Tree then?
Not at first. I went to see some other people. I was sort of holding on to that one. That was my last stop before I was going to say, "Okay, you failed. Now go on back home." I remember going to see Bob Montgomery over at . . . *(pause)*

Goldmine [Music]?
It was Gold something. House of Gold maybe. Bobby Goldsboro ["Honey," "Little Green Apples"] was one of their writers. Anyway, I played the tape for him and he said, "Well, maybe we can get Bobby to work with you a little bit on some of these things." And I just . . .

Couldn't get past the hair? *(laughs)*
I just couldn't get past it. I said, "Okay. Well, thank you." Anyway, I went to a couple of other places, and nobody liked the tape, really. I was striking out with the tape. So I finally called Tree and talked to Larry Henley on the phone.

Now we're talking!
Yeah. And I said, "I'm new in town and I have some songs, and oh, by the way, I know Bob Frank." *(laughs)* So I played my one card. And he said, "You're welcome to come in and play me some stuff. You got a tape?" And I said, "No." It was just instinct talking. By then I knew the tape wasn't doing me any good. So I said, "No, I'm just going to come in and play them for you." So he said, "Well, we don't normally do that. But come on over and I'll listen to a few of your songs."

"Bread and Butter" had already been a hit, right?
Oh yeah. But I didn't know until after I met him that that's who he was. *(sings falsetto)* "I like toast and jam!"

God, I loved that record!

Yeah, me, too. So I went over and played him a couple of songs, and he acted like he liked them. Then he called Buddy Killen [executive vice-president of Tree, later sole owner] down to his office. And Buddy listened to a couple of them and said, "What are you looking for, son?" And I said, "Twenty-five dollars a week," *(laughs)* because I knew that's what Bob Frank was getting. And he said "Well, I think we can do that." And I was just . . . I couldn't believe it. I was stunned. I walked out of there four feet off the ground. It was like, "Holy crap. I'm a songwriter!"

How many days had you been in town?

I'd been there about a week. They even gave me an advance for twenty-five bucks. So I walked on down the Row [Music Row] a little bit. In those days, you know, the publishing companies were all in little houses. And right next to the little houses were these songwriters and rough lower-income people. It was a rough sort of place in those days. And so there were all these rooms for rent.

Did you get you a room?

I got me a room for eleven dollars a week.

Where was it?

1607 16th Avenue South. And you know what? The lady that cuts my hair is David Briggs's girlfriend, and she said he owns that building—1607 16th Avenue South. He hasn't done anything with it yet.

So David Briggs, keyboard player for Area Code 615, the band that inspires you to move to Nashville, ends up owning the building where you first pay rent? That's some serious reverse cosmic shit right there! *(laughs)* **So how long did you live there?**

I was there about two or three months. And then I moved in with a guy I met . . . by then I had met some other songwriters. The place I lived in—actually I was there about six months—there were three other songwriters living there, and there was this lady, you know . . . middle forties, kind of crazy, who lived downstairs.

Was she your landlady?
Well, I never could get that straight what her position was.

You remember her name?
No, I don't. But she was just . . .

Crazy as a bedbug?
Crazy as a loon.

It's amazing how many songwriters I've talked to who lived on Music Row back in the day, and invariably they mention some crazy landlady. Makes me wonder if you all had the same one. *(laughter)* **Okay, let's take a break.**

(Later)
So John, do you remember the first time you ever heard the word "Nashville"?
Hmm . . .

Or the first time you became aware of Nashville?
Well, I knew about Nashville because my favorite radio station was WLAC. So I knew "Get your records at Randy's Record Shop in Gallatin, Tennessee," and "Get your Red Dot baby chicks," and "Send us your poems and a thousand dollars and we'll make a record out of 'em."

You ever send any poems?
No. Never did. But I used to listen to John R and the Hossman. But that wasn't country music. It was R&B. So for years, that's all I knew of Nashville—that they had this R&B station. I knew there was country music down there, but I had no interest in country music, really. And I didn't know that much about it. But WLAC changed my life.

Well . . . *(long pause)* **I think this might be enough.**
Cool beans.

Well, maybe not. *(laughs)* Here's one more: when you were driving down in that Corvair, did you do most of the driving?
I did.

I get the feeling you did *all* the driving.
I did.

Did you drive fast?
(takes a slow puff from his cigar) I was in a reasonable hurry, as I recall.

Would it be safe to say you drove over the speed limit?
No doubt. *(laughs)* And of course, we were thrilled when we got there because the drinking age was eighteen.

Was the Exit/In up and running?
Not really. It got going shortly after I arrived. Ostensibly, they opened it for, you know, sort of weird songwriters like myself.

I remember seeing you perform there.
Yeah . . . those first couple of years had a big impact on me—all those crazy acts like Chris Gantry, and George & the Arizona Star, and Zilch Fletcher . . .

Oh, my God! I loved Zilch!
Yeah, me, too.

He was just so out there!
I still remember his *songs* . . . "Bloody Guts" and "Every Day Is Halloween to You."

Oh, man . . .
(in unison) "I want my baby back / I'm a necrophiliac . . ."

"They took my baby away in a big black Cadillac . . . da-da dum dum . . ." *(laughter)*

I used to get a kick out of taking some of my Vanderbilt English professors to hear Zilch. He used to play this funky hole-in-the-wall place on West End near where Vandyland was. I'm like, "Hey! You guys want to hear a *real* Fugitive poet? Check this guy out!" Then I'd sit back and watch them while he'd sing his songs, and they'd just go nuts!

Oh, man, he used to wear *hard hats* onstage and put the flag on . . . *(pause)* Last year, he came to one of my shows. I got to talk to him. He's a Methodist minister now.

Really? Well when he was in Nashville, I remember he worked in something called "the Blue Unit" at the state mental hospital. Have you seen any of those documentaries Demetria's [Demetria Kalodimos] been making? Like the one she did on George & the Arizona Star? It's called *Pre-Madonna*.

No, I heard it was great.

Yeah, it's on DVD. I'll get you one. She does them as sort of an extension of being a reporter. Sort of like, "Where are they now?" Amazingly, she found both of them.

So what are they doing?

Well, Arizona Star, of course, is living the high life in London like you wouldn't believe.

I believe it.

She still looks like a million dollars. And George is sort of like a street person—but still playing and stuff—in the San Francisco area. There's a club out there that's kind of adopted her. She seems to be doing okay. Doing what she wants to do. But I tell you, that Arizona Star . . . what*ever* she's got going on, it's working for her.

She was a unique talent. No doubt about it.

She had that whole Marilyn Monroe thing going. And nobody could figure the two of them out, you know? Are they straight? Are they gay? Are they from another planet? And every guy with a heartbeat fell for Arizona. Guy Clark even wrote a song about her. Anyway, I didn't mean to go off so, but I wanted to tell you this one thing. When I went to the screening for *Pre-Madonna* at the Belcourt, I met this young man. As it turned out, he was Zilch Fletcher's son! And so he called his dad on his cell phone and I got to talk to him. So how old is the young Fletcher?

He looked like he was . . . I don't know, probably thirty. I mean, everybody seems like they're twenty to me now. Then it turns out they're forty.
Yeah, I know what you mean.

(After a break)
So, John, when did you move back to Nashville?
I moved back in '85. I think it was late summer. My wife's suicide was in April of '85. And so . . . all of a sudden I have this just-shy-of-a-year-old daughter.

You were just a few months out of treatment, right?
Yeah. I got sober in August of 1984. Anyway, by summer, I had to tour. I had to go back to work. And so my older sister, bless her, let me bring Lilly to her place just south of Chicago. So my first sober tour is in Europe, which is where I did some of my worst abusing ever. I'd disappear in those streets of Amsterdam for days.

So you played Amsterdam sober?
Oh, yeah.

"Amsterdam Sober." Sounds like an essay.
That's a book right there. Anyway, all my connections over there would come to these in-stores for the new record, and they'd be slipping little packets of cocaine in my pockets. I'd pull my tour manager aside, and I'd be handling it like it was about a thousand

degrees, and I'd go, "YOU GOTTA TAKE THIS AND DO SOMETHING WITH IT!" *(laughs)*

Anyway, so about halfway through the tour . . . I mean, I had never played sober in my life. And I'd stand on stage every night, and the voices in my head would be talking: "You fake! You phony! You're no good. *They* know it." And this dialogue just went on and on. And then after the shows, of course, we'd all go back to the hotel. And the guys would be hanging out in the bar. And all the chicks, you know. And I wanted to do the same thing, you know. Pick up some girl that would make me feel like I was worth something. But I couldn't. I just couldn't. And so I remember being on my knees in my room, weeping, "God, if I can't do this while I'm working, tell me and I'll go home." And it was like the next night, I'm on stage and the same voices—"You're a fake, you're a phony"—are going. And then about halfway through the set, the voices stopped . . . and I just started playing music. I just remembered the music. And it was like music was being given back to me. It was so powerful. And the voice of the spiritual experience is saying, "Yeah, I gave you this gift. And you've just been trying to kill it . . . with the sideshow. But you can do this, if you want it." It was pretty powerful.

(After another break)
Okay. So you come back from that tour to live, once again, in Nashville. Only this time you have a one-year-old daughter to raise.
Yeah . . . and you know who took me in? Norbert Putnam. He actually put me and Lilly up in their house for about a week or two. They were getting ready to move. He said, "We're moving out in about a week or two. Why don't you guys just stay and wing it?"

So it was just you and Lilly living there?
It was me and Lilly. But there was a succession of nannies, you know, which is a whole 'nother story. *(laughs)* But yeah, it was just us. And then I met Nance, and we fell in love. And the next thing you know . . . she stayed in the house with her son while I was on tour. And she would've taken care of Lilly, but I'd already arranged something. I tried

to talk her into moving in with me, but she wouldn't do it. So I had to marry her. *(laughs)*

Good for her. Okay. Where was Norbert's house?
It was over on Harding Place.

In Belle Meade?
In Belle Meade. 278 Harding Place. We were right by the golf course.

You ever play golf?
Never.

Ashley Cleveland

I FIRST STARTED HEARING ABOUT Ashley Cleveland in the mid-'80s. Whenever a major talent moves to town, it doesn't take long for word to get around. So a year or so before we met, I already knew about this woman with the powerful and soulful voice who also wrote songs.

Before our interview, I emailed Ashley to see if she remembered when we actually met (and to ask when she moved to Nashville). Here's what she had to say: "I don't remember exactly the first time we met. I'm thinking it was either at the Bluebird or the Boardwalk. But I do remember the *feeling* of the first time we met. I was aware of you because I had read about you in the *San Francisco Chronicle* and had been struck by the article. Wherever it was, when you came in the door, it was one of my early experiences of encountering someone who was larger than life. I was sure you were at least seven feet tall. You wore a white Beefy-T, jeans, and a pissed-off look on your face, and I was sold! I also remember my first experiences hearing you perform, watching you prowl and snarl all over the club stages (enlarging them as you went) and then finishing a song with beautiful, perfect French. I minored in French in my oh-so-brief college foray, so that really got my attention. I moved to Nashville August 1, 1984."

I don't remember being pissed off, but if it was the early '80s, I had every reason to be. I'd been touring heavily in late 1979 in support of my third album for Epic. At the dawn of 1980, three things happened within a three-week period that had me reeling: (1) Our equipment was stolen in Cleveland. The headline in the *Plain Dealer* said, "Rock Group Bemoans Theft of Gear Worth $50,000 Here." (2) One of the guys in my band committed suicide, hanging himself from a ceiling

Marshall, Ashley Cleveland, and Emmylou Harris sing the national anthem
at a Vanderbilt women's basketball game, March 2, 2003

light fixture in his father's living room. (3) I was dropped by my record
label (Epic) after three critically acclaimed albums.

A sane person might have taken any one of these events as a sign to
maybe slow down or take a sabbatical. But no. Within a week I was on
a plane to New York, where I signed with a manager who had me back
on the road working nonstop, if only to make payments on a recently
purchased tour bus. The bus experience alone would generate material
for a book, beginning with the opening line: "The two happiest days in
a girl's life are . . . the day she buys her bus and the day she sells it."

That spring—with no record deal—I toured relentlessly. In April alone, we played twenty-eight dates in twenty-two states. By summer, I was an emotional, mental, and physical wreck. Not knowing how to take care of myself, I went home to my family in South Carolina weighing a hundred and twenty pounds. I remember a friend saying, "Chapman, you're so skinny, you'd have to lie down in the shower to get wet!" While in South Carolina, I was hospitalized to have some thyroid nodules removed. The night before I left for South Carolina, the band and I played our last gig at a Nashville club called J. Austin's. My most vivid memory from that evening was a fight in the J. Austin's parking lot, precipitated by my desire to escort the lead guitar player's girlfriend off the bus.

While recuperating at my family's lake house in North Carolina, I overheard my mother discussing the fight incident with my sister Mary.

"Good Lord, Mary, I have never even *seen* a woman hit another woman. Whoever heard of such a thing?"

"Well, you know, Mama, it's a dog-eat-dog world," Mary replied.

At that point, Mother tilted her head thoughtfully to one side. "Well, come to think of it, I've never seen a *dog* eat another dog!"

One thing I can say about my family: they can make me laugh when no one else can. As Dolly Parton said in *Steel Magnolias*, "Laughter through tears is my favorite emotion."

In 1986, while finishing up work on my *Dirty Linen* CD, I called in Ashley to help me lay down some background vocals. As it turned out, the two of us worked well together. My voice has a lot of "air" in it. I'm not a powerful singer. But Ashley is, and our voices blended well together. A few years later, I was honored when Ashley asked me to sing backup on a song that ended up on her *Bus Named Desire* album. Tennessee Williams had *Streetcar Named Desire*, Ashley had *Bus Named Desire*, and I once wrote a song ("Girl in a Bubble") that mentioned "a loveboat named *Desire*." If there's anybody out there with anything else named *Desire*, I'd sure like to know about it. Otherwise, I'm happy to be in this exclusive triumvirate with Ashley and Tennessee. Speaking of Tennessee, one of my all-time favorite lines in country music was written by Bob McDill: "And those Williams boys, they still mean a lot to me—Hank and Tennessee." I've always loved McDill's writing, especially the way he infuses country music with the southern literary thing.

In the late '80s, up until she married rock guitarist-producer Kenny Greenberg in 1991, Ashley lived in an upstairs apartment just down the street from where Chris and I live today. In those days, I was single and used to drift by at about supper time. Ashley was a single mom, living with her five-year-old daughter, Becca. Seemed like every time I dropped by, Ashley would be steaming up some broccoli to go with roast chicken and rice. I remember Becca refused to eat the top part of her broccoli, which she referred to as "hair." She'd only eat the stalks, which was fine with me, as I'd end up eating whatever was left on her plate.

One thing I have always loved about Ashley, besides her musical talent and culinary skills, is her ability to listen. She has always been a good, sympathetic listener. Whenever I'm trying to sort out something in my life, I know I'm safe with Ashley. And believe me, in those days, we had a lot to sort out. Especially in our relationships with men. I remember one song Ashley wrote about this guy who says he's going to call but never does. We laugh about those days now, and often wonder what the odds are for two rockers like us not only to find true love but to find it in the same year. Because that's exactly what happened. In 1991, Ashley fell in love with Kenny and I fell in love with Chris. Now here we are, nearly twenty years later, living lives neither of us could have imagined.

FOR A WHILE, IN THE 1990S, Ashley, Emmylou, and I would sing the national anthem at the final home game of the season for the Vanderbilt women's basketball team. It had become sort of a tradition, until Ashley and Emmy started winning so many Grammys that they had to start bowing out. (The regular season in college basketball winds down in February, which is when the Grammys take place.) I was happy to see Ashley nominated again in 2007 for *Before the Daylight's Shot.*

In 2003, a CD called *SHARE* (*Songs of Hope, Awareness & Recovery for Everyone*) was released to raise funds for the treatment and prevention of alcohol and drug abuse. The album included Ashley singing Neil Young's "Needle and the Damage Done" and me singing my song "Booze in Your Blood." Other performers were John Prine, Travis Tritt,

Ashley Cleveland   179

Martina McBride, Hal Ketchum, BR549, George Jones, and Michael Peterson. After its release, Ashley and I occasionally found ourselves on the road together, playing gigs in Washington, D.C.; Chicago; Denver; Phoenix; and Sedona, Arizona.

Okay, one more flash and we'll get to the interview. When Ahmet Ertegun died in 2006, I emailed Ashley to express my condolences. Ashley may be the only Nashville singer-songwriter ever to be personally signed by the legendary record executive to his Atlantic label. Someone had sent him a tape of Ashley singing with John Hiatt. After listening to the tape, Ertegun inquired, *Who's the girl?*

Ashley's kitchen
Franklin, Tennessee
January 7, 2008

So Ashley, I know you were born in Knoxville, but you came to Nashville from San Francisco, right?
Well, not really. I was born in Knoxville. My parents split up when I was in kindergarten. When I was in third grade, my mother moved to San Francisco with my sister, me, and our black maid, Dorothy. We didn't go anywhere without Dorothy—they were like my two mothers. My mother worked for a company that told her she could live anywhere in the U.S. she wanted, so she picked San Francisco. For me, it was like going to the twilight zone. Like hurtling through a time warp I could not fathom, because they [people in San Francisco] were a good fifteen to twenty years ahead of the South, plus I *talked like this*, you know—with an east Tennessee hillbilly accent. It wasn't the pretty, rolling cadence of the Deep South, and, uh . . . well, I was *really* rejected *(laughs)* when I went out there.

So it was traumatic.
Yes, it was. Plus, I had a chip on my shoulder 'cause my parents had gotten divorced. I mean, it was just the whole thing. So I would spend school months in northern California and summers with my father

in Tennessee. I think the reason I hightailed it back to Tennessee as quickly as I could is because, you know, I had gone out to California under such bleak circumstances, personally.

So you moved back to Knoxville?
Well, I got kicked out of the house in California when I was a junior in high school, so I ended up moving back to Knoxville to finish up high school. Then stayed and went to UT [University of Tennessee] for a couple of years. UT is where I met Pam Tillis.

Pam was a student there, too?
Well, the term "student" is really exaggerating it for both of us. Let's just say we were enrolled and leave it at that. We never went to class. We were always in the clubs, and eventually we crossed paths and decided to put together a folk duo. We played in clubs up and down the Cumberland strip and got to be close friends. This was back in 1977, 1978. Then Pam left school. Both of us had received word from our parents that they were done financing our good times. So we both left school. I went back to California and started playing up and down the northern California coastline.

As a solo act?
Uh-huh. And Pam eventually . . . she spent some time in California, too, living on a houseboat in Sausalito, but we were never there at the same time.

What was the name of your folk duo?
Oh, something unimaginative like Ashley Cleveland and Pam Tillis or Pam Tillis and Ashley Cleveland. Nothing exciting. But we really had a thing singing together. It was really wonderful. So we stayed in touch. And so . . . after I had Rebecca—I was twenty-five, so I had spent a few years playing in clubs *(dog starts barking)* . . . Anyway, I played in clubs up and down the coastline. Then after I had Rebecca, I realized, you know, that I was single and I had this baby and I was going nowhere, and I thought, "I have no idea if I can make a living in the music business. I mean, my life is in shambles, but it's the only

skill I've got." So I figured I'd better go somewhere where they're making music.

Did you do any other jobs, like waiting on tables?
Oh, I worked at a bank for a while. I mean, you know, every job I ever did, I did completely half-assed and was eventually fired from . . . and rightfully so.

What were some of your jobs besides music?
Well, I was a waitress because, you know, one of my best friends, whose brother started Ruby Tuesday's, created . . .

Yeah, in Knoxville, I remember that.
I mean, I couldn't even keep jobs that my friends gave me. *(laughs)* It was like . . . oh, I worked as a waitress, I worked at a music store, I worked at a bank. I just . . . I worked cleaning houses. Now *that* I was quite excellent at. I was a *good* house cleaner. You know, just whatever I could pick up to finance my music career. But mostly I got gigs playing in clubs.

So August 1, 1984, you make the big move.
Yeah, but I had moved back to Knoxville a year before that and worked for my father for a year.

Doing . . .
Oh, he was a big interior designer and had a studio, so I would sort . . . I would go through the fabrics and throw out the discontinued items, just menial . . . nothing. But it was a way to save money. And I reconnected with Pam, and she told me that Becca and I could have a room in her house in Nashville. She had a little house on Branch Creek, right off White Bridge Road. So I came over to visit her right before I moved, you know, to kind of check it out.

Did you bring Becca with you?
Not that first time. I came by myself. My sister and I were roommates in Knoxville, so she took care of Becca, and I came by myself. And

then two things happened. You know, I drove around Nashville while Pam was doing something during the day, and I had no more . . . I mean, I had nothing going for me, I had no prospects, I . . .

Pam was your only Nashville connection?
She was my only connection, and I . . . *(dog starts barking again)* . . . Okay, the two significant things that happened were—the first thing was I'm driving around in this strange city where I hardly know . . .

So you drove to Nashville from Knoxville?
Yeah, I had an old Volvo sedan.

What year?
Lord . . . well, it was probably 1980.

What color was it?
Black.

What color was the interior?
(pause) Tan.

Thank you.
You're really testing my memory bank. *(laughter)*

Inquiring minds must know.
So I drove around, and had the most profound sense of being *home* that I'd ever had. You know, I loved Knoxville—and I had an uneasy alliance with California—but I never . . . I was uprooted early on in life, and then I had lived this dual existence that was so bizarre and so unrelated to anything that I'd known prior—living in Knoxville, Tennessee, and then Marin County, California. The two were so disparate, and the lifestyles were so . . . I mean, it was really like ping-ponging back and forth between two countries. I guess the upshot of it was that I've never had a sense of home or belonging. So I'm driving around Nashville, I know one person, I have nothing going on, I don't even know my way around, but I'm home and I know it. I don't know *why* I know it, but I know it.

Then that night, we went out. Pam said, "You've got to hear some music while you're here." So that night we went out to Bogey's to see Dave Olney, and Pam says, "You've got to hear this guitar player. He's gonna blow your mind." As it turned out, the guitar player was Kenny.

You're kidding! So Kenny played with Dave Olney?
Yes, for years. They even went and got tattoos together. And so I met Kenny that night. He was married to somebody else. He had a very brief early marriage, and so we barely spoke. I mean, he came over and said hello . . . he knew Pam . . . and so he said hello to everybody at the table. But I was so knocked out with his playing that I just never forgot. So, unbeknownst to me, I met my future [husband] my first night in Nashville. *(laughs)* Isn't that crazy?

Unbelievable. So how many nights did you stay in town?
Just that one.

God, that's just too . . . talk about divine providence!
I know, I know. I knew I was supposed to be here, I just didn't know why. And then, you know . . . and then I came back. And I'd been sending these crummy little demo tapes over, thinking maybe I could . . . I mean I was so naïve about how anything in the music business worked. I thought, "Well, maybe I can get some session work or something." And lo and behold, somebody actually . . . this guy called me and said, "You know we got your demo tape and we think we can use you," and gave me the address.

Now when was this?
This was right before I moved here for good. So I came back over and I show up at the session, and he looks at me and he goes, "Who are you?" And I said, "Well, I'm Ashley Cleveland." And he goes, "Oh, we wanted to hire a man."

He thought you were a man?
(laughs) Based on my demos. So I didn't get the gig—the one gig I had!

They wanted you for session vocalist?
Yeah . . . a *male* session vocalist. They heard my tape and thought I was a man.

I hate when that happens.
(laughs) I was crestfallen. It was like my first gig, and then I lost it.

Okay, so you go back to Knoxville, gather up your things . . .
Yeah . . . gathered up my things, and Becca and I came on over hillbilly style.

Then you move in with Pam and her son, Ben. How old was Ben?
He was, like, four or five. And Becca was two.

So what was it like living there?
Well, Pam and I were . . . it was really an ill-fated . . . I mean, I was so type A and she was so type Z. More so than ever back then. I don't think she'd mind my telling this, but, we were just . . . she just really, absolutely dwelled in the right side of her brain, and never came up for air. And I'm very left-brain oriented, I mean very much so for a creative person. It's odd.

I'm that way, too. My brother once told me I was the most left-brain right-brain person he'd ever known. It shocks people to see how organized I am.
(laughs) Yeah, me, too. And so, you know, I come over and Pam is just very freewheeling, but the greatest picture of all that was the time she came in from the grocery store, and she's putting her groceries away, and she says, "I know I've forgotten something, but I can't for the life of me remember what it is." Then she says, "Oh! *Ben!*" Then she runs and jumps in the car and goes back to Kroger where she finds Ben wandering in the cereal aisle.

I love that. Okay. So when did you first hear the word "Nashville"?
Well, let's see. The first time I ever really thought about Nashville was . . . I drove over from Knoxville in high school. I had a little Triumph Spitfire I drove over for a ZZ Top concert.

Was it a convertible?
Yeah. I had the top down and was wearing a bikini to work on my tan, and the truckers went wild.

That's quite an image. So that was your first time in Nashville?
Yes, my first time in Nashville, and I came over . . . actually, no, it was *not* ZZ Top. It was Lynyrd Skynyrd, the Atlanta Rhythm Section, and the Marshall Tucker Band. It was at the fairgrounds.

How old were you?
Seventeen.

Who'd you come over here with?
I came by myself. I don't even know why I did that. But I did.

Did you ever consider moving to New York or Los Angeles?
I did, but I was terrified to try a big city on my own, strapped for cash and with a baby in tow. Nashville was in my home state and felt more friendly to me. Also, I was entirely ignorant as to how record labels worked. I figured Warner Bros. Nashville was the same as Warner Bros. L.A., and that each label location would have different divisions. So I assumed there'd be a rock division at every label in Nashville.

While growing up in San Francisco and Knoxville, were you ever a fan of country music? Or any artists associated with country music?
The two country artists that I loved were Emmy and Rodney Crowell. I wore their early records out. I also had Rosanne's [Rosanne Cash] first record and *The Amazing Rhythm Aces*. That was back when country acts would get airplay on Top Forty, so you would hear some of the more progressive acts.

Okay, one more question, and I'm done. Since you've lived in Nashville, is there an anecdote, a story you could tell, that could only have happened in Nashville?
Let's see . . . yes. In 1992, Kenny was producing Joan Baez with his partner at the time, Wally Wilson. And Joan would not stay in a

conventional hotel where all the windows are hermetically sealed. She could only sleep in a room with an open window.

I can relate.
So she stays at Wally's house, which was around the corner. And then one day she calls me up and . . . Joan Baez is arguably one of the most recognizable people in the world, because she is known internationally, and inter-generationally as well. So anyway, everywhere we went, people would stop their cars in the middle of the street, people would run out of places screaming, "Joan! Joan!"

Did y'all ever go to Kroger?
Oh, yeah. I mean, we'd go out to eat and people would just . . . it'd be a constant line. And she's very gracious, so . . . but anyway, just that recognizability was just so profound with her. And so she calls me up one day, and she says—it was a day they were not recording—and she says, "You know, I noticed you have a lot of leaves in your yard." Then she says, "Well, you know out where I live [northern California], the trees don't really drop many leaves in the fall, and I have a real strong desire to rake. Would you mind if I came over and raked your yard?"

I'm thinking, "Knock yourself out!" because we had a lot of very old trees. So anyway, she comes over and she's in the backyard and our whole—the back of the house has all these picture windows—and I'm inside doing something, and I just laugh the whole day 'cause I'd walk past one of those picture windows, and there'd be Joan Baez raking leaves in my backyard . . . looking just like Joan Baez.

[Shortly after this interview, Ashley won her third Grammy. So I sent her an email. "Congratulations!" it said. "Joan Baez and I are on our way over to prune your trees!"]

Gary Nicholson

GARY CAN PROBABLY TELL YOU, better than I, of our first encounter. But I've heard this story so many times—told by Gary and
others who were there—that I feel confident piecing it together. The
year was 1981. I'd gone to hear Guy Clark at Cantrell's, which was Nashville's only underground club at the time. Guy was backed by a three-
piece band that included Gary Nicholson on lead guitar.

Back in those days, I was known for jumping onstage with musicians whose music I loved. Especially if I'd had a little something to
drink. This night would prove to be no exception. Toward the end of
Guy's set, sure enough, I bounded up on the stage, where I promptly
began singing harmony on the chorus of "Texas Cookin'." I could have
deferentially stepped back down at the close of the chorus, but no-o-o-o
. . . I stayed on for Gary's guitar break, and that's when things got crazy.
I don't know what possessed me, but next thing I know, I'm pumping
Gary's volume pedal with my foot, thinking it was a wah-wah pedal. I
thought I was adding some cool, Tony Joe White funk to the proceed-
ings, when in fact I was causing Gary's guitar to turn off and on repeat-
edly. When I looked over at Guy, he was laughing. I mean, what else
could he do? Mistaking his amusement for encouragement, I stepped
up on my stomping. Gary, meanwhile, was scrambling around, checking his cord connections, trying to figure out what the hell was going
on. But not for long. He soon realized the cause of his problems. *Who
is this woman*, he thought, *and* why *is she doing this to me?*

Later, when we were introduced, Gary was his usual outgoing,
friendly self. He even suggested we get together and write a song.
Sounded good to me. Gary's song "Jukebox Argument" had recently
been recorded by Mickey Gilley. I knew the song and loved the clever

Billy Joe Shaver, Marshall, Gary Nicholson, and Leland Waddell
backstage at the Cactus Café, Austin, Texas, 1989

lyrics—about a couple having an argument while standing at a jukebox,
expressing their feelings through their song selections.

Since that night, Gary and I have written a bunch of songs together, including "The '90s Is the '60s Turned Upside Down," which
has been recorded by Dion, Wynonna, John Jorgenson, and others. After the first George Bush was elected president, we wrote a song called
"The Man Who Would Be B.B. King," which took aim at Bush's cam-
paign manager, Lee Atwater. We felt like Atwater, a fellow South Caro-
linian who played passable R&B guitar, was using his instrument as a

weapon to attract black voters to the Republican Party. We had a ball writing . . .

> *It was time to throw a party*
> *At the Inauguration Ball*
> *You never seen so many black folks*
> *In the whitest house of all*
> *Billy Preston and Bo Diddley*
> *Percy Sledge, to name a few*
> *Then the man behind it all*
> *Got up to get down with them too*
> *But does he really know the song he sings?*
> *This man who would be B.B. King*

Some of the lyrics were downright goofy:

> *Now a Republican singing blues*
> *Is as far-fetched as can be*
> *Like Einstein playing football*
> *It just don't make sense to me*
> *When he's meeting with the President*
> *And planning what to do*
> *Does he think about his brothers*
> *And what they're going through?*
> *Does he really know the song he sings?*
> *This man who would be B.B. King*

A thousand 45-rpm singles were pressed up on Bush League Records with Gary singing under the pseudonym Little Willie Horton and the Weekenders. The cover artwork—a Drew Friedman cartoon that had been published in *Spy* magazine—showed Atwater in Al Jolson black-face holding an electric guitar, surrounded by a group of guffawing fellow Republicans.

Copies of the single were mailed to members of Congress and to the press. The response was staggering. There were write-ups in every major daily in the country, including *USA Today*. There was even a front-page mention in the *International Herald-Tribune*, which caught the attention of my uncle Bob, a conservative Republican from South Carolina who once ran for the U.S. Senate, as he sat reading the newspaper in a café in Belgium, where he was playing in the King Leopold Challenge as a member of the American Seniors Golf Team. The mention inspired him to later write me a letter in which he thanked me for introducing him to B.B. King, whom he had never heard of. "To return the favor," he wrote, "I am sending you a gift subscription to *National Review*." At the time, the only magazine I subscribed to was *Mother Jones*. So when *National Review* started showing up in my mailbox, I became concerned my postman might think I was schizoid.

Letters poured in from all over, including one from Mr. Atwater himself. As fate would have it, Atwater was scheduled to make a stop in Nashville the week "The Man Who Would Be B.B. King" was released. As a result, Gary and I were besieged with calls from the local TV stations. Two sent camera crews to the Chicken Shack to film us singing the song. The Chicken Shack was an old outbuilding behind Gary's house on Cambridge Avenue that served as Gary's writing room, hangout space, and recording studio. It was called the Chicken Shack because it had, in fact, once housed chickens.

My nickname for Gary has always been "Brother G." I'm thinking I was the first to call him this. Gary says it was either me or Lee Roy Parnell. Regardless, it's a fitting moniker as Gary has always been like a brother to me. I could probably write an entire book about some of our exploits, like the time those two women followed us back to our motel in Travelers Rest, South Carolina, after a gig at Al's Pump House in Greenville. Or the night we drove around Nashville in the snow for hours after hearing the tragic news of Eddy Shaver's death. Or that night at the Gentry Center on the Tennessee State University campus when we heard Bobby Blue Bland open for Al Green on Al's fiftieth birthday. Walter "Wolfman" Washington at Antone's in Austin; backstage with the Rolling Stones in Memphis; writing "Daddy's Got a Blues Band (Now Mama's Got the Blues)," which inspired Gary's first home video; songwriter gigs at the Bottom Line and the Birchmere, and those gigs across the Carolinas; Billy Joe Shaver leading Gary to the stage the night we played the Cactus Café in Austin. (There's a snapshot of this somewhere in my house with the caption "The blind leading the blind.")

"Jukebox Argument" was Gary's first cut in the music business. Since then, he's had over four hundred of his songs recorded by everyone from the Dixie Chicks, Vince Gill, Emmylou Harris, and Willie Nelson to B.B. King, Bonnie Raitt, Fleetwood Mac, the Neville Brothers, and the Del McCoury Band, just to name a few. Since 2001, Gary has won two Grammys for co-producing albums for Delbert McClinton.

Gary's house in Nashville
September 17, 2007

So Gary, I've heard you say "Jukebox Argument" was your ticket to Nashville. You want to talk about that for a minute?
Yeah, that's how I got to Nashville, really. I was playing this club in Dallas, six nights a week, from nine 'til two in the morning. I played there for two years. It was a hardcore country gig. Western swing . . . just any kind of country music.

What was the name of the club?
The Country Club.

That spelled with a "K" or a "C"?
With a "C." *(laughs)* Anyway, it was a huge dance hall, people just in there two-stepping and everything. And I was writing songs for the gig. So I had this pile of songs. Then Jim Ed Norman called me from L.A. He was out there having success with Anne Murray and Jennifer Warnes, producing hits like "Right Time of the Night," "You Needed Me," and all that. So Jim Ed was doing that, and I would send him my songs. He had been in my band in California. We made some records . . .

So you were in L.A. before you came to Nashville?
Yeah, I lived out there for three and a half years.

What was the name of your band in California?
Uncle Jim's Music. We made two records for MCA. Don Henley was our drummer on the demos that we got our deal with, so he was our drummer. This was of course before the Eagles.

Were you writing songs for the band?
Yeah, they were all my songs, and I co-wrote some with the bass player, a guy that I'd played with since the eighth-grade talent show.

What was his name?
Wesley Pritchett. He works on Wall Street now. He's one of those guys that does what they do on Wall Street. Key Biscayne, huge house, millions of dollars, and all that. But anyway, Jim Ed was in the band. He was the piano player, I was the lead singer. We had good harmonies and everything. Our band was country rock before the Eagles really defined what Southern California country rock was all about. The Eagles really nailed it.

So you moved to Nashville from Los Angeles?
No, I went back to Texas, played gigs for a while, then moved to Nashville in 1980.

Tell me about your very first night in Nashville.
Well, I flew up with Jim Ed. He'd flown into Dallas from Los Angeles. So I met him at DFW, and we flew to Nashville from there and got a rental.

Where'd you stay?
The Spence Manor.

Anything happen?
Well, yeah, I got in a card game with Sonny Throckmorton, Bobby Bare, and Jim Ed Norman. I had twenty dollars that I had brought from playing six nights a week in a Texas honky-tonk, right? I get a sub to play that weekend, so I could come to Nashville and check it out. So I'd allowed myself to have twenty dollars to spend over the

weekend while I was here. So I sat down to play cards with those guys and after three hands, my twenty dollars was gone. So Jim Ed says, "Here're the keys to the rent car. Drive around and get acquainted with Nashville."

So I got in Jim Ed's rent car and drove up and down Music Row, then drove down to Lower Broad, parked, and walked around. I looked in Tootsie's and all that. I remember seeing a guy that I know from Dallas playing bass in this band, and I was thinking, *Wow! How did that guy get here?* I didn't even speak to him. I was just thinking how terrible the band was. Just horrible. I mean in Texas, we had *amazing* bands, playing Texas swing, Bob Wills, and all that. Anyway, so after that, I drove out Hillsboro Road to this club that was in the basement where the Bluebird is today. I can't remember the name . . .

J. Austin's?
Yeah, J. Austin's, that's it. So I walked in and there was Pebble Daniel and Marcia Routh singing with a band. So I listened to them for a set, then we got to talking. They knew Delbert. They would sing backup with him whenever he played Nashville, and I'd played with him some on the road, so we had that in common. Anyway, I wound up sitting in with them, played a shuffle, whatever.

So you were just here for the weekend with Jim Ed?
Yeah.

Then you went back . . .
Yeah, went back to Texas and got my act together.

So by then, you had decided you were going to move to Nashville for good?
Yeah. There was a big thing in the Garland paper about it. "Local Guy Makes Good" type thing. I remember the picture had me with a full head of hair and my one good Martin guitar. Anyway, at this point Mickey Gilley's recording of "Jukebox Argument" was about to be in the *Urban Cowboy* movie.

So tell me about coming back to Nashville, about moving here.

I got a U-Haul truck. We loaded everything we had in it. I drove up with my friend Roger Hooper, a high school buddy. Barbara came up later with the boys. At that time, we had Nathan, and Travis was a baby. Anyway, we pulled into Nashville. Jim Ed Norman had just bought a house on Richland Avenue, and as part of my publishing draw, I was allowed to live there with my family. We had never seen a house that was as great and grand as that house. We're moving from a cracker-box track house in Garland. Anyway, we drove straight to Jim Ed's house. Walter Campbell met us that night, and the next morning we started unloading everything. You want to hear a good story?

Yes, I do.

We needed a king-sized mattress because we had the two boys, and we were really into co-sleeping with our children. And Barbara, she was nursing the baby. So we look in the classified ads for a king-sized mattress, and I dial this number. The guy picked up the phone at the other end. And I said, "So it's seventy-five dollars, right?" About that time, Sandy Pinkard was at the house—he'd come by just to say hello—and as he strummed a chord on a guitar across the room, the guy on the other end of the phone says, "Did I hear a guitar in the background over there?" And I said, "Yeah, we're just over here fooling around." Then he said, "Well, in that case, make it sixty."

So I drove out to Hendersonville to get this king-sized mattress. And the garage door comes up, and the guy's helping me load it and put it on top of my old Volvo station wagon—it was just so totally Beverly Hillbillies. So I look down as we're tying the mattress on the top of my car, and there's a BMI Award there on the floor of his garage, an engraved plaque with dust all over it. And it says, "Don't Take It Away," which was a *huge* hit for Conway Twitty, a big jukebox hit. And below the title it says, "To Max D. Barnes in recognition, etc." and *that's* who I'm buying the mattress from!

So I say, "Are you the same Max D. Barnes . . ." you know, because I'm writing him a check. "So you wrote this song? You're Max D. Barnes? You wrote 'Don't Take It Away'?" 'Course, I'd never heard of him. He'd written it with Troy Seals. And so he says, "Yeah, I wrote that song. I need to hang that thing up in the house somewhere." You know . . . "I need to get around to puttin' that thing up some time." Then I said, "Yeah, well, I'm a songwriter, too. I just moved here. I have a song in this *Urban Cowboy* movie, and I'm writing for Jim Ed Norman's company." And so we started talking, and he says, "Well, come on in the house." So I went in the house, and in the house there's a lot more awards hanging on the walls and stuff, and I met his wife Patsy, and we talk through the afternoon.

Then the next week after that, I drove back out there and we wrote a song. And the song we wrote was a song that I had already written. It was called "I Just Came Back to Say Goodbye Again." It had been on my Uncle Jim's record, you know, before, but I kept thinking it could be better. And this song, this same song, I had such faith in the title—"I Just Came Back to Say Goodbye Again." I had played the song in Texas, opening a show for Kris [Kristofferson] and Rita [Coolidge], and after the show—we opened the show for Kris and Rita, then went back to the motel where we were staying. My band needed the money so bad that we were playing a gig in the motel lounge where we were staying. So after we opened their show, we tore our stuff down as quick as we could, then raced back over to the motel and set up. So while Kris and Rita are playing their show, we're back over at the motel, setting up in the lounge, and we're playing. So after they get off the gig, they come into this motel lounge where we're playing. And in the process of playing, we do "I Just Came Back to Say Goodbye Again." So the guy that's our manager is the promoter that's booking the Kris and Rita tour, so he introduces me to Kris, and Kris says, "You know, that song, man, that's a great song, 'I Just Came Back to Say Goodbye Again,' that's a good idea for a song. All it needs is a Merle Haggard bridge on it." So I go in this motel room with Kris Kristofferson that night, and we write a bridge for "I Just Came Back to Say Goodbye Again." This was long before I came to Nashville. But anyway, that song was never, you know, it just kind of hung around, and so Max D. and I ended up writing another version of it.

Did that version ever get cut?
The only version that was ever recorded was on the Uncle Jim's record, the very first one I ever did.

Okay. I think I've got enough here. Let me see . . . Oh, yeah.
How long have you lived in Nashville?
Twenty-seven years.

And you moved here from Garland, right?
Right. After moving from Garland to Los Angeles, then back to
Garland, I then moved to Nashville in 1980. I was thirty years old,
married, with two children.

Okay, one more: when did you first hear about Nashville?
Well, it was probably watching *The Porter Wagoner Show* on TV. That
was it.

And what made you move here?
Well, I mean, it was the chance to make a living writing songs instead
of playing honky-tonks.

Anything else you want to tell me?
Well, just before I moved up here, I ran into this guy in Garland who
said, "Man, you've really got a lot of moxie to just pick up and move
to Nashville like that." I didn't even know what "moxie" meant. I had
to look it up.

Beth Nielsen Chapman

I FIRST MET BETH NIELSEN CHAPMAN at the Ryman Auditorium in 1994, at a Shawn Colvin concert. Gary and Barbara Ann Nicholson had a couple of extra tickets. They gave one to Beth, then asked me to join them.

"You need to meet Beth," Gary said.

I had heard of Beth. Waylon Jennings was a big fan of her songwriting, and Willie Nelson had a #1 hit with her song "Nothing I Can Do About It Now," which, quite frankly, had me jealous. I'd always dreamed Willie Nelson would one day cut one of *my* songs, a dream that to this day remains unrealized. So part of me is thinking, *Who is this Beth Nielsen Chapman, and who the hell does she think she is, blowing into town with* my *last name, getting a Willie Nelson cut right off the bat, when I've been wanting him to cut one of my songs for years?! Damn!*

Normally I would have stayed home and pouted. But I'd heard Beth's husband had recently died of cancer, and that had me feeling guilty about my jealousy. I'm thinking maybe the Universe or God or whoever's in charge out there was trying to help me become a bigger person, to rise up out of my pettiness, so to speak. So I accepted Gary's invitation. Sometimes it takes a crowbar to get me out of the house. Unless it's Jerry Lee Lewis, Bobby Blue Bland, Al Green, or a good friend showcasing a new album, my tendency is to stay home. Plus, I had only vaguely heard of Shawn Colvin. I didn't really know her music. So I'm thinking, *Probably some boring folkie.*

Of course, Shawn was great, and I ended up sitting next to Beth in the balcony with Gary and Barbara Ann.

During intermission, Beth and I started talking about our mothers. I said something—I can't remember what—and Beth said, "Oh, we

Clockwise from lower left: Sam Bush, Michael Webb, Tim Krekel, Darius Rucker, Beth Nielsen Chapman, Peter Holsapple, Bill Lloyd, and Marshall at the Bluebird Café, Feb. 1, 2008

should write that!" So a week or so later, we got together for a writing session at her house. At first we worked on the mother idea, but then, as often happens in writing, we went off in a totally different direction.

Mind you, Beth was still grieving her husband's death, whereas I was in the early stages of a relationship with a man I would later marry—a man I am still married to, as of this writing. So perhaps to cheer her up, I started telling Beth stories about this man who seemed totally oblivious to me as far as initiating any sex.

"I know he likes me," I said. "But he just doesn't come on to me like all the other guys I've known. And it's driving me crazy! But, you know, it's also . . . well, kind of a turn-on, actually."

So we started writing "Don't Mind Me," a song that ended up on my *Love Slave* CD, about a woman trying to get her man's attention while he's laid up in bed reading a computer magazine:

Ooh . . . I am so in the mood, babe
I don't mean to be rude, babe
I just thought you should know

I'm . . . gonna try to be smooth, babe
So when I make my move, babe
Even you may not know

So you just keep on reading your magazine
Don't mind me
And while you're lost in cyberspace
I will cast my spell upon you

You . . . often try to ignore me
But I know you adore me
I don't have to behave

I've got the right to want you
Even when you
Don't want me
I've got the right to make
A fool of myself
There's nothing you can do to stop me

We were having a great time. At one point, Beth said, "You know, I've been writing all these sad songs. It's great to get away from all that. This is like being on vacation." So we finished the first verse, the words were flowing, and we were feeling really good about everything, when suddenly, out of nowhere, Beth started weeping.

"I'm so sorry," she said. "I just have to cry. I hope this isn't bothering you."

"Oh, no . . . not at all," I replied. "Go ahead and cry all you want. But if you don't mind, I'll just keep working on the second verse."

I don't know what I was thinking. When you're writing a song, you're often *not* thinking. It's been my experience that things flow better when the brain is out of the way. Anyway, we managed to finish the song, which I credit, in part, to my years in therapy. Otherwise, after the first verse, I might have taken off for Walgreens to buy Beth some Kleenex!

Our paths have crossed a lot since then. Whether it's playing in the round at the Bluebird, doing a benefit, working in the studio, writing songs, or going to parties at Beth's house (Beth throws great parties), being around Beth is always an enlightening experience.

I remember one time spilling out of a Chinese restaurant with Beth and her parents, who were in town for a visit. I stood by in amazement as the three of them proceeded to sing show tunes—complete with choreography—in the parking lot.

Another time, I took Beth to a Vanderbilt women's basketball game. After we settled into our seats, she mentioned it was her first time ever to see a basketball game.

"You never saw a game in junior high or high school?" I asked.

"No," she said.

"Not even on TV?"

"Not even on TV."

I found this hard to believe. How anybody in America could make it to their mid- to late thirties without seeing a basketball game was beyond me. So we're watching the game, and Beth seemed to be enjoying herself. Then a player got fouled and went to the line to shoot a couple of free throws. As the other players lined up and the fouled player prepared to shoot, the gym suddenly got quiet. And at that precise moment when you could've heard a pin drop, Beth leaned over and said, "I don't know what this part is, but it makes me kind of nervous."

I once rode in a van to Memphis with Beth, her son Ernest (who brought along his skateboard), and four or five women songwriter friends to hear Elton John at the Pyramid. We were all sitting with Beth in the audience when Elton John acknowledged her from the stage before singing her song "Sand and Water." This was two months after the death of Princess Diana. Elton had sung a personalized version of "Candle in the Wind" at her funeral, so there was much fan speculation as to which version he would sing for the tour. He finally decided he wouldn't do either version. About that time, someone had given him a copy of Beth's *Sand and Water* CD. When he heard the title song, he knew he had found the perfect song to commemorate not only Diana but his friends who had recently died of AIDS.

Of course, Beth had never met Elton John and had no idea he knew her or her music. So one day, she's at home minding her own business, when the phone rings. "Hello, Beth? It's Elton," said the voice on the other end. As Beth stood there trying to figure out which one of her friends was playing a trick, the voice with the English accent continued. "Listen, I really love your song 'Sand and Water' and would like to include it in my show. And oh, by the way, would you mind coming down to Atlanta while we're rehearsing?"

Then Beth realized, *Oh my God, it's really Elton John!*

BETH HAS BEEN THROUGH MORE than most. Not long after her husband died of cancer, she was diagnosed with breast cancer. After the surgery, Chris and I were in her hospital room, along with Annie Roboff, Kimmie Rhodes, Gary and Barbara Ann Nicholson, and four or five others. None of us could say a word—not that we would have known what to say—because Beth, still under the influence of the anesthesia and probably giddy that she'd survived the procedure, well, she just could not stop talking!

Beth is more than a survivor. Today, she is one of the most vibrantly productive people I know. Her latest CD, *Prism: The Human Family Songbook*, is a double-disc set that features chants and songs of devotion from different cultures. As a songwriter, her best-known hit is probably "This Kiss" (co-written with Annie Roboff and Robin Lerner), which was a monster hit for Faith Hill.

I was playing the Bluebird recently with Bill Lloyd, Tim Krekel, Darius Rucker, and Peter Holsapple, when Beth breezed in with a film crew from the Al Jazeera news network.

To say the girl gets around would be an understatement.

My house in Nashville
February 7, 2008

So Beth, let's talk about Nashville a minute. You moved here when?
1985.

You remember the date?
Hmm . . . whatever day was the biggest snowstorm in years.
You remember?

I can remember trying to get out of town during a big snowstorm in mid-January of '85.
Yeah, that sounds right. Anyway, so we drive up. We were living in Mobile, so it was about eight hours from Mobile. My parents—my family—lived in Montgomery, so we'd stopped there to spend the night. It was me, my husband Ernest, and our young son "Ernesto," who was five. My husband had been trying to get me to move to Nashville for a couple of years.

Were you and Ernest working together in music?
No, he was the director of a treatment facility for adolescents. He had a private practice as a counselor, and I had stopped writing about this time. My first record came out in 1980. Barry Beckett produced it. It was recorded at Muscle Shoals Sound. I was living in Mobile at the time and had no idea, you know, I didn't know you had to have a manager and all sorts of other things. So it came out and then disco hit right about the same time—the same week, actually. "Disco Duck" and my record came out the same week. *(laughs)* And so, you know, I had great reviews. Things like, "Wow, what a beautiful record. Too bad she didn't do it ten years ago." *(laughs)* "Kind of like Carole King." You know. But now Donna Summer was going, *(sings)* "Love to love ya, bay-bee!"

"Beep-beep, toot-toot, hey-hey . . ."
Exactly. So anyway, I felt this *huge* door slamming. At that time, I was signed to Screen Gems as a songwriter.

In Nashville?
Yeah. But then as soon as my record didn't do anything, they dropped me. So I got dropped from the label, dropped from my publishing deal . . . so that was 1980.

So, before you ever came to Nashville, you had already been dropped by a record label? What label?
Capitol.

That's major.
I mean, my experience was, I assumed it was all going to be just fine, because everything up until that point had come to me so easily. Major publishing deal, major label, and all that. So I'm thinking, Okay, the record will come out, I'll have a big hit off it, then I'll be touring, and everything's going to be perfect. So, for the first time in my life since I was eleven, when I decided I was going to be a famous singer-songwriter and then everything would unfold perfectly, I realized that I had made a mistake, that I must not be very good, because they hate me, nobody cares. You know, if I had been on some little tiny label, just eking my way along, and didn't have any success, I could've said, "Well, it's because I'm not on a major label." But in my mind I had everything, I had a label, I had gone to L.A. to do the strings, I had met all these famous people, and everybody was waiting for my big thing to happen. And then when it came out and didn't stick to the wall, Capitol was like . . .

Next!
Yeah . . . we'll just go roll the dice with somebody else. But *my* perception was that it was all because I was not good enough. That was what I believed. I was like a little kid that walks in and suddenly realizes that her shoes suck compared to everybody else's shoes, that she really should be ashamed for thinking that they were good enough. So I went into this huge crisis of confidence. For the first time, really. And I went, "Well, screw that, I'm just going to start my family, and I'm not going to write songs. I obviously made a mistake and need to find out what I'm really supposed to be doing." So I denied the songwriter in me any access to the light of day for about three years.

So that record came out . . . when?

That record came out in 1980. Then in 1981, I had a son. And all my creative energy went into Play-Doh, and making mobiles for his crib, and learning to bake homemade teething biscuits. And all my friendships changed 'cause I was no longer going to be a successful person in the music business. So the people I had started to get to know in the music business—that was too painful for me. I was more interested in learning what Lavinia down the street—who had a child my child's age—what she thought was the best way to make pie. So I started to try and find my way in the community of young mothers. And I discovered that, not only were they not impressed that I was a singer-songwriter, but they were kind of like, That's weird! So I retreated even more.

Then about three years into that, I had been working on a series of Play-Doh heads, like, I was sculpting these heads. And I'm sitting there at three in the morning, which is the only time I had to sculpt my Play-Doh heads. It had become this addiction. I mean, I was doing artistic things all day long, 'cause I wasn't writing, you know? Creative energy has to go somewhere.

Exactly.

That is, if you don't drink yourself under the table or something, you've got to . . .

Oh, yeah, when I'm not writing, I compulsively garden.

Right! So anyway, it's three in the morning, and my husband comes up and puts his hands on my shoulders—I was trying to get this nose just right on this Play-Doh head—and he says, "Honey, I think it's time for you to start writing songs." And this cry came out of me, like I had not cried in years. And I put my head down and just started sobbing . . . just sobbing and sobbing. And it was the songwriter in me going, "Thank God, somebody's getting me out of prison!"

Not long after that, I started writing songs again. The first several I wrote were so bad, they were like me trying—and at that time, Emmylou Harris was just popping onto pop radio. *(sings)* "If I could only win your love . . ." Then, like, in '83, somewhere around there, Rosanne [Cash] and Rodney [Crowell] were making those great records, and I was starting to listen to country radio a lot. And I was, of course, a huge Willie fan. I had all his records. I still loved to listen to music, but as I started to re-emerge as a songwriter, I'm thinking, "I want to write *those* kinds of songs—the kind *other* artists will record, because obviously, I suck as a recording artist, nobody will ever want me again, so I'd better start thinking about what makes a song flexible enough to go into different people's vocal cords and work." So I started studying. And I was playing in little bars, you know, all those bars in Mobile and Montgomery. And I learned all these songs from the '20s, '30s, '40s, '50s, all the way through the '80s. You know, like I learned the greatest songs of each era, which was the best songwriting college I could have ever gone to. And then I started writing these really, really, *really* bad country try-to, want-to-be songs, where I was writing from a character's point of view.

At this point, were you thinking you would be going to Nashville?
Well, my husband said, "You need to . . . we need to move to Nashville or get you out of Mobile. Nothing's going to happen here." And I was like, "Just let me see if I can ever even remember how to write. And then we'll see." I was very hesitant.

So between him saying, "We need to move to Nashville," and you actually moving, how much time elapsed?
Well, I didn't really get serious about moving to Nashville until after a couple of years of him pestering me. But he was helping me, he was mentoring me through the process. Ernest was a very good writer. He didn't write songs, but he wrote poetry and prose. He was very astute. He would say, "Your melodies are really good, but your writing . . . I'm not connecting with this writing. You need to write something that you feel—not something you think. And not clever." And I was like, "I DON'T KNOW . . . I DON'T KNOW HOW TO DO THAT!" And we had this huge fight and stuff. *(laughs)*

In the TV movie of my life, the scene with the Play-Doh will be in there, and the scene where he's screaming at me, trying to get me confident again. But the truth is, he wasn't an authority to me, because he wasn't in the music business.

What did he know?

(laughs) He didn't know shit. But then one night, the Beach Boys came to Mobile. And they stayed in the Riverview Plaza Hotel, where I had been singing solo for two years, six nights a week. So the Beach Boys were staying in the hotel, and I could see them in those big glass elevators. And I kept watching them, thinking, "Maybe one of the Beach Boys will come over here." I had written this new song called "Five Minutes" and a couple of other songs. I was starting to get good at the country songs. I had seen *Coal Miner's Daughter*. Seeing that movie was like, Oh, I get it! You mean I can exist in a country song? Okay. So now all I have to learn is how to get *me* in a country song, instead of writing how *they* would sing it. So "Five Minutes" was a breakthrough song in that respect.

So that night, there's this guy sitting there in front of me listening, and he's going, "Play another song you wrote . . . play another song you wrote." Finally at the end of my set, I'm packing up and he comes over and goes, "Well, first of all . . . let me tell you a couple of things: first of all, your speakers are out of phase." And I'm like, "And *who* are you?" And he goes, "I'm actually one of the Beach Boys." And it was Bruce Johnston, the guy that plays keyboards. And he says, "Okay, you played four original songs. Two of them sound like #1 hit songs. I know, because I wrote 'I Write the Songs.'" And I'm like, "Okay." And I'm thinking, "Is this really that guy?" 'Cause I really couldn't tell.

Which one of my friends is playing a trick on me now?

Right! *(laughs)* So I went home and woke Ernest up and jumped on the bed and threw all my tip money on his face and said, "We're moving to Nashville." Because finally a person with authority had said it was okay. So then Ernest sat up in bed and said, "Well, that's just real fine. Finally somebody that knows something agrees with me. Now maybe you can see what I was trying to say."

So anyway, long story short: we end up moving to Nashville on the day of the worst winter storm ever. And we're eking along on ice-patched I-65 north toward Birmingham, and it was getting to be about four-thirty, five o'clock in the afternoon. It was getting dark, and those poor suckers on the other side of the interstate—for ten miles it was a parking lot. People were getting out of their cars. Then all of a sudden, our lane stopped, and we sat there for like an hour. And I remember Ernest saying, "You know, when you make it really big in Nashville, I want us to always remember this day." We had this little five-year-old kid in the car; it was really very unnerving. We finally got into town, and Mac McAnally was a great help to me. He walked me around.

You knew Mac from Alabama?

I knew him because he had played guitar on my record. Barry Beckett was also really helpful. He let Jim Ed Norman [head of Warner Bros. Nashville] and some other people know, "Hey, there's this artist-songwriter, she's coming, she's moving to town."

So you didn't just show up cold. I mean, other than the snow. You had connections because of your record.

Right. All those things I thought meant nothing turned out to be very important to me.

So that record was your calling card.

Yeah. Then I started meeting people that actually *knew* my record, that had actually bought it. I had been so divorced from that record. All I knew is that Capitol didn't sell enough for me to count, so they dropped me. So as far as I was concerned, nobody even knew it existed.

Is that record available now?

No. You can't get it. In fact, the masters were drowned in a flood in the basement of Muscle Shoals Sound. And they were returned to me, but they are these buckled-up 24-track tapes that I guess you can bake or something. But they're pretty much destroyed. And even if they weren't destroyed, they don't belong to me. Capitol owns them.

Anyway, that record opened some doors, but it still took me five years to get anything going. The song "Five Minutes"—I had three publishers fighting over that song. I was tempted. One guy wanted to give me five thousand dollars for that one song.

And I'm saying, "Man, we could really use that money." But Ernest said, "No. We need a publishing deal. You need a family. You need a business." So we held out. And so we ended up signing with MTM. They'd just signed Bill Lloyd, Radney Foster . . . there was this little pack of kids. Trisha Yearwood was the receptionist. Alan . . . oh, you know . . . Alan . . .

Reynolds?
No . . . Alan . . . the songwriter . . .

Shamblin?
No. The tall one . . . big artist . . . Alan . . .

Jackson?
Jackson, yes, thank you! [Undergoing] chemo just blew out the name department in my brain.

They say after fifty, proper nouns are the first to go.
Oh, *(laughs)* I hadn't heard that one. Anyway, Alan Jackson was working in the mailroom at TNN [The Nashville Network]. It was just this whole . . . you had no idea these people were going to end up being who they are. Whenever I teach now, when I do songwriting classes and stuff, I always hear people say, "How do I get to meet this or that producer?" And I say, "Well, you just look to your left and to your right, because the people you fell off the turnip truck with are going to be all the people that you're going to need. It's okay to have a few mentors, but basically your camp is already established."

And it was amazing, because I went with MTM, in part, because Meredith Stewart was heading up their publishing department. As it turned out, her mother's best friend was Loretta Lynn! I can remember unpacking boxes, waiting for the phone to ring—again, absolutely convinced that as soon as Loretta Lynn heard "Five Minutes," she would cut it. Because it was written for her. It's about a woman who's leaving at the very moment her husband's coming home. He's walking in the door while she's walking out. And she's saying, "You look like you can't believe I'm leaving. And you've had all this time to learn how to love me. Now my cab is on the way. So you've got five minutes to figure out how to get me to stay." And that's the song. And I just *knew* Loretta Lynn would cut it. There was no question in my mind. I was already figuring out how I was going to celebrate. Then the phone rings, and it's Meredith calling me from back at the office, and she says, "Well, I called Loretta. You know, I played her the song . . ."

And I went, "Okay, *great* . . . so . . ."

Then Meredith says, "Well, she passed."

I couldn't believe my ears! I just couldn't believe it. It was like a bad flashback to when they dropped me from my label. I was like, "Well, I guess I'm not supposed to be doing this." And I had a *big* tumbling back . . . like, "Oh, I never should have moved here! Oh, my God! That was my big song!" It was like *Cut!* I went into this whole panic. And my husband was like, "Puh-*leeze*." And I was like, "No, you don't understand! This is it!" I mean it was like, "If Loretta Lynn won't cut 'Five Minutes,' I don't have any business here!"

So did anybody ever cut it?
Yes. Pam Tillis cut it. Barry Beckett was producing a record on Pam. But then it didn't end up on her record.

I hate when that happens.
But then five years later, Lorrie Morgan cut it and it went to #1.

Well, there you go.
In the meantime, I ended up working . . . worming my way into the Bluebird scene. One night Don Schlitz ["The Gambler"] asked me to get up and sit in at an in-the-round, the Golden Round, *(laughs)* and I sang a couple of songs that I wrote. Then he asked me to write with him. That was a great breakthrough, because we wrote "Strong Enough to Bend" in, like, twenty minutes.

Tanya [Tucker] recorded that.
It still took two years, though, from when we wrote it. But nobody tells you that. Nobody tells you these things take time. You know? So when I teach songwriting, I tell every single person . . . I go through all my hit songs. They think that you walk out of the writing room with "This Kiss," and everybody goes, "Oh my God, that's a smash. Let's do it now!" And what happens is, it takes two years.

Yeah, I remember you guys kept re-cutting that song, using different singers.
Yeah. There's just so much . . . waiting. Every song I've ever had any success with has sat around for at least a year, if not two or more. Where you send it to all the obvious people and they pass. And then you go, "Wha . . . ?

Now, Beth. I've got some questions here.
Okay.

I'm going down my little list here. So you moved to Nashville in 1985. So that means you have lived here for twenty-three years. *(whispers)* That's amazing.

It *is* amazing. Sometimes life goes by so fast I get windburns. *(laughs)* Okay. **And so you moved here from Mobile. Can you remember the first time you heard the word "Nashville"? Or when you first became aware of Nashville?**
Well, my impressions of Nashville—if I go back into my foggy memory—were mostly Grand Ole Opry, like Patsy Cline. I'd read some biographies about Willie, and that gave me a little more of a fleshed-out picture of at least what it was like in the early days, you know, with Kris Kristofferson, Willie, and all those guys hanging out. And I was a little intimidated by the idea of people assuming that I was now going to be "country" if I came to Nashville.

But do you remember hearing about Nashville, like on a TV show . . . somebody saying the word "Nashville," or just . . .
Well, I think I attributed a bit of the *Hee Haw* culture . . . you know, like, if you'd have asked me . . . I don't remember a particular moment where I heard "Nashville" and I had some kind of a . . . it was sort of an accumulated sensibility about it.

An accumulative awareness.
(laughs) Accumulated . . . like little pieces of hay that start to accumulate into a hay *(pauses)* . . .

... bale? *(more laughter)*

Anyway, as I've moved here and watched it grow and seen all the parameters that it has, I'm put off by people's interpretation of Nashville. In fact, when I was interviewed at length by Al Jazeera last week, they wanted to go to the Grand Ole Opry, they wanted to go . . . I said, "Great. You should go to the Grand Ole Opry, and you should go to the Bible center where they make millions of Bibles. But you should also go to the Hindu temple, because there's a humongous Hindu temple here. And there's also a very large Indian community," and so on. Then there's the music business, which has also splintered off in all these directions. And now everybody's definition for everything has changed. But Nashville to me has always been, at its core . . . Mayberry. I had a feeling it was my Mayberry.

I remember the first time we came up here. It was me, my husband, and our bonking-around-in-the-hotel-room, bouncing-off-the-walls five-year-old child. We stayed at the Vanderbilt Holiday Inn right across from the Parthenon, where my son would run and play. He called it "the Squirrel Park." Near where my husband had gone to Vanderbilt Law School years and years and years before.

So he knew Nashville.
He knew Nashville. He had a scholarship for a couple of years. And when his father died, he went back home and he never finished law school.

So Beth, let me ask you another question. Before you guys drove up in the snowstorm in 1985, had you ever been to Nashville before?
I had been to Nashville, because I got signed to Screen Gems. And they flew me up a couple of times.

When was that?
That would have been . . . 1980? '79 maybe?

So that was your very first time to come to Nashville?
'79, '80 . . . like those two years when I was making my record. The first time I came to Nashville, Gail Davies was just getting signed and

a lot of attention. I remember I went to dinner with Gail Davies and the guys from Screen Gems, Charlie Feldman . . . Screen Gems had bought out this really bad contract that I signed when I was eighteen. My dad had co-signed it. This guy in Birmingham had a studio, and basically I would drive up to Birmingham all through when I was seventeen, eighteen, nineteen years old, and I would just play all my songs into his microphone, and he would hit "play/record" and then "stop," and he accumulated about fifty songs. And so Screen Gems ended up buying those fifty songs from him for twelve thousand dollars. And to me, that was like a fortune. And I was trying to get out of this contract so I could do the record with Barry [Beckett], but I couldn't. The guy in Birmingham wouldn't let me go, and he had done nothing. I'd signed this five-year slave contract.

How did this guy know about you?
Well, I was in this band that was the most popular band in Montgomery, Alabama—this was before I moved to Mobile. We got signed by Terry Woodford in Muscle Shoals. So we were getting ready to cut a record, and half the songs were mine. I was talking to the producer one day in the studio, with Mac McAnally and Clayton Ivey doing overdubs, and I dropped this piece of information. I had totally forgot I had signed this contract with the guy in Birmingham, because I hadn't been in touch with him in over two years because he never did anything. So I said, "You know, I signed this contract with this guy . . ." And he goes, "Contract?" So I showed him the contract, and I remember he put his head down on the board, and he said, "We can't do any of your songs. You can't even be on this record. You've got to get out of this contract."

Did you get out of it?
Well, I threatened to sue. And then he got scared because it was such a bad contract that if I had gotten a lawyer and spent the money, I could have gotten my songs back. But it would have cost me a lot of money, and I wasn't in a position to do that. But I didn't let *him* know that. I just called him up and said, "I want out." And he said, "Well, you know, I've invested a lot." And I said, "You've invested nothing but

tape. I'll buy the tapes from you." And he said, "No, I've invested in helping you create your songwriting career, blah, blah, blah."

So anyway, he contacted Screen Gems and said, "I want to sell this catalog I own." And they bought the catalog under the condition that I would consider coming to sign with them. 'Course, I was so thrilled to meet somebody real, you know, that was a real, legitimate company. They signed me right away. And he let me go. I later found out that they had given him a buyout of twelve thousand dollars. So that was my first wake-up call as a writer. Where I actually got a punch in the stomach about, This shit's actually valuable! You know? I'd never even had a hit. As for my Screen Gems catalog, you can just hear somebody trying to learn how to write songs. There's a lot of little moments here and there. There's one really good song that was cut years later by Crystal Gayle called "When Love Is New," that I wrote when I was, like, seventeen.

So the first night you spent in Nashville was to come up about the Screen Gems deal. How old were you then?
I was, ah, let's see . . . it was '79?

Were you with Ernest?
Yeah. I had just met Ernest.

Were you married?
No. I got married in '79. So Screen Gems kind of came around '78. And around the time I met Ernest, I was put in touch with Screen Gems. 'Cause I got kicked out of the band.

So you're kicked out of your band, 'cause you were under contract to this guy, and then he sells it to Screen Gems, so that's really how you end up in Nashville?
Yeah. And Charlie Feldman said, "Hey, we love your writing! And we want you in our family!" And all they had to tell me was they published Carole King, and it was like, "I'm in!" Then they told me they were going to pay me a . . .

So Screen Gems had Carole King.
Yeah. I think they did her early catalog.

They have the songs on *Tapestry*?
Goffin and King . . . yeah, they did all that early stuff. And you know, they were very respected and knew how to deal with writers, and I just was so thrilled. And then I met this fabulous guy and I was getting married. And all this stuff was happening at the same time. So I was making trips up to Nashville. I probably went up there two or three times in '78 and then, you know, in '79, I went up there a couple of times. And they were harvesting through my songs, and all the while, I was writing.

Where'd you stay when you came up then? Do you remember?
They put me in some hotel. I didn't stay with people, 'cause I didn't really know anybody. You know, I'd just stay like at the . . .

Spence Manor? Across from BMI?
I stayed there one time. Yeah. 'Cause I didn't have a car either. I just walked everywhere. And it was like Mayberry. And then when they dropped me . . . the minute my record didn't do well, they decided not to pick up my option. Then I got pregnant right around the time my record didn't do well. I was like, "Let's just start a family." I got pregnant right away. And I was so excited. I called Screen Gems and said, "Hey, I'm going to have a baby!" My option was up, and they were like, "She's going to have a baby, she just got dropped by her label, and she doesn't live here." So they let me go. That was toward the end of 1980. The record came out, flopped, I got pregnant, and Screen Gems dropped me—all in 1980.

So you spend the next five years going through your Play-Doh period.
Yes. My creative-frustration period.

So when you first came to Nashville, Screen Gems flew you up? They paid your airfare?
Yes, but first they flew to Mobile and came to this little club I was singing in.

Oh, so Nashville came to you, before you came to Nashville. *(laughs)*
Yeah, Charlie Feldman and the other guy that ran the L.A. office or the New York office . . . Paul Tannen. They flew into Mobile to hear me.

So the first time Screen Gems flew you to Nashville, did somebody pick you up at the airport?
Yeah, they picked me up at the airport. I just felt like . . . you know . . . I had this odd sense of entitlement. It was weird. When I found out that they paid that guy twelve thousand dollars for my catalog, I suddenly felt like I was somebody. I must be good. And this was before I found out I wasn't good. This was before I had no reason to believe I wasn't fabulous. Oh, the guy in Birmingham. Of course he wants me. Yes, I'll sign that. Where do I sign? Muscle Shoals? Of course they want me, but they can't have me because I'm stuck with this guy. Then here come these other people. Of course they want me. And then they fly me up . . . you know? And then I'm . . . you know . . . but I wasn't grandiose. But then again, I *was* kind of grandiose about it. I had no idea how unusual and how lucky and . . . I also didn't really know my own strength as a talented person. I was still in and out. But that gave me great support. So I'd go up there and just write, you know, and I wasn't really co-writing with anyone yet, but I was inspired. I was writing a lot, and I was in love, and I was getting married, and it was all great. When I called and told them I was pregnant, I thought they were going to be happy for me, you know?

That's like telling a publisher you're in a band. They're like, "We don't want her rehearsing with a band when she could be writing songs!"
Exactly.

Okay, so I think I've got what made you move here—your husband!
Well, my husband threatened to start smoking again.

***(laughs)* See, that's the kind of thing I want.**
But I've got to back up. Before the Beach Boys, there was this whole year where he would get mad at me every time we would talk about songwriting. Finally we broke through the anger thing. But I would keep bringing him songs I was writing, and they were bad, they were really uninteresting. I mean, they just missed the mark. And he knew what a good writer I was. He really believed in me, way before I did. But he didn't have good bedside manner. He'd just get frustrated, and he'd go, "Just fucking write! Just do it! You can do it!" And I'm like, "LEAVE ME ALONE! I DON'T WANT TO WRITE!" And round and round we'd go. Finally he said, "Just write something you know."

One time we had this big fight. I was nursing my son and I was sobbing. And I'm like, "I'M NOT WRITING ANY MORE! IT'S TOO PAINFUL!" And the milk is going . . . and my kid is like *kuwhaah!* 'Cause when you cry and you're nursing at the same time, the milk . . .

It doesn't work.
The milk was just running down on his chin. And Ernest said, "Write what you know." And I said, "*This* is what I know! How 'bout a song about *breast-feeding*?!" He went, "Great! Write a song about breast-feeding." And I went, "Okay! I'll show you. I'll write a song about breast-feeding." So that's what I did. About a week later, I played him this song about what it felt like to breast-feed.

What was it called?
I could just imagine how good this was going to sound on country radio.

Hey, they played "The Pill." So what was it called?
I can't remember. I think it was called "My Heart" or something. It was just this whole beautiful, intimate thing. The La Leche League would have loved it for their theme song. So Ernest listened to this song, and he said, "Okay. This song is extremely well written. I totally

hear your voice as a writer. You're right, it's not useful outside of a certain kind of niche marketing, but this is what I'm talking about." And that got me a little thread that I could follow. It was just a little thread. So then in six months, I started writing without us screaming back and forth. We were kind of vulnerable with each other, so we had all these rules. I had written out RULES FOR LISTENING TO MY SONGS: (1) You cannot yell. (2) You must listen to the whole song before you start commenting—because Ernest was a critic. He was like . . . *(makes ripping noise)*. And (3) you have to start with the things that are *good* about it.

Anyway, he was really good. Then for about six months we worked really well together, and I kept bringing him new songs, and they were getting there. I started writing about falling in love with him, and started writing about things in my childhood, and I started working on a song called "Child Again," which was really an important song for me. Because it was the first really grown-up song I wrote for me as an artist.

It's a song about my grandmother when I was in high school. But I didn't know that's what it was about. I started it in 1981 and finished it in 1987. So I was working on this song. It was this thing I kept following . . . this sort of misty . . . like I had a verse, and I had a chorus, and I just loved it, but I didn't know what happened in the second verse for two more years. You know . . . *that* sort of thing. And I remember sitting in an oyster bar in Mobile, and finally writing the last piece of it. They had an old player piano, and I got up from my oysters and went over there, and I figured out a way to overlay these two nursery rhymes and change key. And I was so excited that I had finally finished the song!

Actually, that was after I had moved to Nashville. We had come back down and were having dinner with Ernest's family in Mobile. So I started it in Mobile and finished it in Mobile. But anyway, that song started right in that six-month period of vulnerability of trusting that I could do this again. And then that's when I started writing songs like "Five Minutes." And then I had about four or five songs that he thought were fucking great. Then he started getting his other hat on like, "Beth, you need to get these to Nashville." It was like a monster starting to appear, that was putting pressure on me to take my babies outside the house, which was a huge mistake on his part, because I was just starting to like writing again. The last thing I needed was some jerk with a size-twelve shoe to go, *(stomps floor)* "SUCKS!"

So you weren't ready.
"I don't even need to ever take them out of the house. I need to write. You're right. I need to write. Because otherwise I'll just be sculpting Play-Doh. But I don't need . . . I don't need the accolades, I don't need the headaches, I don't need the money, I'll do something else. I don't want to do it!" And he's like, "You're absolutely wrong. You're being obstinate . . . blah, blah, blah." So that became our new thing to argue about. We didn't argue about whether I was confident in my writing.

You'd reached a new level of arguing.
We went to a whole other argument, which was, When are you going to send a tape to Nashville?

Now, Beth. I've got one more question, then we're done.
Are you kidding?

No. I've got enough, really.
Well, I've got to tell you this one thing. He threatened to start smoking again if I didn't send tapes of my songs to Nashville. I had a deadline and everything. It was that Friday. I had to have all the tapes in. I had to send the tapes with letters to Roger Sovine, and then Mac McAnally. Anyway, so . . .

Okay. Now, Beth! Tell me one thing that's happened since you've lived in Nashville that only could have happened in Nashville.
Okay. *(pause)* There was this French photographer named Michel Arnaud—a friend of Robert Hicks—that came to town several years ago. He was doing a book on Nashville. So Michel and I end up going to the Cracker Barrel—the one out on Charlotte Pike. He had photographed me and had photographed my son, Ernest. He was getting photographs of all these quirky people in Nashville for this

really cool book. One of the people he really wanted to photograph was Chet Atkins. So I called David Conrad and said, "I've got to find Chet, because there's this really fantastic photographer who wants to photograph him." And David says, "Well, I'm meeting Chet for breakfast. We meet every Saturday morning down here at the Cracker Barrel. I'll tell him that you're going to bring a photographer, and if it's all right with him . . . ," you know. And so he called me back and said, "Yeah, it's all right. Chet said, 'Bring it on.'"

So I walk into the Cracker Barrel with the French photographer, who was so delighted to meet Chet. But before that, as we're pulling up to the Cracker Barrel, who should walk out the door, but Donna Summer! So I say, "Oh, look! There's Donna Summer!" And he goes, *(French accent)* "Donna Summer? Donna Summer . . . *Donna Summer?*"

So the French photographer can't believe Donna Summer is in the same restaurant with Chet Atkins. And I say, "Well, you just never know what's gonna happen." So we walk in, and Chet—there's this little flurry of activity. He takes us out on the porch. They get a guitar. Michel takes some pictures. Then, as Chet and David Conrad go back in to finish their breakfast, they invite us to join them. So while we're eating breakfast with Chet, I happen to look across the restaurant, and there's Leon Russell. So by this time, Michel is . . .

He's on overload.
He's going, *(French accent)* "I can't believe this. I can't believe it!" Now I don't really know Leon, but I walk over and say, "Leon, I'm here with this French photographer. We came here to photograph Chet Atkins. He's really great. He's doing this book. And by the way, I'm a huge fan," you know. And Leon says, "Sure, you can take some pictures, but I'd rather do it over at my house." So we get in a caravan. It was me, the photographer, and Leon. Chet stayed at the Cracker Barrel. So we caravanned over to Leon's, which wasn't too far away. Meanwhile, Michel is just shaking his head. He can't believe it. So we get to Leon's house. He brings us down into his basement. Have you been to Leon's?

I have not.

Well, his studio has pink and white shag carpeting all up the walls. Albert Lee's guitar is mounted on a mannequin. It's just goose pimples for somebody like this photographer. So Michel takes a bunch of pictures. And I end up staying for another couple of hours, hanging out with Leon. And we start writing a couple of songs. I still have the work tape. For years, I've thought about tracking him down to finish those songs.

Marshall and Willie Nelson in Nashville, ca. 1984

$\mathcal{W}$illie $\mathcal{N}$elson

I FIRST MET WILLIE NELSON in Nashville in the fall of 1973. I'd gone to a party at Rick Sanjek's house up on Overlook Drive, a few blocks south of the Vanderbilt campus. Rick was general manager of Atlantic Records' Nashville office, which had been open for about a year. Willie was the first artist signed to the label.

Rick's house was a brick-and-stone Tudor revival that he and his buddies had named Snake Haven Manor, after a neighbor had complained about the overgrown conditions in his yard. My date for the party was an aspiring photographer-writer named James Carson. I use the term "date" loosely here, only because James had picked me up in his velvet blue 1972 Audi 100. I remember the car because it was my first time to ride in an Audi.

James and I were friends, running in a crowd that included artist Paul Harmon, filmmaker Coke Sams, and writer Joy Wahl (who later became my manager). So it wasn't like I had the hots for James or vice versa. In fact, James had the hots for Rick's secretary, Pam. But then Pam had the hots for Paul, who had the hots for Joy and Pam and every other beautiful woman he came into contact with. I mean, these were freewheeling times.

So James was my date. But by the end of the evening, "chauffeur" might have been a more accurate description. Because when it came time to leave, there was another passenger in the car.

WHEN WE ARRIVED AT THE PARTY, Snake Haven Manor was packed with people milling around, drinking beer and shooting pool. We hadn't been there long when I spied a man with shoulder-length red hair sitting in a chair off to the left. He was playing a beat-up guitar and singing songs he had written. Not everyone was listening, but I was intrigued, so I ambled over and sat down at his feet. He acknowledged my presence with a smile as he continued to sing. The lyrics of his songs, and just his whole persona, got my attention right away. "Shotgun Willie sits around in his underwear / Biting on a bullet and pulling out all of his hair." *Whoa! Wait a minute. Where is* this *shit coming from?* To say I was completely blown away would be an understatement.

I hadn't been that affected by a performer since seeing Elvis from the colored balcony back in Spartanburg when I was seven years old. I was twenty-four now, but I might as well have been that seven-year-old back in Spartanburg. Nothing I'd experienced could have prepared me for this Willie Nelson. These songs were *real,* by God. And this man had obviously lived them. "Bloody Mary Morning," "Sister's Coming Home," "Pick Up the Tempo," "Shotgun Willie," "It's Not Supposed to Be That Way" . . . the songs just kept on coming. I was smitten.

When James drove me home later that night, I was no longer riding shotgun in the front seat; I was riding with Shotgun Willie in the back. To this day, I can still see James smiling at us from his rearview mirror, his face aglow in the dashboard lights.

WHEN I THINK BACK ON THOSE TIMES, much is a blur. But there are moments of total clarity. Here are some things I remember:

Mario's Restaurant
October 1973

IT WAS DURING THE ANNUAL disc jockey convention in Nashville, otherwise known as DJ Week. I was having dinner at Mario's with my good friends Betty and Bobby Herbert and Jane and Vereen Bell. We were getting primed for a concert later that evening at the old Sheraton Hotel ballroom (across from Union Station). Willie Nelson was scheduled to perform, along with Troy Seals, Sammi Smith, and Waylon Jennings. Of course, none of us knew it at the time, but this industry-crowd concert would later become known as the night the Outlaws officially served notice there was going to be a changing of the guard in country music.

So we're sitting there enjoying our spaghetti Bolognese with glasses of Chianti wine, when suddenly I noticed Willie Nelson and his wife Connie having dinner about four tables away.

"Don't look now," I said to Betty, "but Willie Nelson and his wife are over there having dinner."

Somebody at our table had just mentioned that we'd best get moving if we wanted to catch Willie's performance. But with him sitting four tables away, there was no way we were going to miss anything. So we relaxed and enjoyed the rest of our meal, which included coffee and dessert.

Afterward, while standing out front waiting for Bobby to bring the car around, someone in our party—it may have been Vereen—noticed Willie and Connie standing there beside us. The doorman was about to call them a cab when Vereen said, "Hey, we're going to the concert. Y'all want to ride with us?"

Willie, being Willie, smiled and nodded, then said, "Could we stop by Ernest Tubb Record Shop first? I need to get a guitar strap."

About that time, Bobby pulled up in his red two-door Jeep Commando. Don't ask me how, but the seven of us managed to squeeze ourselves in. As I recall, Willie, Connie, and I were crammed in the very back, with Betty and Bobby in the front and Jane and Vereen on the middle bench seat. Everyone was in high spirits as we headed downtown.

When we arrived at the Sheraton, Sammi Smith was finishing up her set, singing "Help Me Make It Through the Night." Since Atlantic was sponsoring the concert, we were in luck as far as seating. As soon as Rick Sanjek spotted us, he waved us to some seats in the second row.

When Willie took the stage, he immediately looked down and smiled at us—his fellow diners from Mario's, the ones who'd given him a ride downtown to buy the guitar strap he was now using. This was my first time seeing him live onstage with his band, and I was beside myself. Every time he looked at me and smiled, which was often, everything inside of me just melted. I couldn't take my eyes off him. Nothing else in the world mattered in that moment but this red-headed man and his music. I mean, I was totally in love with the guy.

Nugget Recording Studio
Goodlettsville, Tennessee
November 1973

I ONCE ASKED WILLIE—THIS WAS in the mid-1980s—
what his favorite album was that he ever recorded. "Oh, probably *Phases
and Stages*," he answered.

Most people don't know this, but *Phases and Stages* (Atlantic, 1974)
was recorded twice. Once with Jerry Wexler in Muscle Shoals, and a
few weeks later with Fred Carter Jr. and Rick Sanjek at Nugget Studio
in Goodlettsville, just north of Nashville. There are many versions of
the story. The one I heard goes like this: after the Muscle Shoals sessions, Willie told Sanjek he wanted to re-record the album using his
band. (Wexler had used the Muscle Shoals rhythm section, which included veteran session musicians David Hood, Roger Hawkins, Pete
Carr, and Barry Beckett.) So Sanjek booked Nugget, which was owned
by Fred Carter, and for three nights—November 19–21, 1973—Willie
and his band (sister Bobbie, Paul English, Bee Spears, and newcomer
Mickey Raphael) and a few guest musicians (Texas fiddler Johnny Gimble, Bobby Thompson, and Grady Martin) re-recorded the songs from
Phases and Stages.

I was there for every one of those Goodlettsville sessions. In fact,
I was sort of Willie's unofficial chauffeur. My car in those days was the
infamous "Whitetrash," my 1961 Ford Galaxie—white with red interior—that I'd bought for two hundred dollars from a Church of Christ
lady who'd never driven anywhere but to church.

My four most vivid memories from those sessions are (1) watching Paul English role a Texas-sized joint—basically the size of a huge
cigar—which he then passed around; (2) driving back to Nashville
late one night with my car windows rolled down and Willie curled up
asleep in the front seat with his head resting on my lap; (3) hearing Fred
Carter Jr. say—with a touch of wonder and parental pride: "Man, my
little daughter can really sing!" Twenty-three years later I was reminded
of those words when Deana Carter burst on the scene with "Strawberry
Wine," the #1 single from her debut album, *Did I Shave My Legs for
This?*; and (4) singing background vocals with Jeannie Seely and Hank

Cochran on "Bloody Mary Morning," "No Love Around," and "Pick Up the Tempo."

When it came time to release *Phases and Stages* in early 1974, Atlantic went with the Wexler-produced version. The decision was contentious, and some heads rolled, but Wexler ultimately prevailed. Frankly, I loved both versions. I mean, how could you go wrong? To my ear, the Muscle Shoals sessions sounded a bit crisper. But the Goodlettsville sessions had a warmth and intimacy that was magical.

I always thought the Goodlettsville sessions would remain forever buried in a vault. But in 2006, Rhino (in conjunction with Atlantic) released a three-disc set called *Willie Nelson: The Complete Atlantic Sessions* that included ten bonus tracks, which turned out to be the ones from Goodlettsville. There were quite a few omissions in the liner-note credits, namely Johnny Gimble's fiddle, Bobby Thompson's banjo on "Bloody Mary Morning," our background vocals on the three aforementioned songs, and Cam Mullins's string arrangements on the ballads ("I'm Falling in Love Again," "It's Not Supposed to Be That Way," and "I Still Can't Believe You're Gone"). But the songs were all there, just as I remembered them.

Halloween night at the Troubadour
Los Angeles, 1974

IN THE FALL OF 1974, I toured New Zealand and Australia as a background singer with the Roger Miller Show. Roger's regular singer, Marie Cain, was unable to make the trip, so I was her replacement. If I ever write about that tour, it would have to be fiction or nobody would believe it.

Once back in the States, I hung around Los Angeles for a while, staying with friends Bill Nelson (no relation to Willie) and Mary Craven in their garage apartment. Bill was a film editor and Mary an aspiring actress and playwright. Mary had a five-year-old son, Gregor, who called me "Martian" because he couldn't pronounce Marshall. Somehow that seemed appropriate for L.A.

Bill was usually working, so Mary and I were always going out to hear music or take in a movie. For my last night in town—which happened to be Halloween—Mary and I went to the Troubadour to hear Willie and his band. I remember being backstage before the show, talking with Paul English. Then we took our seats. The Troubadour was packed to the gills that night—the buzz so thick you could cut it with a knife. Robert Hilburn from the *L.A. Times* was there, along with a scattering of movie stars. This was two months before the release of *Red Headed Stranger*, the album that sent Willie's career soaring into the stratosphere.

When Willie took the stage, he immediately launched into "Whiskey River." Later in the set he announced, "I've got a lot of friends here tonight. Bob Dylan's here. Roger Miller . . . Kris Kristofferson . . . and Marshall Chapman, a girl singer from Nashville." It was surreal, hearing my name mentioned in the same breath with those guys. But it was nothing compared to what happened later that night.

In those days I was just starting to write songs, so I kept a spiral notebook handy for jotting down lyrics and song ideas. I'd had it with me a few weeks earlier during the long flight from Los Angeles to New Zealand with the Roger Miller Show. I was sitting back in coach with the band, minding my own business, when Roger strolled back to see how everybody was doing. (Roger and his manager, Dann Moss, always rode first class.) We were about ten hours into the flight, and everybody was starting to get a little squirrelly. I was jotting down something in my notebook when suddenly someone snatched it out of my hands. I looked up to see Roger scribbling something on the cover. I had a moment of panic, thinking he might read something I'd written, but he just handed it back and moved on. I still have that cover in a scrapbook somewhere. The words are faded but still legible: "Marshall—When your toes and fingers fail you, you can always count on me. R.M."

That night at the Troubadour, Roger was sitting in the row in front of me, a few seats down. When Willie mentioned our names from the stage, Roger turned around and gave me a look that said, *Where does it say background singer's name gets mentioned in the same breath as big-time superstar?* Actually, we had become friends during the tour. He was always teasing me, saying, "Hey! Where does it say background singer gets to ride in limousine with big-time superstar?" or "Hey! Where does it say background singer gets corner table?" "Hey! Where does it say . . ." this or that. It had become sort of a joke between us. Roger knew I wasn't a background singer. I imagine on some level he knew I had other aspirations, and he seemed to respect that. But the teasing never stopped.

After Willie's show at the Troubadour, about twenty of us (including Willie) ended up at Roger's house in Beverly Hills. At that time, Roger was living in the Aviary on the old John Barrymore estate. The Aviary had originally been exactly that—an aviary . . . you know, with exotic birds flitting around. Later, it was converted to a screening room before finally being remodeled for living quarters. Former occupants included Katharine Hepburn, Marlon Brando, and, most recently, Candice Bergen.

From the road, the Aviary looked like a Spanish tower, nestled among the pine and cypress trees. The front entrance opened into a small, sunken living room where a massive iron chandelier hung down twenty-five feet from a domed ceiling, which was studded with stained-glass windows depicting scenes from John Barrymore's films. There was no furniture to speak of—other than a Persian carpet with ten or twelve throw pillows scattered about. A fireplace stood at one end of the room. It was chilly that night, so Roger had a fire going. At least he *thought* he had a fire going. Problem was, it kept going out. At one point, he was jabbing at the logs with a poker. He was starting to get a little exasperated, so the room got real quiet. About that time, Willie said, "Jiggle it a little, it'll open!" which cracked everybody up. (*Jiggle it a little, it'll open* was the second line in Roger's most recent single, "Open Up Your Heart.")

So we're all sitting around on the floor, when suddenly a guitar materialized, as so often happens whenever songwriters are gathered together. This particular guitar was an old Washburn gut string from the 1920s. I remember the name "Louise" was inlaid in mother-of-pearl across one of the frets, very discreetly, in a plain cursive script. I couldn't help but wonder about Louise. Was she some unobtainable object of desire for the guitar's original owner? Some woman he could never have, so he had her name inlaid in mother-of-pearl, high up on the neck, where it would rarely be touched by human hands?

When the guitar got to Willie, he pulled out a crumpled piece of paper where he'd recently scribbled some lyrics to a new song. "I think this one has the same melody as another one I wrote," he said, laughing. "Can't nobody arrest you for stealing from yourself, right?" When the guitar got to me, I sang "A Woman's Heart (Is a Handy Place to Be)." My own heart was pounding a mile a minute, but I managed to make it through. After I finished, Roger turned to Willie and said, "'Running from a friend to find a stranger'? *That* ain't bad," as they both nodded in agreement.

Over the years, I'm often asked, "When did you first realize you had the talent to write songs?" It's hard to say, really. But I'll go with that moment in the Aviary.

South Carolina
December 1978

I AM HOME VISITING MY PARENTS in Spartanburg. My father and I are sitting in the den listening to *Stardust,* Willie's 1978 album—the one where he sings pop standards from the 1930s and '40s. Songs like "Georgia on My Mind," "All of Me," and "Blue Skies." Songs Willie has loved since childhood.

My father has recently purchased a cassette copy of the album, and now he can't stop playing it. Just for the record, my parents are *not* country music fans. Their preference has always been classical, opera, show tunes, Glenn Miller, Benny Goodman, and the like. So it was quite a departure for my father to be listening to Willie Nelson. Willie was my bag, not his. But my father loved those old jazzy songs, so Willie's album forged sort of a musical bond between us.

At Amazon.com, one of the customer reviews for *Stardust* says, "I really don't like country music, but I *love* this album." When Willie first decided to record *Stardust,* a lot of people—including many at his record label—thought he was crazy. After all, he was the hottest thing in country music. Why would he want to ruin his career by recording an album of old standards? "Career suicide!" they all shouted behind his back. But Willie, being Willie, stuck to his guns and came out smelling like a rose. *Stardust* is his all-time best-selling album, having sold over five million copies.

So Dad and I are sitting in the den listening to *Stardust*, when suddenly we notice Mother standing in the doorway. Now anyone who knows my mother knows it's a rare thing indeed for her to stand still, much less listen to anything. But there she was, listening. Dad and I couldn't believe it. We just sat there mesmerized, waiting to see what would happen next. With Mother, something *always* happens next. So while Willie's singing, "All of me / Why not take all of me," Mother's standing there listening with a quizzical look on her face. When the song ended, Dad and I looked up at Mother. "That man can't sing," she announced. Then, looking even more confused, she added, "But I *like* it."

WILLIE IS IN HIS SEVENTIES NOW and still going strong. His most recent album, *Two Men with the Blues*, was recorded live with Wynton Marsalis at Lincoln Center in New York. As of this writing (2008), it's #1 on the jazz charts.

The next time I saw Willie was during Farm Aid 1996 at William Brice Stadium in Columbia, South Carolina. I was a performer that year, having just released a new album (*Love Slave*) on Margaritaville/Island Records. My band and I had left Nashville at midnight in a customized tour bus, arriving in Columbia that next morning. No sooner had we checked into our hotel than I was whisked off to a press conference by a record company rep. While en route, the rep informed me that each performer was expected to make a brief statement about the plight of the American farmer.

The press conference was like something out of a Fellini movie. There were TV cameras and bright lights everywhere. I was feeling a little fuzzy, having traveled all night through the mountains. But the minute I saw Neil Young, I felt better. I'm not sure the word exists to describe his appearance. Somehow *disheveled* falls way short. I didn't recognize him at first. I thought he was some homeless guy who'd wandered in off the street. But the minute he spoke, I recognized his voice and thought, *Oh my God, that's Neil Young.*

Others in the room included Willie, some of the guys from Hootie

& the Blowfish, two Native Americans in full headdress, Steve Earle, a couple of Beach Boys (not Brian), an assortment of politicians looking out of their element, Freddy Fender and Doug Sahm from the Texas Tornados, Jewel, the guys from Son Volt, and of course members of the press, which included all the local TV stations, *USA Today*, the *New York Times*, *Rolling Stone*, the *Charlotte Observer*, *The State*, the *Atlanta Journal-Constitution*, and so on.

When I told my mother that I was playing Farm Aid and that it was going to be in Columbia, her first words were, "Oh, you'll probably run into my friend Les Tindal, who runs the Department of Agriculture." (For the record, my mother is a major player when it comes to South Carolina politics. She was the first female to serve on the State Development Board *and* the State Election Commission. She also served on the State Health Coordinating Commission, the Palmetto Conservation Foundation, and the South Carolina Mining Council, and was chairman of Governor Jim Edwards's inaugural ball.) As it turned out, Commissioner Tindal was standing right behind Willie and one of the Native Americans, looking very Republican in his suit and tie.

When it came time for each performer to make a "brief statement," I must admit, some of the ones in the early going weren't very brief. In fact, they were downright longwinded. I won't name any names, but by the time it came my turn to speak, I couldn't think of anything to say that hadn't already been said. So with Willie, God, and everybody else looking my way, I just said, "Is Les Tindal here?" Everyone kind of looked around nervously like, *What is she doing?* Finally, the Republican-looking man in the suit behind Willie said, "Yes, I'm Les Tindal." "Oh, great!" I said. "Mama told me to tell you to do whatever Willie wants you to do, okay?" At that, Willie broke into a big smile and a few people laughed. Mind you, this was a tough room. These people were serious and angry about what was happening to the American farmer, and rightfully so. But hey, we all have to do what we have to do. I then looked at Willie and said, "Hi, Willie. Thanks for having me."

THE NEXT TIME I *TALKED* TO WILLIE was four years later. I was at home in Nashville, checking my phone messages, when I heard this voice say, "Hey, Marshall, it's Willie." At first, I wasn't sure who it was. But it's hard not to recognize that Texas hill country drawl. *Oh my god, that's Willie!* I thought. He left a number, so I dialed it and we had a nice conversation. He mentioned something about my coming down. I thought he meant to Austin, so I politely declined, thinking he was pulling my leg. I later learned he was on his tour bus behind the Ryman Auditorium in Nashville. Tommy Spurlock had been hanging with him that night. Tommy and I had recently been doing some recording, so I figured Tommy had given him my number. Anyway, Willie asked how I was doing. I told him I was doing good, that I'd finally found someone, and we'd bought a house together, that I was writing a book, mostly staying home, life was sweet, and so on. Then Willie said, "Well, there's an old proverb that says, 'If you build a house of quality in the woods, the world will beat a path to your door.'"

I thought about that for a moment, then said, "Well, I like the *first* half of that."

OKAY. HERE'S HOW IT STANDS: a transcript of my live interview with Willie was to begin at this point. That was the plan. But as Robert Burns once wrote, "The best-laid plans of mice and men often go awry." Here's what happened.

The Willie "interview"
Memphis/Beaumont/Austin
August 2–4, 2008

AT FIRST, I TRIED GOING through proper channels. I put in an interview request with Willie's publicist in California. She emailed me back saying she was "not adding anything to Willie's schedule." Okay. Forget proper channels. I've never been a proper-channels kind of girl anyway. So I emailed my buddy Mickey Raphael, who plays harmonica in Willie's band. Mickey suggested I contact Willie directly and gave me his personal email address. *Willie does email?* I couldn't believe it. So after I calmed down, I emailed the Red Headed Stranger:

Hey Willie—

Any chance I could come to wherever you are to ask you six questions for a book I'm working on? I'll even bring my golf clubs. Call me and I'll fill you in.

Lots of love,
Marshall

Six days went by with no response. Then I got another email from Mickey:

Willie got your email. Try him again.

This was Wednesday, July 30, 2008. I went to Willie's website and saw where they were on the road in Maryland and would be playing Danville, Virginia, the next night (Thursday), Louisville the night after that (Friday), and Memphis after that (Saturday). I didn't need my Rand McNally to know they'd be passing within a three-wood shot of my house after the Louisville show. Things were looking up.

I also noticed that Memphis and Beaumont were the last two stops of their current tour, followed by a three-week break. Maybe I could catch Willie during the break. Wait a week or so, fly to Austin, stay with my friend Jane Hilfer who lives on the road that goes out to Willie's ranch, do the interview, then fly home. That seemed like the best scenario. So I emailed Willie again:

Hey Willie—

Will you be in Austin during your next break? I have a good friend who lets me stay in her guest house off Bee Caves Road. I could fly down any time between August 11 and 20. I'd like to sit down with you for thirty minutes or so and talk about your early days in Nashville. Call me and I'll fill you in. (615) xxx-xxxx.

Love,
Marshall

The next day, after running errands, I came home to find a voice message on my phone: "Hey, Marshall, this is Willie. Give me a call at (512) xxx-xxxx. Bye!" I immediately went for a walk around the neighborhood to ground myself. Then I dialed the number.

"Hello."

"Hey, Willie. It's Marshall Chapman."

"Well, hey there, good-looking!"

He sounded youthful and alert. The antithesis of a seventy-five-year-old pothead. He asked about my book. I told him that it was about Nashville and that I'd love to interview him about his early days here. "It's not a kiss-and-tell," I added.

"Oh, I'm not worried about that," he said. "My reputation is the kind you can't ruin."

I mentioned flying to Austin some time between August 10 and 20.

"I'll be in Maui then," he said. "Why don't you just come on out on the road and hang with us for a while?"

My heart froze. *Did I just hear what I just heard? So what are you afraid of, girl?* The truth is, I was terrified. There were just too many unknowns. Especially for a quasi-agoraphobe like myself. The only tour bus I'd ever been on was my own, other than a brief run on Emmylou's. Trying to sound nonchalant, I said, "Well, there's no rush really. Any time within the next year will probably do."

"The next year?" Willie said. "Oh . . ."

His voice trailed off. Was it my imagination, or did I detect a trace of disappointment?

After we hung up, I called my husband. When I told Chris what I'd said, he came alive.

"You call Willie back right now and tell him you'd love to ride with him. Damn it, Marshall! This is a once-in-a-lifetime opportunity. You've got to strike while the iron's hot!"

"But it's the end of the tour and he's probably exhausted," I said.

"Promise me one thing," Chris said.

"What's that?"

"That you won't make any decisions based on co-dependency. Willie's a grown man. He can take care of himself. If he's invited you to ride on his bus, then take him at his word. Now you call him back right now and tell him you're going!"

Our conversation was beginning to remind me of the last scene in *Casablanca*—the one where Rick orders Ilsa on the plane. Only this was *Casablanca* in reverse: instead of Outlaw ordering Love Interest to go with Honorable Husband, Honorable Husband is ordering Love Interest to go with Outlaw. *If that bus leaves and you're not on it with Willie, you'll regret it. Maybe not today. Maybe not tomorrow. But* soon, *and for the rest of your life!*

So I picked up the phone and dialed Willie's number . . . again.

"Hello."

"Willie, it's Marshall Chapman. Remember me?"

"Well, yeah," he said, laughing.

"Listen, I've had a change of heart. I think I *will* come hang with you guys."

We then discussed logistics. I mentioned they would be passing within a stone's throw of my house in Nashville after the Louisville show, but Willie was concerned about the hour, that he might be asleep and signals would get crossed and I'd end up stranded on the side of the road. So it was agreed I would hook up with them in either Louisville or Memphis.

Sounding every bit like my mother, I asked:

"Now, Willie, I have to ask you one thing."

"What's that?"

"Is there cigarette smoking on your bus?"

"Nah," he said. "No cigarette smoking permitted."

"Good!" I said. "Because cigarette smoke gives me a terrible headache. Now marijuana smoke, I don't mind. In fact, I love the smell of marijuana."

There was a momentary pause. Then Willie said, "Me, too!" as we both burst out laughing.

After we hung up, I called Chris at work.

"Okay, I talked to Willie and I'm meeting up with them in either Louisville or Memphis."

"Great!"

"Will you do me a favor?"

"Sure."

"Will you call your probation officer as soon as we hang up and see if he'll give you special permission to drive me to Memphis Saturday? Meanwhile, I'll call Tim Krekel about Louisville. Who knows? Maybe Tim's in Nashville and I can catch a ride to Louisville with him."

Just for the record, my husband is a recovering drug addict with over eight years' sobriety. In September 2005, he pled guilty to a misdemeanor stemming from a self-prescribing incident from 1999. He was fined and placed on three years' probation, which means he has to get permission *two weeks in advance* to travel anywhere outside the Middle Tennessee Judicial District.

There are many advantages to having a husband on probation. One is, you're absolved from having to deal with a certain stratum of society—namely the one I was born into, the one where propriety often takes precedence over reality. So in many ways, Chris's situation has been a blessing. "I'm sorry, but my husband's on probation and we won't be able to attend." To which Mrs. Propriety replies, "Oh, well . . . ah . . . I'm just so *sorry!*" all the while thinking, *Probation? Good Lord, what was I thinking inviting these people?* Word gets out and the phone stops ringing.

Okay. So I called Tim Krekel. As it turned out Tim was in Maine and wouldn't be back in Louisville for a week or so. He was sorry to miss the show, but excited I was going to spend some time with Willie. "Be sure and give him my best," he said.

I was just starting to think that Memphis might be my best bet, when the phone rang. It was Chris.

"I talked to Denny Boguskie" (Chris's probation officer).

"And?"

"He said I could drive you to Memphis. But when I told him you were hooking up with Willie, he said, 'Chris, I'm going to give you permission to drive your wife to Memphis. But you are *not,* I repeat, *not* to set foot on Willie Nelson's bus, you hear me? You just drop her off, then drive straight on back to Nashville.'"

I couldn't believe it.

"Oh wow, that's great!" I said. "Should I still look into renting a car?"

"Nah, I'll drive you."

TWO DAYS LATER, CHRIS AND I are cruising along I-40 toward Memphis. It was Saturday afternoon, and we must've been a sight. Chris was wearing a surgical mask, as he was coming down with some sort of respiratory infection and didn't want his germs getting on me. I was feeling a little under the weather myself, having spent a sleepless night following intense negotiations with a magazine editor, while trying to pack and get focused on Willie. Meanwhile, I'd booked a return flight and made arrangements to stay with Jane after Willie's bus got to Austin. I figured by then, I'd need a few days of rehab.

"What time will you be arriving?" Jane asked.

"I have no idea," I said. "I imagine they'll leave for Austin right after the Beaumont show. It could be early in the morning. I'll call you when I get in."

AS CHRIS AND I APPROACHED the outskirts of Memphis, I could feel my entire life as I had known it up until then begin to fade away. I checked my cell. There was a message from Mickey:

Marshall, it's a zoo down here [AutoZone Park]. Your best bet is to go directly to the hotel. It's the Holiday Inn on Poplar. Willie's bus should be there. They don't leave until six o'clock. The crew and band busses are already here [at the venue]. Just make sure you're on Willie's bus. It has four bunks, but you should be able to grab one of the front couches. We've been out three weeks and it's getting crazy. The band bus is wall-to-wall bodies—girlfriends, wives, you name it. I'm stepping over bodies to get to my bunk. And the crew bus, forget it. It's chain-smoking heart attacks waiting to happen.

The minute we turned into the Holiday Inn parking lot, I spotted Willie's bus. It was hard to miss, as it was parked in front of the hotel entrance. I knew it was Willie's bus because the back windows had been painted over with an airbrushed mural of Willie's eyes superimposed over the eyes of an eagle. I recognized the artwork from his *Spirit* album.

Willie had told me to call him when I got in. "But what if you're taking a nap?" I said. "I'd hate to wake you up before a show. Why don't you give me David's cell." So that's what he did.

David is David Anderson. As best I can tell, he is Willie's personal assistant. He's been with Willie since 1974. We exchanged emails five years ago when I was getting reprint permissions for my first book. As far as I know, this would be my first time to meet him in person.

David has the perfect gatekeeper personality—intimidating, always lurking, never offering anything. He reminds me of Lurch from *The Addams Family*. Only Lurch would be considered loquacious compared to David.

I had called David the night before while packing. Our conversation went like this:

Ring . . . ring . . .

"Yeah," answered a voice completely devoid of expression.

"Oh, hi, David, it's Marshall Chapman."

(silence)

"I'm riding from Memphis to Austin with you guys. Listen, is there anything I need to bring?"

(more silence)

"I mean, I was thinking it might be cold on the bus and was wondering . . ."

"Dress warmly." *Click.*

ORDINARILY, SIX PEOPLE RIDE on Willie's bus: Willie, David, Willie's sister Bobbie (who plays piano in his band), his daughter Lana Nelson (who makes sure everyone is fed and happy), and the two drivers—Gator and Tony. All have been with Willie for over thirty years. In fact everyone I meet, from the crew to the band, seems to have been with Willie for over thirty years. The whole operation has the feel of a family circus on wheels. But I'm getting ahead of myself.

Back to the Holiday Inn. David comes out and loads my suitcase in one of the bins underneath the bus. I hug Chris goodbye, then turn and climb on board. The bus door closes behind me, and I step through the heavy curtain that stays closed behind the driver's seat. It takes a while for my eyes to adjust to the dim lighting. As I ease myself down onto a tufted leather couch, a young woman smiles at me from across the aisle. She is drop-dead gorgeous, her smile dazzling. A large flat-screen TV broadcasts MSNBC in silence. The tufted leather couch is comfortable. A good thing, I note, since I'll probably be sleeping on it later tonight, if indeed I sleep at all.

Bobbie Nelson gets on the bus. She looks radiant and ready for the show. She's wearing high heels and a flowing dress to go with her long, flowing hair. She smiles and says hello.

"Hi, Bobbie," I say. "I met you thirty-five years ago at Fred Carter's studio."

She acts as if that were only yesterday, and we exchange pleasantries. I feel like I just got dropped off at summer camp and Bobbie Nelson is my new best friend.

More people get on the bus. A beautiful young couple who seem to be in love. The young woman is Amy Nelson, Willie's daughter with Connie. The young man is Cyrus Spears, son of Bee Spears, Willie's longtime bass player. Lana Nelson gets on and we're ready to roll. As the bus pulls away from the curb, somewhere in the dark recesses of my mind, I hear Sly Stone singing, "It's a family affair . . ."

Willie emerges from the back, and we exchange warm greetings and hugs. "Did you meet Eva?" he says, gesturing to the beautiful woman sitting across from me.

Eva is Eva Hassmann, an aspiring filmmaker and actress from Germany. She met Willie through Peter Bogdanovich, who reportedly is financing a film she's making called *Willie and Me*. The film's title brings to mind a song by David Allan Coe called "Willie, Waylon, and Me." I miss Waylon. Somehow, the universe seems a little tilted without him.

Speaking of Eva: have you ever been in a room with someone of the same sex—in this case, female—who is so incredibly glamorous and beautiful, so undulating and sexy, you can't help but think, *My God! If this is a* woman, *then what am I, an orangutan?* I mean, I'm no slouch, okay? But this Eva Hassmann is *beyond* good looking. Doe-eyed with light brown hair, she reminds me of Marilyn Monroe (in the way she moves) with a little bit of Marlene Dietrich (the younger version) thrown in.

It's obvious Willie is taken with her. I mean, what man with a heartbeat wouldn't be?

Willie slides into the booth across the aisle from the little kitchen area. An open laptop sits on the table in front of him, along with books, CDs, and other paraphernalia. Eva moves into the seat across from Willie. At one point, Lurch appears from the back of the bus. He stands next to Willie like he's waiting for something. Willie looks up and says, "Is everything out of control?"

Lurch raises an eyebrow.

"Good!" Willie says, giving me a wink. "'Cause that's the way we like it."

AS THE BUS ROLLS ALONG Poplar Avenue toward AutoZone Park, my cell rings. It's Chris. "You okay?"

"I think so," I answer. "Here. Talk to Bobbie. She's Willie's sister."

I hand my cell to Bobbie. "Here. Talk to Chris. He's my husband. He's also an angel."

I figure whatever Bobbie says to Chris will be better than anything anybody else could say.

"We *love* Marshall," she says. I can feel Chris breathing a sigh of relief from wherever he is. He and Bobbie talk for a minute. Then she hands my cell back over, but it cuts off before Chris and I can say good-bye. My cell phone hasn't been worth a damn since I ran over it with my car. But that's another story.

Bobbie shows me where she recently had a pacemaker put in after suffering two strokes. The pacemaker feels like a little box of matches placed beneath the skin just below her collarbone. It's hard to believe Bobbie is seventy-eight. Her brown hair, which falls well below her waist, has the luster of an eighteen-year-old's with just a few specks of gray. Willie's hair is the same, only his is red. Lana's hair is a striking iron gray. It's not quite as long as her father's or Bobbie's—it's somewhat thicker and wavier—but its luster and length are just as remarkable. Later, I say to Willie, "You Nelsons sure got the hair gene."

"Must be that Cherokee blood," he replies. (Willie and Bobbie are one-fourth Cherokee. Lana's mother, Martha, was full-blooded.)

Willie plays a DVD of the opening scene from *Willie and Me*. We all watch as Eva's character, Greta, tries to make her way into a concert hall where Willie and his band are playing. She tries one entrance after another, but all doors are locked. Not to be deterred, she crawls—in a pair of high heels—up a drain pipe and out onto a roof, where she peers down through a window at Willie while he sings "Always on My Mind." She is totally enthralled. At one point, one of her high heels comes loose and goes clattering down the roof before falling to the ground. Later, as Willie and his entourage are leaving the concert hall, they stumble upon the high heel. Willie reaches down to pick it up. When he looks up, Greta is standing before him so starstruck she can barely speak. After much hemming and hawing (and undulation), she manages to ask Willie for his autograph. He graciously obliges. But then he keeps misspelling her name. It's a cute scene. Eva is as beautiful onscreen as she is off. As far as I can tell, Greta is Eva and Eva is Greta—just like Willie is Willie.

Willie announces that he and Eva have written a song called "It Is What It Is (Says Love)."

"Well, *he* wrote practically all of it," she later confides to me. "I was just in the room."

"That counts," I say. "Had you not been in the room, it never would have been."

Willie plays a recording of the song. Eva's voice has a sexy, breathless quality that reminds me of Marilyn Monroe singing "Happy Birthday" to President Kennedy. Technically speaking, she can't sing. But who cares? A lot of people thought Willie couldn't sing. The contrast between their voices has a certain *je ne sais quoi* that's appealing. I'll take Eva over a thousand Celine Dions any day.

"You guys should put this out," I say.

Eva is no bimbo. As my mother would say, she's "dumb like a fox." She's got moxie, and an honesty that can at times be disarming. I try to imagine what it would be like to go through life that physically beautiful, having people react only to that.

IT'S HOT AS HELL IN MEMPHIS. By late afternoon, we're told the heat index at the AutoZone infield is 118 degrees. Willie is scheduled to go on at seven, followed by the Dave Matthews Band.

AutoZone Park is a minor-league baseball stadium located in the heart of downtown Memphis. It's home to the Memphis Redbirds, the Triple-A affiliate of the St. Louis Cardinals. For tonight's concert, a massive stage has been set up in the outfield facing the stands. By the time we arrive, the field and stands are a solid mass of humanity.

Willie's bus is directed to a spot on South 4th Street behind the outfield about twenty yards from the stage. From inside the bus, we hear the whoops and hollers of Saturday-night revelers. High-rise condominiums with people partying on balconies surround the bus on three sides. A Texas flag hangs from a balcony rail, as do a couple of overzealous fans.

The minute Willie steps off the bus, the air fills with an electric charge, like you feel in the summer before lightning strikes. Willie is wearing a black T-shirt with dark jeans, running shoes, and a black cowboy hat. His trademark braid of red hair falls to just below his waist. He's unmistakably Willie. The crowd chants, "Wil-*lee!* Wil-*lee!*" Without a word being spoken, Eva takes his left hand and I take his right. With Lurch and Tony leading the way, we begin making our way toward the stage. Willie's hand feels warm and calm. At one point, I let go so he and Eva can step down some narrow stairs. When they reach the bottom, Willie reaches back and I again take his hand. Wolf whistles cut through the intensifying noise of the crowd. Someone shouts, "HEY, WILLIE, WHERE'D YOU GET THOSE BABES!?" I can see the headline now: "Amazon Rocker Authoress and Fräulein Movie Goddess Lead Texas's Greatest Gift to the World to the Stage."

The view from the stage is breathtaking. The lingering late-August light softens everything. Just outside the park, glimmering skyscrapers rise dramatically into the twilight, none more dramatic than the Peabody Hotel with its huge red neon sign, THE PEABODY, towering from its roof.

Several portable machines blow cool air out onto the stage. I station myself in front of one and proceed to watch the show. Willie opens with "Whiskey River" and never looks back. The crowd is young. Most have come to hear Dave Matthews, but you'd never know it. They shout in unison during "Beer for My Horses" and clap along when Bobbie plays "Down Yonder." I particularly enjoy hearing the older stuff—songs like "Me and Paul" and "Night Life." Willie's band consists of Bobbie on piano, Paul English on drums (snare only), Billy English

(Paul's brother) on percussion, Bee Spears on bass, and Mickey on harmonica.

The band and crew depart for Beaumont immediately following Willie's set. Willie stays behind so he can sing "Gravedigger" with Dave Matthews later on. Meanwhile, we all sit around on his bus listening to music. At one point, I hand Willie a reissue CD of my Rounder album, *Take It On Home*, which has a cover version of his song "Pick Up the Tempo." Willie originally recorded it as a waltz. My version is straight-ahead rock & roll. He seems to get a kick out of it, but it's hard to tell, really, what Willie thinks about *anything*. My Austin friend Sarah Bird perhaps said it best: "Willie World has its own gravity."

A part of me wishes I could smoke weed just to be sociable, but weed was never my thing. The few times I've smoked it, I ended up paranoid, locking myself in a room with a bag of tortilla chips, or driving twenty miles an hour on the interstate, thinking I'm speeding.

I give Willie a CD of some of my newer songs. When "I Love Everybody (I Love Everything)" comes on, everybody starts grooving. Before it ends, however, Lurch is there to take Willie back out to the stage. It's amazing how Willie seems to take everything in stride. One minute he's hanging out on his bus playing the CD of an old friend he hasn't seen in over ten years. Then he's singing and playing "Gravedigger" with Dave Matthews in front of twenty thousand screaming fans. I doubt his blood pressure ever changes.

WHILE STANDING IN THE WINGS watching the Dave Matthews Band, I can't help but notice their trumpet player. He reminds me of William "The Refrigerator" Perry as far as sheer physical size. He is, by far, the largest musician I have ever seen. He's out there blowing in the heat and the lights, and the sweat is just pouring off his huge body. His neck is wider than my waist. I am fascinated by his size. There's something beautiful and strong about him. Being onstage makes performers seem larger than life, but this guy gives the expression new meaning.

As we make our way back to the bus, Lurch and Tony stand by patiently while Willie signs autographs. A wire fence separates Willie from a gathering throng of fans. Many hold up camera phones, hoping to transmit Willie's image back to God-only-knows where. A young girl hands Willie her cell phone. "It's my mama!" she exclaims. Willie takes the phone and says hi to Mom. Pretty soon, it's a cell phone frenzy. "Hey, Willie! Talk to my girlfriend! She don't love me no more!"

BACK ON THE BUS, EVERYONE is in high spirits as we all settle in for the six-hundred-mile ride to Beaumont. I compliment Bobbie on her rendition of "Down Yonder." "Well, you know, my style is pretty much Baptist honky-tonk," she says, laughing. I tell her "Down Yonder" is the first song I remember hearing as a child. As the bus rolls south through Mississippi, I present Willie with a DVD of *Hush Hoggies Hush,* a four-minute documentary about a man in Yazoo County, Mississippi, who has trained his pigs to pray before they eat. Willie seems pleased. But then again, it's hard to really tell.

Willie plays some recordings by his sons, Lukas and Micah, who have a band; Lukas plays lead guitar and Micah plays drums. Their music has a sort of West Coast, Stevie Ray Vaughan vibe.

Later on, Willie plays a recording of himself singing hymns with the Jordanaires. It's just them singing with no instrumentation, and it's magical.

"Man, that's great!" I exclaim. "Has it ever been released?"

It has not. And may never be. Without mentioning names, I get the impression the producer of the session and Willie's management are in some sort of dispute. Oh, well. What the world doesn't know, it won't miss.

AS THE BUS KEEPS ROLLING south toward Louisiana, one by one, people drift off to try and get some sleep. I have no idea what time it is, nor do I care. Pretty soon, it's just Willie and me sitting across from each other in his booth. I ask if he'd like to read the fourteen-page intro I've written for our interview. He smiles and nods yes. "If there are any inaccuracies or anything that makes you cringe, I want to know about it," I say.

Willie puts on his reading glasses. I watch him while he reads. At one point he laughs.

"Where are you?" I ask.

"Roger Miller," he says.

He continues reading. A minute later, he laughs again. Every time he laughs, I can't help it; I ask, "Where are you?" I do the same thing whenever Chris reads anything I've written. Why should Willie be any different? *It is what it is, says Love.*

"Where are you?" I ask.

"Your mama," he answers.

Afterward, he points out that I've misquoted the proverb—the one about building a house of quality in the woods.

"Oh, how does it go?" I scrounge around for my pen, which seems to have disappeared. "Here. Say it into this." I hold out my Sony voice-recorder as Willie leans in and quotes the proverb.

LATER, I WILL LOOK BACK on this moment and think, *Oh my God. I should have tried for the interview then. That was the time!* Easy to say, once you're far removed from Willie World. But when you're sitting across from Willie, as I was in that moment, this seventy-five-year-old who, thirty-five years earlier, inspired me to become a songwriter, who has since become an American icon, not to mention Texas's Greatest Gift to the World . . . well, it just seems like it would have been *sacrilegious* at that point to press things.

So we just sit there and talk about our lives. I tell him about Chris, and he tells me what a good job Annie has done raising their boys. After a while, we stand up and say goodnight. Willie retreats into the back of the bus, and I stretch out on the tufted leather couch, hoping to get some sleep. When it doesn't come, I just lie there with my eyes closed, trying to focus on my breathing.

IT'S AFTER SUN-UP WHEN WE pull into the Holiday Inn Beaumont. This is my third day with no sleep, but I am not overly concerned. As long as I stay relaxed and eat well, I know I'll be okay.

I've always considered sleep the most overrated of bodily needs. You can die of starvation, right? But who ever heard of anybody dying from being awake? As far as I'm concerned, we can all sleep when we're dead.

Some of my most magical life experiences have occurred when I was sleep deprived. I have this theory that sleep deprivation somehow destroys ego energy, thus freeing your soul to do whatever needs to be done: dance, sing, laugh, cry, make love, create, emote . . . the possibilities are endless. As long as you don't fight it, sleep deprivation can be your friend.

As if to prove my theory, some words start formulating in my brain. *Are they lyrics?* I'm not sure. I take a scrap of paper from my carry-on bag and begin writing:

When everything's swirling around out of control
And everybody's down to their very soul
Dancing to the rhythm of the universal whole
That's the way I like it

Keep moving forward, baby, don't you look back
The journey never ends when you're running with the pack
This train's moving fast and there ain't no track
That's the way I like it

That's the way I like it
That's the way it goes
The more love you give away
The more love grows
Where it all ends up
Nobody knows . . .
That's the way I like it
That's the way it goes

Next thing I know, Gator is handing me my room key. "Your bag should be in your room," he says.

At the top of the scrap of paper, I write, *Hey Willie—What do you think? xox, Marshall.* I place it on Willie's desk. But in doing so, I notice something printed on the other side. It's my seven interview questions—the ones I use to guide me during interviews for this book. I'm thinking, *Oh, well. I'll just leave it to fate. If Willie happens to see the questions, maybe it'll remind him of our interview and help him prepare.*

And if he doesn't see the questions, but sees the lyrics, who knows? Maybe he'll feel inspired to jump in and finish the song. When it comes down to it, *if I had to choose between interviewing Willie or writing a song with him, the song's gonna win out every time. Then again, he may never see any of this, and that's okay too! I'm just chairman of the doing-the-best-I-can committee—I am not chairman of the results. Now, on to the next moment.*

THE WEATHER IN BEAUMONT IS surprisingly pleasant, especially after the stifling heat in Memphis. The air here is actually *moving.* It's like God is saying, *Here! Let me help you breathe!* Also, the temperature is much cooler, which is surprising considering we just drove six hundred miles south. *Must be those breezes coming in off the Gulf.* I close my eyes and take in a long deep breath. The salt air tastes good and reminds me of childhood summers at Pawley's Island.

Someone mentions there's a hurricane—Hurricane Edouard—brewing out in the Gulf. Forecasts call for it to hit the Beaumont area an hour or so after the show tonight.

BEYOND THE HOLIDAY INN PARKING LOT, across Interstate 10, a yellow WAFFLE HOUSE sign beckons. *Ah, yes! Eggs, sausage, protein, here we come!* But first, I go to my room to unload and freshen up.

My room is on the seventh floor toward the back of the hotel, beyond the atrium with its huge cascading waterfall and giant American and Texas flags hanging from the ceiling. It's hard to tell whether my room is a room or a suite. I guess you could call it a suite, if you count the windowless room between the front door and bedroom. I check the window in the bedroom to see if it's operable. It looks like it was operable at one time, but that was many renovations ago. I have a well-documented phobia about being in hermetically sealed hotel rooms.

The clean white sheets on the king-sized bed look inviting. I run a hot tub, sprinkling lavender bath salts into the rising water underneath the faucet. I always carry little packets of lavender bath salts whenever I travel. Some people never leave home without their American Express card. I never leave home without my lavender bath salts.

After bathing, I feel restored. I put on a clean pair of shorts, clean T-shirt, fresh socks, and my New Balance running shoes. I then tie a light-cotton hoodie around my waist, strap on my fanny pack, and pull my black visor down over my forehead. Before heading out the door, I grab my room key and a bottle of Evian.

It feels good to walk in full stride across the parking lot. However, once I reach Walden Road—which is really more of a four-lane super-highway—walking becomes more of a challenge. It's obvious this area was not built with pedestrians in mind. Everything I see makes me acutely aware that I'm in Texas—big cars whizzing by on big concrete highways with big signs overhead, the big underpass running underneath big-ass Interstate 10—all of it starting to simmer, as the sun climbs into that great big Texas sky. I suddenly think of Cormac McCarthy's *The Road* and try to envision what this will all look like after the apocalypse, when there's no more fossil fuel. Concrete, weeds, and sky. We're almost there.

On the other side of Interstate 10, I spot a Cracker Barrel straight ahead. Since the Waffle House is further down, I opt for the Cracker Barrel. There are no sidewalks anywhere. A big-ass pick-up truck full of yahoos whizzes by. They honk and yell like they've never seen a pedestrian. *Just wait,* I think. *Your time will come. I'll still be walking, and you'll be trying to drive that big-ass truck on fossil fumes.* I smile as that Aesop's fable comes to mind—the one about the tortoise and the hare.

Cracker Barrel delivers, as always. Scrambled eggs and sausage never tasted so good.

Back at the hotel, I go to the front desk to pay for my room. The desk clerk tells me it's been taken care of. "They're all on American Express," she says. I then ask for a couple of sheets of stationery. "We don't have any stationery in this hotel," she replies. "I may have some Xerox paper in the back." I stand there in silence, lamenting yet another nail in the coffin of American culture: the replacement of hotel stationery with Internet access. *Why can't they offer both?* I wonder. The desk clerk reappears with several sheets of white paper. "Thank you," I say, then head for the elevators.

Back in my room or suite or whatever it is, I sit at the desk in the windowless front room and write down the lyrics to "The Way I Like It (Riding with Willie)"—at least what I have so far. It may need another verse. I remember all the words, which is always a good sign when you're writing a song.

I try to call Chris, but my cell is acting weird. The hotel phone is turned off, so I give up and slide into bed. As I lie there between the cool clean sheets, I try not to think about the quality of the air I'm breathing or where it's coming from. But I'm having a hard time, as I always do in these hermetically sealed hotels. Before I know it, my mind has drifted into the long, dark duct system that brings air to my room. *God only knows what's in those ducts*, I think. *Probably mold.* I start to feel panicky. So I try to not think about anything. The only way I can do this is to concentrate on my breathing. So I just lie there and breathe . . . in . . . then out . . . in . . . then out . . . in . . . Finally, after being awake four days and three nights, I drift off to sleep.

Two and a half hours later, I wake up. It's about noon and I'm starving. *Plus, I have an interview to do!* So I get up and dress and again walk across the hotel parking lot. Earlier that morning while walking to the Cracker Barrel, I had noticed a restaurant with a Cajun-sounding name directly across the highway. It had been closed that morning, but now it was open.

PAPPADEAUX SEAFOOD KITCHEN IS a chain of restaurants out of Houston. I normally shy away from chains, but sometimes on the road you have to go with what's available. Feeling skeptical but hopeful, I head for Pappadeaux.

Once inside, I sit down at the bar. When the bartender comes over, I order a mixed green salad with a bowl of oyster gumbo. And for my beverage, a glass of unsweetened iced tea mixed with lemonade. "Oh, you mean an Arnold Palmer?" the bartender says. "Yes!" I say. "But most people don't know it's called that."

I've been drinking Arnold Palmers for years. Only I didn't know they were called Arnold Palmers until summer before last. Until then, I must confess—I thought *I* had invented this beverage. It was kind of hard for me to accept at first, that someone else had beat me to the punch. Even if that someone was a world-famous golfer. But since Arnold is twenty years older than I am, I concede that it's possible, even probable, that he, not I, invented this refreshing summertime beverage.

Of course, my version of the Arnold Palmer is by far the best you will find anywhere. The traditional Arnold Palmer is half-tea, half-lemonade. I make mine with about three-quarters tea (preferably Arizona Diet Green Tea with Ginseng) and just enough lemonade ("All Natural" Simply Lemonade) to act as a sweetener. I then add a couple of good-sized sprigs of fresh mint, which I pummel into the crushed ice with the blunt end of a chop stick until the mint flavor runs all through the liquid. I'm serious: I'll put my Arnold Palmer up against anybody's.

Once I accepted the fact that Arnold Palmer invented the Arnold Palmer, I began to groove on the idea that Arnold and I have something else in common besides a love for the game of golf. When it comes to golf, however, one thing we don't have in common is our handicaps. Arnold probably doesn't have one. And if he ever did, it was probably single-digit until he was well into his seventies. But even taking into account his advanced age (Palmer is in his eighties now), it is probably safe to say our handicaps are light-years apart. By the way, whenever anyone asks what my handicap is, I always say, "My brain."

AFTER LUNCH, I STOP BY the front desk at the Holiday Inn. "Hi, I need a room list for the Willie Nelson group," I hear myself say. Somewhere in the dark recesses of my mind, the voice of Vince Lombardi is saying, *Act like you belong.*

The desk clerk prints out a room list. "Here you go," she says cheerfully. I look at the sheet and notice nearly all the rooms are on the seventh floor. I also notice that Willie's name is not on the list, but that doesn't surprise me. If he indeed has a room, surely it's listed under another name. The only names I recognize are David Anderson, Lana Nelson, Bobbie Nelson, Tony Sizemore (Willie's driver), and Gates Moore (Gator). Next stop: Lana Nelson.

I first met Lana in the summer of 1987, when I was a Coral Reefer in Jimmy Buffett's band. We were playing a private party somewhere in Connecticut, and Lana was in the audience. We had a nice visit after the show.

At this point, I'm thinking I need to talk to *somebody* about my interview with Willie, and Lana looks to be my best bet.

So I knock on her door.

"Hey, Lana. It's Marshall. You got a minute?"

"Sure. Come on in."

"Listen, I don't know if your father told you or not, but he knows—or at least he knew at one time—that I'm hoping to interview him for my book. Tonight's the last show, and I'm thinking this afternoon would be the best time. It'd be great if we could sit down somewhere quiet for thirty minutes or so. What do you think?"

"I was just with him on the bus," she said. "If you go down there now, he's there."

"Doesn't he have a room in the hotel?"

"Nah, he pretty much stays on the bus."

"Where's the bus?"

"It's parked behind the hotel, back in the far corner."

We sit and talk for a few minutes, mainly about our mutual friend Virginia Team. When I mention that Virginia is being honored in a couple of weeks at some big gala in Nashville recognizing women in country music, Lana says something about sending her some flowers. I promise to send her information regarding this event. I also offer to pay for my room.

"Oh, don't worry about it," she says. "It's just a drop in the bucket."

"Oh, okay. Well . . . thanks! I guess I'll see you later."

I SWING BY MY ROOM and grab my little Sony voice-recorder (along with a backup), making sure all batteries are in working order before slipping the recorders into my pocket. I then head for the elevators.

Once outside, I walk around to the other side of the hotel. Willie's bus is in the far back corner of the parking lot, just as Lana had said.

The bus door is unlocked, so I open it and climb aboard. Lurch is standing next to Amy Nelson, who sits at Willie's laptop writing a letter. They seem intensely engaged in this activity. I get the impression the letter is being written to a lawyer, as Lurch seems well versed in legalese. I sit down on the tufted leather couch. Lurch, being Lurch, doesn't acknowledge my presence.

After a while, I mention something about my interview with Willie.

"He's chillin'," Lurch says.

"Should I come back later?" I ask.

(silence)

I'm starting to get a sinking feeling in my stomach.

"Should I just knock on the door?"

"Not when he's chillin'," Lurch says.

I don't make a move. The bus isn't scheduled to leave for a couple of hours. I'm thinking I'll just stay put until it's time to go clear out of my room.

About that time, Willie comes out from the back of the bus, looking vibrant and alert, not at all like someone who's been chillin'. He smiles and hands me a white sheet of paper with something written on it. He seems happy and kind of pleased with himself, like a kid in school who just handed in a paper he was proud of. I glance down at the sheet and damned if there aren't seven—they were even numbered—*handwritten* answers to my seven interview questions, the ones that happened to be printed on the back of the scrap of paper containing the lyrics to "The Way I Like It (Riding with Willie)," the paper I'd left on Willie's desk earlier that morning, which in this moment seems twenty lifetimes ago. I am speechless. I again look at the seven answers that have been scrawled out with a black Sharpie pen, obviously in Willie's hand.

I manage to mumble something like, "Oh, thanks!" all the while thinking, *What the fuck!*

Then Willie looks me right in the eye. "Those lyrics you wrote are really good," he says. Then just like that, he's gone.

AMY NELSON IS THE FIRST to speak.

"You know . . ." she begins. "I don't think my dad likes doing live interviews."

Is it my imagination, or is Lurch suppressing a grin?

"One time somebody was interviewing him," she continues, "and they asked, 'Which comes first, the music or the words?' Do you know what Dad said?"

I can't imagine.

"'Yes,'" she says. "That's all he said—'Yes.'"

We both agree "yes" was the perfect answer to the question every songwriter gets asked a thousand times in his or her career, and that whenever an interview starts off with the "Which comes first . . ." question, it usually signals the beginning of a bad interview.

Amy looks at the sheet I'm holding, the one with her dad's handwritten answers, and exclaims, "That's really great! I've never seen him do anything like that before!"

Maybe she was trying to cheer me up or just speaking the truth or both. Who knows?

At this point, the only thing I know for sure is I need to be alone. I also sense a big-time attitude adjustment heading my way like Hurricane Edouard out in the Gulf.

"Hey, thanks, I'll see you guys later," I say.

BACK IN THE SAFE CONFINES of my room, I completely fall apart. I am crying great, heaving sobs, all the while talking to myself, saying things my husband would say if he were here: *Marshall, you precious thing, you are the* most *precious thing in the world. Yes, you are precious, and don't you ever forget it.* I keep telling myself this over and over. (You'd have to have grown up in my family of origin to understand why.) Meanwhile, my heart is breaking. It looks like I am *not* going to get my Willie Nelson interview. Not now. Not on this trip. Not on tape like all the other interviews. Not as I had hoped.

I call Chris and I am inconsolable. Keep in mind, I'm running on three and a half hours of sleep in four and a half days. Let's hear it for sleep deprivation! My soul is obviously having its way.

Out of nowhere, I start thinking about my father, who's been dead for over twenty-five years. I can see him as clearly as if he were standing here. I am ten years old in a room with him, my sisters, and a cousin. He is talking, but he's not talking to me. He's talking *about* me like I'm not in the room, even though I am.

"Marshall never wants little things," he begins. "She'll never nickel-and-dime you in the checkout line at the grocery store, wanting candy, chewing gum, and whatnot—not like you girls," he says, looking at my sisters. "Marshall just bides her time until she does want something. And when that happens, look out! Because it will be *big* and she will want it *bad*!"

Truer words were never spoken.

It's time to board the bus, but how can I, crying like this? I again start talking to myself, but this time it's more like a prayer. *Oh God, please don't let me cry on Willie's bus. Please, please, I beg you. Don't let me cry on Willie's bus. He has been nothing but generous and kind. I'm begging you, God. Please, PLEASE . . . DON'T LET ME CRY ON THAT BUS!*

Suddenly, I feel a strength well up inside me, like a pot of liquid iron about to boil over. It's a strength I have never known. My brain is not speaking to me, so the only thing I can hear is the universe. Without intellect, desire, longing, fear, and judgment, I have only my soul as I pass into that biblical state known as the Peace That Passeth All Understanding. It's a place I recognize, but in feeling only. Everything else is a brave new world. Whatever this is, it's bigger than the Pentagon, bigger than Wall Street, bigger than the Kremlin, bigger than sex, bigger than Ecstasy, and yes, bigger than Willie World. My soul has found bedrock at last. I am now ready to board the bus.

WILLIE'S SHOW TONIGHT is in the newly refurbished Julie Rogers Theatre in downtown Beaumont. The Julie Rogers is one of those grand old theaters built in the 1920s (in this case, 1927) with a proscenium stage, balcony, exquisite chandeliers, the works. It seats about seventeen hundred, and tonight's show is sold out.

Willie and band are scheduled to perform for two hours or so. There is no opening act. It's all Willie.

Upon arrival, Lana leaves the bus and returns with plates of hot food for Willie and Bobbie. After they're taken care of, she leads Eva, me, and Amy Nelson to catering, which has been set up in a hallway beyond the dressing rooms above the backstage area.

I load my plate with comfort food—namely black-eyed peas and mashed potatoes. The black-eyed peas are out of this world. It's amazing how much better food tastes when you're in that place of Peace That Passeth All Understanding. Not to mention, when you're near the Gulf.

After the meal, I run into Mickey Raphael. It's the first time I've actually seen Mickey face to face since I came on board, which is entirely understandable since he rides on the band bus. Willie World is literally a three-bus circus, and it's been my observation that the only time the inhabitants of one bus see the inhabitants of another is at the show.

Earlier, I had run into Poodie Locke, Willie's longtime stage manager, and we reminisced about the old days. Poodie reminded me that I had played his club in Austin in the early 1980s.

Mickey and I shoot the breeze for a minute. I present him with a DVD of *Hush Hoggies Hush* just as the show begins. I had brought along an extra copy for the band bus. It's my firm belief that every rock & roll tour bus should have this DVD. Anything to help lighten the load when you're out on the road.

Mickey sets the DVD on his amp as the band kicks off with the opening riff to "Whiskey River." As Willie begins singing, "Whiskey River, take my mind . . . ," a gigantic Texas flag drops down behind the band. The crowd is on their feet.

I am standing in the wings behind the man running the monitor board. A couple of older guys are standing behind me. They look like old ranchers straight out of the movie *Hud.* Everyone is tapping their feet, smiling, and swaying along to the music. Willie sings "Beer for My Horses," and the younger members of the audience shout in unison during the chorus. Then he sings a medley of his classics, "Funny How Time Slips Away," "Crazy," and "Night Life." I am totally into the moment and the music. When he introduces "Good Hearted Woman," saying, "I'd like to dedicate this to my friend Waylon Jennings," I'm thinking, *Shit, I know Waylon's part like I know the back of my hand!* About that time, I notice the tall mic stand at the front of the stage— the one just this side of Willie's, the one reserved for Mickey when he's not blowing into his handheld mic.

I step up next to the man running the monitor board.

"Is that mic on?" I ask.

The monitor man is big and burly. Not somebody you'd want to trifle with. He turns and seems somewhat taken aback.

"Who are you?" he says.

"It's all right," I say. "Just make sure that mic's on. I'm going out to sing with Willie on the next chorus."

He looks a little nervous.

"Hey, Mickey!" I say just loud enough for Mickey to hear.

Mickey turns around.

I point to my mouth, then point to the tall mic.

"I'm coming out to sing," I say, mouthing the words in an exaggerated manner so he can read my lips.

Mickey smiles and nods. Willie is singing the first verse, totally oblivious to what's going on at our end of the stage. I'm beginning to wonder if the spirit of Waylon Jennings himself hasn't suddenly inhabited my body. My don't-give-a-shit gauge is completely maxed out.

Willie doesn't see me walk out on the stage. As I pass Mickey, I shrug my shoulders and say:

"What's he gonna do? . . . Fire me?"

Mickey laughs.

I reach the tall mic just in time to sing the first line of the chorus.

She's a good-hearted woman
in love with a good-timing man . . .

My mic is turned up. (Thank you, monitor man!) I can hear my voice out in the auditorium blending with Willie's. The audience acknowledges my presence. I have never played Beaumont, and I imagine some in the audience are thinking, *Who in the hell is this honky Amazon in the baggy shorts and pink flip-flops?* Willie turns around, his soulful eyes wide with surprise. Then he breaks into a big smile. For a brief shining moment, I'm in love again.

She loves him in spite of his wicked way
she don't understand . . .

After Willie sings the second verse, I come in again on the chorus. Willie's phrasing can get funky, but I stay with him because I am watching his mouth. As they say back in South Carolina, I am on him like white on rice, even as we modulate going into the last chorus.

To hell with a damn interview! Nothing is better than this! I am singing with Willie Goddamn Nelson, and any thought of an interview can just go fuck itself for all I care! This is music, for chrissakes! This is life! This is God-stuff! And if the Devil doesn't like it, he can sit on a tack!

At the end of the song, Willie and I bump fists. Then I respectfully do a little bow from the waist with my eyes closed and my hands pressed together as if in prayer—first to Willie, then to the audience—before making my exit.

"That was Marshall Chapman!" Willie says to the audience. I can't remember if he said anything else, and it really doesn't matter. I am walking on air. When I get back to my post between the sound guy and the two old men, one of the old men gives me his business card. His name is Wayne. He's from Lafayette, Louisiana. He's tall and lanky and seems to have gotten a lot cuter since I sang with Willie. Later, I take his hand and we slow dance while Willie sings, "All of me . . . why not take all of me?" Everyone around us is smiling.

Later, the band does a smoking version of "Bloody Mary Morning." Bee Spears and Willie bring the crowd to their feet as they lock into the bass riff, building it to a crescendo before releasing for the last verse. During the next song, Billy English takes over bass-playing duties so Bee can take a break. Bee saunters over to where I'm standing and says, "That was *great*, man!" I assume he's talking about "Bloody Mary Morning."

"Yeah, that was really great, man. You guys were so locked in!" I say.

"No, I mean your singing."

"Oh, thanks!" I say.

I barely recognize Bee. We're all getting older, but Bee is a far cry from the skinny, long-haired, bearded hippie dude I remember from the 1970s. His hair is short and gray, and the beard is gone. The only remaining sign of funkiness is the soul patch growing under his bottom lip.

"Bee, you almost look respectable!" I say, laughing.

Everyone is in high spirits. Beaumont is the last show before everyone heads for home. It's also the only show played on Texas soil during this three-week run. Willie is loved all over the world, but here in Texas, the love seems to spring from a deeper source. The next day's *Beaumont Enterprise* quotes a member of the audience saying, "Willie Nelson *is* Texas. He could be on the flag. He could be governor if he wanted." They love him here like they love the air they breathe.

After the show, Willie's bus heads for Austin. Lurch is no longer with us, as he is on the band bus, which is going to Dallas. Lurch, Paul, and Billy all live in the Dallas–Ft. Worth area. Mickey and Bee will fly out of DFW to Nashville.

Willie's bus has a new passenger—a cherubic-looking, bright-eyed kid with curly brown hair. I had noticed him passing through my peripheral vision a time or two backstage in Beaumont. His name is Gabriel Barreto. As it turns out, he's the eighteen-year-old son of actress Amy Irving and Brazilian film director Bruno Barreto. I get the impression his mother sent him to Willie to learn a few life lessons working as a roadie. Before the Beaumont show, the crew hog-tied him with duct tape as sort of an initiation send-off. I imagine this is not the sort of thing young Gabriel would experience clubbing with his showbiz friends in Manhattan or Hollywood. Amy Irving and Willie remain friends after a much-publicized affair that started during the filming of *Honeysuckle Rose*, the 1980 movie in which they co-starred. The affair temporarily broke up Irving's relationship with Steven Spielberg, whom she later married. I have heard that Amy Irving was "the love of Willie's life." Regardless, one thing is always true: once Willie loves you, you never leave the circle.

Taking into consideration the length of tonight's show, which is three hours if you count all the handshaking and autograph-signing that follows, and Willie's age (which is seventy-five, and I know I've already mentioned it, but that still doesn't make it any easier to believe), I figure Willie will crash once we're on the bus. But once again, I forget that there's no space or time in Willie World.

Once we're rolling, Willie appears from the back of the bus, freshly showered and ready to rock. Wearing a huge black Snoop Dogg T-shirt that falls practically to his knees and a fresh pair of socks, and carrying his old gut-string Martin, he joins us at the front of the bus.

Willie's guitar is called "Trigger," and it seems to be the only guitar he plays anymore. It's beat-up and ragged-looking, just like Willie. Trigger has two sound holes—the round one made by the manufacturer, and a ragged one where the pick guard used to be, if indeed his guitar ever had one. The ragged hole has obviously evolved from years of heavy strumming. Scrawled all over the body of the guitar are names of musician friends Willie has known over the years. The most prominent—*Roger Miller*—is inscribed just below the bridge.

Willie sits on the couch directly across from sister Bobbie and me. Someone brings out a little electric keyboard and sets it down across my and Bobbie's laps. I hold it steady as the bus barrels along a bumpy stretch of Interstate 10.

Gabe Barreto seems to have an encyclopedic knowledge of every song Willie has ever recorded. So with Gabe egging them on, Willie and Bobbie proceed to play instrumental after instrumental, including some they haven't played in a while—like "Spirit in E9" from his *Spirit* CD.

This is Willie World at its deepest, most soulful level. It is after midnight and I'm rolling along a highway somewhere in southeast Texas, moving through the great American night, listening to music that is beyond sacred. When Willie plays the jazzy Django Reinhardt classic "Nuages" (French for "clouds"), Bobbie never misses a chord or a beat. The bond between these two runs deeper than deep. I'm thinking the whole "Willie Nelson & Family" phenomenon begins right here with these two siblings. Whenever Willie writes a new song, Bobbie is usually the first to hear it. And, more often than not, they're the first to work it up.

While Willie and Bobbie continue playing "Nuages," I manage to slide my little Sony cassette recorder from my pocket and hit the record button. The recorder is geared for the human speaking voice, and I wonder if the quality will be listenable. As usual, my worries are unfounded. The recording is amazingly clear. Even now, as I listen to it—just that minute-and-a-half segment—I am taken back to that moment on the bus. There's more than music on this little slice of tape. Life, love, hope, faith, endurance—it's all there, the rolling sound of the highway a perfect backdrop.

This impromptu concert lasts for a couple of hours. At one point Willie gets up to go to the bathroom and gives the guitar to Gabe. He plays it for a while, then passes it along to me. I notice the action is set up pretty high. It's all my rangy fingers can do to make a chord. I strum a few jazz chords, then segue into Cindy Walker's "Going Away Party." Willie comes back out and stands there while I finish the song.

Lee Smith (the novelist) once told me she had actually ridden Misty, the real live pony that inspired the children's classic *Misty of*

Chincoteague. When Lee told me that, I was mightily impressed, as I read and loved that book as a child. What a thing to be able to say! The only comparable claim I can ever make is that I once played Trigger on Willie Nelson's bus.

After Willie and Bobbie finish playing, Lana opens up a bottle of wine. "I believe I'll have a glass of wine with you ladies," Willie says, as he offers a toast to Lana, Eva, Bobbie, and me. By then, Gabe is stretched out asleep on one of the couches. I imagine being hog-tied by Willie's crew can take it out of you.

I can't remember what all happens after that, other than at one point, Willie pulls up one of my all-time favorite recordings, which is Gram Parsons and Emmylou Harris singing "Love Hurts." When the acoustic guitar intro begins, Willie is sitting at his desk and I am sitting on the aisle floor next to his leg. By now, it's probably safe to say I am feeling the effects of the wine. Hopefully, everyone else is too. Because as soon as Emmylou Harris and Gram Parsons begin to sing "Love hurts, love scars / Love wounds and mars . . ." I begin *lip-synching* the lyrics (in a rather dramatic fashion) while holding onto Willie's leg like it's a microphone. Eva and Bobbie are the only ones who see me do this, and they are laughing, which only encourages me. Every now and then I turn around and look at Willie, who is reading something and seems totally oblivious to what's going on.

Some fools think of happiness, blissfulness, togetherness
Some fools fool themselves I guess, but they're not fooling me!

I continue my pantomime, complete with an air-guitar rendition of James Burton's killer guitar licks at the end. By now, Bobbie and Eva are really cracking up, while Willie remains oblivious. Or maybe he's choosing to ignore us? As usual, it's hard to tell.

LATER ON, AFTER EVERYONE DRIFTS OFF and the interior lights have been dimmed, I wander to the front of the bus, where I sit down next to Tony, the driver. There's been a wreck and Interstate 10 is a parking lot. Tony says it's been like this for almost an hour. Finally, things start loosening up and we're rolling again.

"What do you like most about driving this bus?" I ask.

"I've got the best seat in the house!" he replies.

We talk about everything under the sun—well, Tony does most of the talking. I mostly sit there and listen as he talks about biodiesel, the drug bust in Louisiana the year before (Tony was driving), and "quick red lights," which I learn are the bane of every big-rig driver's existence. A quick red light is actually a quick *yellow* light, which causes the light to turn red before a big rig like Willie's bus can come to a stop, at least without slamming on the brakes.

"You don't want to turn your sleepers back there into an accordion," Tony says as we run a quick red light near Bastrop. A few cars honk their horns in protest as the bus barrels through the intersection. Tony flashes the headlights and never touches the brakes.

WEST OF AUSTIN, WE TURN off Highway 71 onto Pace Bend Road. The bus passes a gravel parking lot where some patrons are leaving a roadhouse. By now it's a little after two in the morning. Somebody recognizes Willie's bus, and before long, people are honking their horns and waving as if welcoming home a conquering hero. For a mile or so, carloads of late-night revelers follow us, honking and flashing their lights. Finally, on a straightaway, one of the cars swings out to pass. A voice yells, WE LOVE YOU, WILLIE! as the car goes careening by, its taillights disappearing in the distance.

After a few more miles, the bus pulls up to a gate at Willie's ranch. Tony gives me the four-digit security number, so I step out and punch it in. The gate begins to open as I jump back into the bus. We climb a little hill before coming to a complete stop. Home at last.

A few passengers begin stirring around, looking like zombies, their eyes glazed with sleep. At one point Willie comes from the back and looks right at me with his big soulful eyes.

"Did you get what you needed?" he asks.

His question takes me by surprise. Is he referring to our live interview? The one that never was?

"I got a lot of things, Willie," I say finally. "It's been great and I appreciate everything . . . I'll be in touch."

"All right, then," Willie says. "Well, Gator is going to give you a ride to wherever you need to go."

As Willie turns to leave, I call out, "Hey, Willie!"

He turns around.

"Don't give up on me," I say. I want to add, ". . . because I'm a work-in-progress," but I let it go.

Willie's smile turns serious. "Don't give up on me!" he says.

That was our last exchange.

I **STEP DOWN FROM THE BUS**. It feels good to be walking on solid ground again. I look around, trying to see through the dark. Everything seems dusty and dry. Some horses move around in a nearby paddock. One of them whinnies softly. Soon Gator and Tony are loading my bag and Bobbie's luggage into the back of a big pick-up truck.

The truck is a beat-up red 1991 Chevrolet Suburban named "Hank." Tony dusts off the seats, then opens a door for Bobbie before opening one for me in an unexpected but appreciated display of gallantry. Then Gator slides in behind the wheel. I'm riding shotgun, with Tony and Bobbie in the back seat. Gator turns the ignition and Hank's motor rumbles into action, sounding like one of those badass trucks in *No Country for Old Men*.

Bobbie's house is just down the road. After we pull up, Tony and Gator carry her luggage through an open garage. Bobbie has a lot of luggage. I imagine Elizabeth Taylor has nothing on Bobbie Nelson when it comes to luggage.

There are no cars in her garage—just racks and racks of clothes hanging everywhere.

"Looks like you're getting ready to have a garage sale," I say.

"Oh, you know I love to shop," Bobbie says, smiling. "Those are just clothes I can't fit in my closet."

Her living room/kitchen area is undergoing a renovation. Bobbie seems pleased with the progress that's been made since she was last home. A picture of Willie from his younger days hangs over the fireplace. After a while, we say our goodbyes.

Now it's just Gator, Tony, and me barreling along Pace Bend Road toward Highway 71. I am starting to feel like Katharine Ross in *Butch Cassidy & the Sundance Kid.*

"I'd better call Jane," I announce.

"Who's Jane?" asks Tony from the back seat.

"Jane's my friend. I'm staying at her house off Bee Caves Road."

"Is she single?" Tony continues.

"Well, yeah," I answer. "Actually she's recently widowed."

Tony seems undeterred. "How old is she?"

"She's about my age," I say, laughing. I dial Jane's number and brace myself, as I imagine I am waking her from a deep sleep.

Someone picks up the phone, but doesn't answer.

"Is she cute?" Tony continues from the back seat.

"Hey, Jane! It's Marshall. Are you there?"

I turn around to Tony, "Hell yeah, she's cute!"

Jane mumbles something I can't quite understand.

"Hey, Jane . . . listen, I'm so sorry to be waking you up. I just wanted to let you know I'm about ten minutes away."

"Oh . . ." Jane says, sounding fuzzy and far away. "I wasn't sure who you were." Later Jane tells me that when the phone rang, she was so deep in sleep, she had forgotten all about my visit and was wondering, *What kind of pervert would call here at three o'clock in the morning?*

"So what do you boys want for breakfast?" I say jokingly to Tony and Gator.

My comment is met with dead silence, at least from Jane's end.

I sense her rising apprehension though the phone, as she's thinking, *Holy shit!* Surely *they don't expect me to get up and fix breakfast for them!?*

"Tell her I want to check her for ticks!" Tony shouts from the back seat.

Finally, I hear Jane laughing. Then the line goes dead.

This damn cell phone! As soon as I get back to Nashville, I've got *to get a new one.* (Which of course I haven't done as of this writing.)

As we near Jane's drive, I ask Gator to make a dramatic show as we pull in. I envision myself stepping from a big cloud of dust with my bags, like some gunslinger in a Western movie. Gator hits the accelerator. Hank's wheels spew gravel as we lunge into Jane's driveway without hitting the antique wrought-iron fence on either side, or the stack of clay gardening pots to the right. A big cloud of dust billows up as we skid across the gravel to a stop.

"That good enough?" Gator says, laughing.

I give him a thumbs-up.

I look around and am suddenly aware of how *civilized* everything seems. Especially compared to where I've just been. I feel like Dorothy in *The Wizard of Oz*, only in reverse. One thing's for sure: I am no longer in Willie World.

Jane's world is like something out of *Architectural Digest*, with its manicured lawns and landscaped gardens with olive trees planted in huge Italian pots. Her house is the antithesis of a McMansion. Built of fieldstone in the 1890s, it is grand in an understated, old-world kind of way. Inside, airy rooms filled with books and art await.

Gator takes my bag down from the back of the truck. It's not that heavy.

"I think I can handle it from here," I say.

Jane stands just inside the door, wearing her bathrobe.

"Hey, Jane!" I call out. "Meet Tony and Gator. Tony, Gator, meet Jane."

"You sure you don't want me to check you for ticks?" Tony calls out from across the yard.

We all laugh and wave goodbye. Gator expertly backs Hank back down the drive in another cloud of gravel and dust.

"Sorry about the pots!" he yells out. Then just like that, they roar off into the night and are gone.

I AM NOW ENTERING DAY FIVE on three and a half hours' sleep.

"The things we do for art!" I exclaim, as I step into the house.

We walk back to the kitchen, where I pour myself a glass of fat-free milk while Jane starts making almond-butter toast. Then we go sit on the sofa in the upstairs reading room.

"I want to hear all about it," Jane says.

The Willie "interview"
Beaumont, Texas
August 3, 2008

1. How long have you lived (or did you live) in Nashville?
I lived in Nashville 10 years—1961–1971

2. Where did you live before?
Texas—Oregon, Washington

3. When did you first hear about Nashville?
all my life WSM

4. What made you move here?
I knew this was the market place to sell your music.

5. What mode of transportation brought you?
1951 Buick

6. Did you ever consider Los Angeles or New York?
I ran Pamper Music in L.A. for a while

7. Describe your first 24 hours, your first day or night, or just recount an early experience that stands out in your mind, maybe something that could *only* have happened in Nashville.
I got drunk—layed down in the middle of Broadway.

1. I Lived in Nashville
   10 years - 1961-1971
2. Texas - one. Utah.
3. all my life WSM
4. I Knew this was
   the market place.
   to sell your music.
5. 1951 Buie
6. I Ran Pamper music
   in L.A. for a while
7. I got drunk - layed
   down in the middle of
   Broadway -

NOTE: A year later (August 9, 2009) I finished "The Way I Like It (Riding with Willie)." Here are the last two verses:

Big wheels rolling down Interstate 10
I haven't slept since I don't know when
I couldn't really tell you what state I'm in
That's the way I like it

Bobbie and Willie play music all night
Sister and brother, what a beautiful sight
Songs long forgotten now seeing the light
That's the way I like it

I emailed Willie the finished lyrics, not knowing if his email had changed. A few hours later, I received the following, sent from his iPhone: "Thanks great song. Love Willie."

Acknowledgments

I'D LIKE TO THANK ALL my songwriter friends, including the ones featured in this book, for all the inspiration; Jay Orr, for believing; John Gouge, LeAnn Bennett, Liz Thiels, Tina Wright, Michael Gray, and Kyle Young at the Country Music Hall of Fame and Museum; Eli Bortz, Sue Havlish, Dariel Mayer, Betsy Phillips, Ed Huddleston, Jenna Phillips, and Jessie Hunnicutt at Vanderbilt University Press; and Peter Guralnick, Barry Mazor, Chet Flippo, William McKeen, Chris Fletcher, Matt Timm, Dave Hickey, Kim Harrelson, Lee Smith, Phil Sparks (the Grammar Doctor), and Ronnie Pugh (at the Nashville Public Library). Also, Dick and Annie Bower (AnDix Indexing Associates) and Becky Brawner (Unlikely Suburban Design).

Also, thanks to Georgia Rae Hiatt (that's her foot on the cover), Margaret Ellis, Anthony Scarlati, David Climer, Brandon Barca, Tamara Saviano, Lisa Kristofferson, Donnie Fritts, Fred Foster, Jack Clement, John White, Katherine Chrisman, Doug Jeffords, Walter and Kitty Forbes, Mac Gayden, Rod Williamson, Carmi Murphy, Jerry Southwood, Kenny Gibbs, Al Clayton, Officer Chez of the L.A. County Sheriff's Department (Malibu/Lost Hills station), the man at the LAX Hertz return lot, Claudia Church, David Martin, Jill McCorkle, Matraca Berg, Fayssoux Starling McLean, Virginia Team, Diana Haig, Carol Campbell, Genia Harris, Rutland Harris, Hallie Slocum, Tom Comet, Chuck and Beth Flood, Danny Flowers, Yvonne Groenendijk, Jeannie Bare, Jordan Powell, Sid Evans, Holly Gleason, Kelly Hobbs, Marion Kraft, Bev Lambert, Edie Hartwick, Melanie Heeran, Beth Thomas, Roy Neel, Rose Drake, Nancy Hiatt, Tracy Nelson, Travis Rivers, Jon Vance, Garry Velletri, Clara at the Marion County (Indiana) Sheriff's Department, Tom Bailey (University School of Nashville), Mary Chapman Webster, Mama, Dorothy Chapman Josey, Hon.

Robert F. Chapman, John Jeter, Jane Hilfer, Denny Boguskie, David Anderson, Rick Sanjek, Tim Wipperman, Paul Harmon, Coke Sams, James Carson, Jennifer Herbert Vick, Jane and Vereen Bell, Bill Nelson, Mickey Raphael, George Gruhn, Gates "Gator" Moore, Lana Nelson, Eva Hassmann, Bobbie Nelson, Amy Nelson, Tony Sizemore, Tim Corbin, and Mark Arrington.

Gone but not forgotten . . .
Tim Krekel, Jackie Street, Mary Craven, Stephen Bruton, Merlin Littlefield, Randall "Poodie" Locke, John Stewart, Hoyet Henry, W. Gilbert Templeton, Tony Hilfer, Bob Mercer, Phil Walden, and Jerry Wexler.

Credits

Photo Credits

Frontispiece: Courtesy of Gaylord Entertainment
Page 5: Chris Fletcher
Page 9: Courtesy of Gaylord Entertainment
Page 31: Ramcey Rodriguez
Page 41: Claudia Church
Page 61: Glen Rose
Page 80: Chris Fletcher
Page 95: Squire Fox/ *Garden & Gun*
Page 105: Donn Jones
Page 115: Edie Hartwick
Page 123: Melanie Heeran
Page 139: Courtesy of the author
Page 157: Marshall Fallwell Jr.
Page 177: Neil Brake/Vanderbilt University
Page 189: Courtesy of the author
Page 199: Lance Cowan
Page 222: Courtesy of the author
Page 267: Courtesy of the author

Index

Page numbers in bold refer to photographs.

Blake, Norman, 6
Bland, Bobby Blue, 156,
   191, 198
"Blood Red and Going
   Down," 148
"Bloody Guts," 171
"Bloody Mary Morning,"
   224, 227, 258
"Blowin' in the Wind," 117
"Blue," 99
Blue Jean Country Queen, 151
"Blue Skies," 230
Bluebird Café, **31**, 40, 78,
   105–6, 124, 125, 137, 146,
   176, 194, **199**, 201, 202,
   210
BMI, 11, 79, 195, 215
Boardwalk, 176
Bobby Bare & Friends, 81
"Bobby McGee." *See* "Me
   and Bobby McGee"
Bogdanovich, Peter, 240
Bogey's, **123**, 184
Bogguss, Suzy, 160
Boguskie, Denny, 237
Bon Jovi, Jon, 153
Bongo Java, 61
"Booze in Your Blood," 179
Boston, Massachusetts, 32, 33,
   34–35, 73, 76
Bottom Line, 191
Bourgoise, Dan and Fred,
   158–59
BR549, 180
Braddock, Bobby, 104–11,
   105, 153
Braddock, Lauren, 105
Bradley, Harold, 20, 79
Bradley, Owen, 79, 106
"Brand New Key," 116
Brando, Marlon, 229
"Bread and Butter," 168–69
Briggs, David, 163, 169
"Brilliant Conversationalist,"
   137
Bring the Family, 159–60
Bromberg, David, 69
Brooks, Garth, 37
Brown, James, 156
Bruton, Stephen, 13, 270
Bryant, Jimmy, 84

Buckingham, Steve, 135
Buffett, Jimmy, 126, 251
Bug Music, 133–34, 158–59,
   160
Buried Alive (Friedman),
   155–56
Burnett, T-Bone, 159
Burns, Robert, 233
Burton, James, 59, 261
Burton, Richard, 40
Bus Named Desire, 178
Bush, George H. W., 189–91
Bush, Sam, **199**
Bush League Records, 190
*Butch Cassidy & the Sundance
   Kid*, 263

Caccavale, Tony, 126
Cactus Café, **189**, 191
Cain, Marie, 227
Campbell, Walter, 195
Campbell, Will, 21–24, 26
Canadian Country Music
   Awards, 121
Canadian magazine, 62
"Candle in the Wind," 201
Cannons in the Rain, 108
Cantrell's, 131, 188
Capitol Records, 84, 204, 208
Carlson, Harry and Louise,
   90
Carolina Theater, vii
Carothers, Craig, 152
Carr, Pete, 226
Carson, James, 223
Carter, Carlene, 57
Carter, Deana, 226
Carter, Fred, Jr., 226, 240
Carter, June, 55, 92
Casablanca, 236
Cash, Johnny, 10, 18–19, 24–
   26, 27, 51, 55–58, 114, 153
Cash, Rosanne, 39–40, 55, 57,
   75, 186, 205
Cathedral of the Incarnation,
   128
CBS Records, 20, 135
Cedarwood Publishing
   Company, 16
Centennial Park, 48, 166
Central Songs, 90

Channel, Bruce, 12
Chapman, Beth Nielsen, 28,
   61, 198–221, **199**
Chapman, Ernest (Beth's
   husband), 203, 206–8,
   214, 217–19
Chapman, Ernest (Beth's
   son), 201, 203, 219
Chapman, Hon. Robert F.
   (uncle), 191
Chapman, James A.
   (grandfather), 6
Chapman, James A., Jr.
   (father), 4, 6, 230–31, 254
Chapman, Marshall
   Aix-en-Provence, 156–57
   and Angel, 122–26, **123**
   and Bare, 79–81, **80**
   Beaumont concert with
      Willie Nelson, 255–58
   and Beth Nielsen
      Chapman, 198–202,
      199
   Bluebird Café, **31**, 40, **199**
   and Braddock, 104–6, **105**
   and Buffett, 251
   Bug Music, 134
   car incident, 61–63
   and Clark, 112, **115**
   and Cleveland, 176–80,
      177
   at the Cockeyed Camel,
      139
   and Crowell, 38–42, **41**
   Dirty Linen, 124
   "The Earth Is a Dog,"
      139–40
   Epic Records, 60, 63, 81,
      140, 145, 176, 177
   equipment theft, 176
   Farm Aid 1996, 231–32
   and Fletcher, 235–39
   and Gauthier, 28–29, **31**
   and Harris, 59–65, **61**, **177**
   and Henry, 137–40, **139**
   and Hiatt, 155–62
   and Hilfer, 234, 238,
      264–65
   and Howard, 37, **123**
   Inside Job, 125
   and Kristofferson, 3–15, **5**

They Came to Nashville